Legacies of VALOR

TRAITS OF CHARACTER:
THE NOBLE & THE NOTABLE

DAVID C. HAMMOND

WestBow
PRESS
A DIVISION OF THOMAS NELSON

WestBow Press books may be ordered through booksellers or by contacting:

WestBow Press
A Division of Thomas Nelson
1663 Liberty Drive
Bloomington, IN 47403
www.westbowpress.com
1-(866) 928-1240

ISBN: 978-1-4497-4855-5 (e)
ISBN: 978-1-4497-4856-2 (sc)
ISBN: 978-1-4497-4857-9 (hc)

Library of Congress Control Number: 2012908109

Printed in the United States of America

WestBow Press rev. date: 07/19/2012

CONTENTS

Finally, be strong in the Lord, and in the strength of His might. Put on the full armor of God, that you may be able to stand firm against the schemes of the devil. For our struggle is not against flesh and blood, but against the rulers, against the powers, against the world forces of darkness, against spiritual forces of wickedness in the heavenly places.

Therefore, take up the full armor of God, that you may be able to resist in the evil day, and having done everything, to stand firm.

Stand firm therefore, having girded your loins with truth, and having put on the breastplate of righteousness, and having shod your feet with the preparation of the Gospel of Peace.

Take up the shield of faith with which you will be able to extinguish all the flaming missiles of the evil one, and take the helmet of salvation, and the sword of the Spirit, which is the word of God.

—Ephesians 6:10-17

ACKNOWLEDGMENTS

First and foremost, I would like to thank my wife, Linda, for encouraging me to write. Without her support and encouragement, *Legacies of Valor* would never have found its way out of the margins of my Bible and into your hands.

An expression of deep gratitude goes out to my parents, who made sure I was fed a steady diet of positive encouragement, church attendance, and live examples of Christian character worthy of following.

I would also like to recognize and thank all the pastors, preachers, teachers, and Sunday school leaders who shared their personal Bible studies and lessons with me through their sermons, writings, and teachings. Many of their personal revelations from years of study are captured in this book, but without individual credit given, as it would be extremely difficult to determine who shared what, and when.

Last, I dedicate this book to my daughters, Kelly and Grace. It is my hope that someday they will share this book with their children, that they may gain insight into who their father was and what fueled me over the years, and most importantly, that they may come to know as I have the joy and peace that comes from knowing our heavenly Father and friend—a relationship built one step at a time.

FOREWORD

My purpose in writing *Legacies of Valor*, which contains the most significant Bible lessons and observations I've enjoyed over the years, is to provide a single reference for folks like you to be able to read, consider, and learn from the insights and interpretations that I have been afforded through others. These insights have helped me better understand who I am in Christ and what God Himself has to say about each of us.

While my personal story may pale in comparison to someone more notable or more famous, I believe that the principles of valor and the trials and journeys of others, including myself, may strike a chord of similar circumstance with many readers.

When my daughters were young, my wife and I would take them to church and drop them off at Sunday school. Then we would head off to our adult class, and then on to "big church," where we would listen intently for sound bites of wisdom and guidance from the pulpit to encourage us over the coming week.

We would take notes, jotting down new epiphanies and pearls of wisdom in the margins of our Bibles and highlighting verses with whatever color of pen we had. If you looked at one of my Bibles today, you would see that I have often highlighted my highlights from previous sermons, noting a different observation the second or third time around.

All these insights and revelations marked in my Bible started to minister to me. It started rather selfishly. I thought, *when I pass on, which daughter do I give my most marked-up Bible to? Maybe I should buy another Bible, highlight it to match the other and write in all my marginal notes and references so that both girls will have the benefit of possessing the principles that guided me through both good and rough times.*

Then it hit me. *I'm too young to think like that!* Another light bulb popped on. How many others might benefit from the same information? Why not assemble this information in such a way that others might also enjoy reading and considering new or maybe just slightly different interpretations and perspectives from pastors and teachers they might not have heard of.

I quickly dispelled the notion that our personal Bible studies and notes are supposed to be kept personal, noting that that was probably the voice of the enemy trying to dissuade me from sharing truths about God.

Kids, family, friends, and coworkers are not always receptive to our words of wisdom or "preachy sermonettes." Sometimes the best way to reach out to others, to share thoughts, advice, and pearls of insight, is to use more subtle and less threatening channels. It is truly my prayer that after reading *Legacies of Valor*, you too will find its contents worthy of sharing with your kids, friends, and others; I hope that this book might serve as your voice, as you reach out and begin your own campaign to pay God's wisdom forward.

INTRODUCTION

The lessons, observations and stories captured in *Legacies of Valor* have been collected over thirty-five years of study and walking with God. The principles applied within have been tested by adversity, trials, and struggles that I believe many will be able to identify with. Today, over fifteen million people are unemployed, suffering in solitude from rejection, frustration, and depression. I can most certainly relate to these folks.

But I alone cannot reach out to encourage all these people, not without your help. We all know someone, a family member, a neighbor, or a distant relative, who is currently going through unemployment, or under-employment, which seems to define a whole new category of discouraged people. I'm hoping that after you finish reading *Legacies of Valor*, you will go out and buy another copy and give it to one of these people who are currently out of work and could benefit greatly from a few words of encouragement. Maybe you'll see that my story—God's story—might be just what they need to hear right now to stay in the hunt and in the fight. Consider it your pay-it-forward opportunity to be a blessing to someone in need.

I was raised a Southern Baptist, but the lessons and sermon notes in this book come from many points of view and denominations. Over the years, Linda and I have had the joy of living in many different places. We moved quite often for my career as a marketing consultant for many different companies. Once we had settled into our new digs, wherever they might have been, we would venture out in search for a church, which met the needs of our family at the time. We've enjoyed attending the churches of and learning from the Baptists, Lutherans, Presbyterians, Methodists, and many non-denominational Bible-based churches as well.

It should be noted that this book does not favor one denomination over another, but instead is focused on the personal insights and revelations gained by digging deeper into what the Bible has to say on any given topic. For me, it is all about simplicity of message. At a very early age I learned that it is childlike faith that moves mountains and is the attribute God first seeks in each of us; it is an unquestioned faith that we can trust in Him as a child trusts a parent. I always felt that if following God became complicated or legalistic, something wasn't right.

Therefore, the structure of this book was designed with simplicity in mind. The first half of the book attempts to lay down some basic principles from the Bible such as acquiring wisdom, understanding and defining character, building faith, and establishing a habit of prayer. The second half of the book takes a closer look into the lives and stories of faith and failure of some of the Bible's most noble and worthy characters and some less worthy yet notable characters.

In my quest to find shining examples of valor, and attributes of success that could be easily applied to my life, I learned that, often, the well-known classic Bible tales about valiant characters are only part of the story. In fact, many, if not most of these characters are plagued with heartache, disappointment, bad decisions, and temptation. At the end of the day, these mighty warriors for the King are human, just like you and me, and their real stories aren't about their victories as much as they are about their journeying through their valleys.

I have incorporated the full scriptural quotations within each chapter so that you do not have to get up to reference your Bible, or, if this book makes its way to other parts of the world, as I hope it will, for the benefit of readers who may not have access to a Bible.

Within many of the scriptural references, I've highlighted key words and phrases which we often skim over but which I believe to be profound and crucial bringing the verse to life. I've also provided observations and little epiphanies of insight from the margins of my Bible; I found these helpful in solving a problem or interpreting a Scripture.

Last, I've kept the commentary light and conversational to mimic the style of dialogue most common in Bible studies, where an open exchange of ideas, thoughts, and interpretations are welcome. I've also layered in a bit of humor with the hope of demonstrating that as we journey through life and strive to be more like our Savior, we need to enjoy the journey, taking time to laugh, to do that thing with the roses, and to enjoy the adventure.

At the end of the day, when all is said and done, what we leave behind is our character, the essence of who we were, what we believed in, and for what we fought. And hopefully, those remaining behind will have been blessed, encouraged, and strengthened by our actions of faith and our words of encouragement. Hopefully, they will be inspired to pay it forward and share our essence with others.

ACQUIRING WISDOM:
GETTING UNDERSTANDING

To receive instruction in wise behavior, righteousness, justice and equity; to give prudence to the naïve, to the youth knowledge and discretion, a wise man will hear and increase in learning, and a man of understanding will acquire wise counsel.

—PROVERBS 1:3-5

Let's face it: we like hanging around people who are confident, knowledgeable, and enjoyable to be around. No one likes hanging around someone who is wrong more often than not, gives bad advice, or is quick to judge. To avoid being one of these well-intentioned but often wrong individuals, we would be wise to consider the writings of Solomon, as captured in the book of Proverbs. Proverbs is an excellent place to begin the search for wisdom and understanding. There are thirty-one chapters in Proverbs, one chapter to read for each day of the month—this would be a great discipline to begin today. (A chapter a day keeps stupid at bay.)

As in life, the truths revealed within Proverbs are taught, and hopefully learned, through contrasting views, experiences, and encounters. You'll see that quite often, in a single verse, there is a statement of correct behavior, followed by a contrasting truth about an incorrect behavior;

it is a simple comparison between right and wrong, or good and evil. One day you can be on top of the world, feeling wonderful about receiving great news from a friend; on the very next day, you may find yourself forcing a smile after learning a coworker has shared something inaccurate about you with others.

> The beginning of wisdom is: Acquire wisdom; and with all your acquiring, get understanding. Prize her, and she will exalt you; She will honor you if you embrace her.
> —Proverbs 4:7-8

In some of the verses in this book, you'll note that I italicized some phrases for emphasis. I have found it helpful to break down Scriptures to make them easier to understand. Over the years, I've found simple formulas or equations that make some verses easier to grasp. In the example above, the word "is" functions as an equals sign. Thus, the beginning of wisdom equals acquiring wisdom. To put it another way, you are acquiring the moment you begin.

This is an important observation, as many new Christians get overwhelmed with all the new things they are learning about their God, their walk, and the life lessons of others in the Bible. It's often difficult to understand much when we first take on a new task or learn a new language, but if we continue to pursue the principles with diligence, we will achieve understanding.

There is also a cause-and-effect principle at play here. "She [wisdom] will honor you, if you embrace her." This is a simple if-then principle. If we do this, then such-and-such will happen. If we are sincere about gaining knowledge and understanding, we will be diligent in pursuing it wholeheartedly, without wavering. And if we do this, we have the assurance that we will find understanding and answers to our questions.

However, there is much more at play here than just gaining a better understanding of something. Gaining understanding not only gives us insight into a matter, but also produces favor, as noted in the Scripture below.

> Good understanding produces favor, but the way of the treacherous is hard.
> —Proverbs 13:15

Gaining or having favor, both in God's sight and in our everyday lives, is very important to being effective both for God and for others. We will explore the essence and value of favor in greater detail later in the book. For now it is noteworthy that understanding produces (or equals) favor, as noted in the Scripture above. Vice versa: favor produces understanding.

In other words, the more understanding we acquire of God's Word, the more favor we have in His sight because we are pursuing the right thing. Likewise, the more favor we have in God's sight, the more understanding or insight into His word we will acquire.

> A man will be satisfied with good by the fruit of his words,
> and the deeds of a man's hands will return to him.
> —Proverbs 12:14

With more insight into God's Word and His principles for dealing with life and with those around us comes satisfaction with good things happening in our lives because of the good fruit (encouraging words of wisdom) from within us.

The Bible says that not only do we enjoy a more satisfied life, but also even our enemies will be at peace with us.

> When a man's ways are pleasing to the Lord, He makes
> even his enemies to be at peace with him.
>
> —PROVERBS 17:7

The verse above is an excellent display of the cause-and-effect principle. Just knowing that there is a formula or principle at work that can keep our enemies at bay—and, moreover, at peace with us—is all the motivation we should need to live happier, more fulfilled lives. Knowing what pleases God is just as important as knowing what displeases Him. If we conduct our business in a way that displeases God, how can we boldly approach the throne of God in prayer and expect to receive anything we've asked for?

> In whom we have boldness and confident access through
> faith in Him.
>
> —EPHESIANS 3:12

> Now to Him who is able to do exceeding abundantly
> beyond all that we ask or think, according to the power
> that works within us.
>
> —EPHESIANS 3:20

God can not only hear the prayers of those praying in faith and believing that He is who and what He promises to be, and that he answers all that we ask through prayer; God can also answer what we think, even, exceedingly and abundantly, beyond our wildest imaginations!

> Let us therefore draw near with confidence to the throne
> of grace, that we may receive mercy and may find grace to
> help in time of need.
>
> —HEBREWS 4:16

There are a great many advantages in initiating a search for wisdom. If we are persistent, we are promised understanding. We gain favor in His sight. We are promised a satisfying and fulfilled life. Even our enemies will be at peace with us. And all that we can ask or even think will be granted far beyond what we might imagine.

But for these truths to manifest in our lives, we must approach the throne in faith and with confidence that He is who He says He is.

> And without faith it is impossible to please Him, for he who comes to God must believe that He is, and that He is a rewarder of those who diligently seek Him.
>
> —HEBREWS 11:6

Simply put, it is impossible to please God without faith, because faith honors God and God always honors faith. So what is faith and how do we obtain it?

> Now faith is the assurance [substance] of things hoped for, the conviction [evidence] of things not seen.
>
> —HEBREWS 11:1

Let's take a closer look at this passage to see if there is any deeper understanding to glean. Consider the first two words of the passage above. Faith is the now which we stand upon while we wait for the evidence to manifest. The term *assurance* is the substance or ingredient that mixes in the formula for hope.

According to sermon notes scratched within the margins of my Bible, hope is the "confident expectation of a soon-coming good." To keep with the baking analogy, we don't have a cake yet, but because we followed the recipe and have assurance and confidence in the ingredients we've used, we are confidently expecting a tasty cake very soon.

But it's important to note that you must also be hopeful and firmly planted in belief to be in faith. In other words, it's hard to cook if you aren't in the kitchen.

So how do we obtain this faith?

> Be imitators of those who through faith and patience inherit the promises.
> —HEBREWS 6:12

> So faith comes from hearing, and hearing by the word of Christ.
> —ROMANS 10:17

> Now we who are strong ought to bear the weaknesses of those without strength and not just please ourselves . . . for what was written in earlier times was written for our instruction, that through perseverance and the encouragement of the Scriptures we might have hope.
> —ROMANS 15:1-4

Job, one of the Bible characters in the Old Testament, searched long and hard for wisdom. He experienced some pretty tough times, as did many other characters we'll learn about in this book. In the Judean hillsides, David found God and developed his giant-slaying faith, confidence, and trust in the Lord. He went on to experience great suffering and tragedy when wisdom departed and disobedience took residence. While our discussion thus far has hopefully been enlightening to some, it only begins to scratch the surface of true wisdom. Its value and correct application are described further in Job 28:12-28. We are reminded of the simplest truth about wisdom:

> And to man He said, "Behold, the fear of the Lord, that is wisdom; And to depart from evil is understanding."
> —JOB 28:28

SIGNIFICANT OBSERVATIONS:

1. Acquiring wisdom is the beginning of understanding.
2. Hearing, reading, and studying the Word is the way to acquire wisdom.
3. If we are persistent in our quest, we are promised greater understanding.
4. We gain favor in God's sight.
5. We are promised a satisfying and fulfilled life.
6. Even our enemies will be at peace with us.
7. All that we can ask or even think will be granted.
8. Without faith, it is impossible to please Him.
9. Faith comes by hearing the Word and by imitating those who walk by faith.
10. In faith, we can approach the throne with boldness and confidence.

WITHOUT REPROACH:
UNDERSTANDING GOD'S CHARACTER

*But if any of you lacks wisdom, let him ask of God, who
gives to all men generously and without reproach, and it
will be given to him. But let him ask in faith without any
doubting, for the one who doubts is like the surf of the sea
driven and tossed by the wind.*

—JAMES 1:5-6

What an excellent verse to meditate on. Notice that this verse starts out
with the words, "if any of you lacks wisdom." Let's stop right there.
Notice the verse doesn't say, "only after you have said ten Hail Marys,"
or "only priests and ministers," or "only those found worthy may ask for
wisdom." No, it states quite clearly that "if *any* [anyone at any time] . . .
lacks wisdom, let him ask of God, who gives to *all* men generously and
without reproach, and it will be given to him."

All of us come from different backgrounds, have experienced different
upbringings, and may have emotional baggage from parents, ministers,
or others that may need to be checked for a season if we are going to
be open enough to consider personal and practical interpretations of
Scripture. It is not my intention to belittle or undermine denominational
traditions or religious rituals that prescribe certain practices to
approaching God. Rather, my objective here is to simply point out that

the Bible prescribes a personal and intimate relationship between God and man, a relationship, which promises that if we simply ask, we will receive. Herein lies our first glimpse into God's character.

God gives to *all men, generously and without reproach*. While the Bible does say in this passage that "in the counsel of many, wisdom is established," here James is talking about how to obtain wisdom one-on-one with God. Not only is wisdom given to all generously, it is also given without reproach. Without reproach means without criticism, without accusation, without reprimands and without blame.

I think James chose these words carefully, knowing that most folks would rather pass on asking for wisdom, or anything for that matter, if they thought they would be reprimanded for previous bad decisions or accused of not being worthy enough in the first place. Fortunately, God operates completely differently than most people in the world we live in. In today's society, knowledge is power. In the corporate world, your boss might not be quick to give you all his insights, because if he did, he might end up working for you someday. It's unfortunate that many climbing the corporate ladder are misled by their superiors and coworkers simply because these "mentors" are insecure in their own right.

It's perfectly normal for parents to respond with a no when children ask for things they either don't need or couldn't handle. But what parent wouldn't respond favorably to a genuine request for greater understanding?

In today's hi-tech world of unlimited access to information via the Internet and search applications like Google, if you can form a question, you can easily obtain access to a wealth of resources that will shed light on your inquiry. Here's an interesting analogy for you to consider: like God, an Internet search will give to all men generously and without reproach.

So if you have made mistakes in the past—and by the way, we all have—here's some good news: neither the Internet nor God judges your worthiness to begin a search for knowledge. To get started or to ask God for insight into understanding wisdom more deeply, *all we have to do is ask*. This is the first baby step we have to initiate on our own.

The second instruction in this passage states that we must "ask in faith without any doubting." To be honest, this can be hard to do. Sometimes, when it is unclear whether our requests accord with God's will or simply our own, it can be difficult to ask in faith without doubting. Why? Because we aren't sure if what we are asking is God's will. But it shouldn't require a lot of faith to ask God for wisdom. We already know that *it is His will for us to have wisdom*, so there should be no doubting from the get-go that we are "asking according to His will." The Scripture tells us in advance that *He will give us wisdom,* and that *He will give it generously,* without rebuke or criticism.

To be able to confidently ask in faith without doubting requires only two things. First, a request must be generated. Second, we need strong confidence in the One in whom *we are placing our faith*. I'm sure you have friends and acquaintances whom you have no doubt could and would deliver if you asked them to do something. You know them and can trust them to handle your request. You wouldn't leave your children in the care of your auto mechanic while you went to work; likewise, it wouldn't be wise to expect your local butcher to be able to file your taxes. We call on friends or engage the services of others because of their expertise, their ability to deliver, and their availability to assist.

So when it comes to placing faith in matters of the heart or in our spiritual well-being, it is wise to seek and trust God, who is both an expert in handling such affairs, and is always available.

Legacies of Valor is all about obtaining a deeper understanding of biblical characters, both their most noble traits and their less notable character flaws. This book is intended to help us conduct a self-awareness expedition into *who we are in Christ*. To do this, we must examine and understand what God has to say about us, how He sees us, and what we need to know about Him. Over the next few chapters we are going to look more closely at what character is. Where does it come from? Why do we need it? How do we get it?

Character defines who we are, what we value in life, and how we prioritize and manage our affairs. I realize that not everyone experienced the same upbringing as I did; I was raised in the south, brought up in a Christian home by two God-loving parents. We'll need to step out of ourselves for a moment to establish a baseline for understanding how to define good character. Maybe you were raised by a single parent, or on the streets with little to no parental influences in your life. Maybe those who helped you establish a firm footing in life and an understanding of right and wrong had little wisdom to offer you because they were themselves abused as children, or victim to addictions beyond their personal control. We all come from different walks of life, different cultures, and different experiences. Let's take a closer look at God's attributes in order to establish our baseline. In the next chapter we will examine how our individual characters are established, shaped, refined, and polished.

God is best defined and understood in terms of attributes. You could write multiple novels about the attributes of God, or study the Bible over and over, year after year, for a lifetime, and still you would not be able to comprehend all that He is. That said, let's limit our discussion to a handful of manageable attributes of God that confirm and assure us that He is the only one with whom we can entrust our deepest fears and concerns.

God is all-powerful. In the beginning God alone created the heavens and the earth. God alone spoke light into existence when the earth was void and dark. In a word, an expanse between the waters and land was created. And the expanse above the waters and land He called heaven. At His command, the earth sprouted vegetation, plants, seedlings producing fruit; living creators beneath the seas; and birds to roam the skies. Then cattle and creeping things to roam the earth, and from the dust of the ground, He created man. "Impossible" is not in God's vocabulary. He created all things and sustains all things. Who, if not God, could do such things?

> The Everlasting God, the Lord, the Creator of the ends of the earth does not become weary or tired. His understanding is inscrutable. He gives strength to the weary, and to him who lacks might He increases power.
>
> —ISAIAH 40:28-29

> Whatever the Lord pleases, He does, in heaven and in earth, in the seas and in all depths.
>
> —PSALM 135:6

> Great is our Lord, and abundant in strength; His understanding is infinite.
>
> —PSALM 147:5

If we believe and accept these truths about God, then it should be a no-brainer for us to turn to Him as the ultimate mentor and provider when we grow weary from trying to carry the burdens of life by ourselves, or when we need strength to carry on, or when we need deeper insights into handling life's curveballs.

God is all-knowing. His understanding is infinite. As the Creator of our universe and everything within it and beyond it, only God knows how the dawn rolls into place and where to hide the sun when dusk gives way to twinkling stars. Only He commands the winds and calms the seas. Consider the beautiful detail of the butterfly's wings. Who but God can change the colors of the chameleon to protect it from predators? Consider the array of life and beauty beneath the seas, the color of Caribbean waters.

Who but God has a color palette so deep and rich? Consider the majesty of mountain ranges, far and wide. Who, if not God, places life and breath into the embryo, defines the growth, the nature, and character of every living thing?

> Have you ever in your life commanded the morning, and caused the dawn to know its place. Have you understood the expanse of the earth? Tell Me, if you know all this.
> —Job 38:12, 18

God is everywhere and God is eternal. God is not confined to any particular point in time; past, present and future. Nor is He confined to any part of the universe, but is present at every moment in time, at any point in space, and despite the surround-sound noise of life, He hears our every prayer.

> I am the Alpha and the Omega," says the Lord God, "who is and who was and who is to come, the Almighty.
> —Revelation 1:8

> We know that God does not hear sinners; but *if anyone is God-fearing*, and does His will, *He hears them*.
> —John 9:31

God is holy and perfectly righteous in all His ways. God is loving and kind. He is near to all who call upon Him and a rewarder of those who diligently seek Him.

> The Lord is righteous in all His ways, and kind in all His deeds. The Lord is near to all who call upon Him, to all who call upon Him in truth.
> —Psalms 145:17-18

> Let us love one another, for love is from God; and everyone
> who loves is born of God and knows God. The one who
> does not love does not know God, for God is love.
> —1 JOHN 4:7-8

None of us could begin to boast of speaking things into place, as described above. *But God has placed attributes of His nature within our grasp.* We can be imitators of Him and freely share love with others, both those whom we find easy to cherish and those who persecute us at every turn. It may not be easy to love this way, but it can be practiced. We can call out to the Lord and be near Him if we call upon Him in truth. We can share His passions and compassions with those around us who are struggling, and speak light and hope in the dark crevices of their heavy hearts. We can share with all those who will listen that *God is everywhere*; He is available to hear their cries anytime, anywhere.

While we may not be able to speak colorful hues of hope into tomorrow's rainbow, we can speak hope, faith, and encouragement into the lives of those whose storm has yet to pass. And when we grow tired and weary, beat down and spent, we know that we can ask God for renewed strength; when we have a lack, He will increase our power.

Like God, we can be generous to all men, without reproach. Whenever possible, we can financially assist those who are out of work or struggling in this area. We can generously give encouragement and share the knowledge we have gained in studying the Word to those who have not yet heard it or who have simply lost their way. We can do these things and many more, all without judging, rebuking, or criticizing those around us.

> Do nothing from selfishness or empty conceit, but with
> humility of mind let each of you regard one another as more
> important than himself; do not merely look out for your
> own personal interests, but also for the interests of others.
> —PHILIPPIANS 2:3

SIGNIFICANT OBSERVATIONS:

1. God gives wisdom to all, generously and without reproach.
2. All we have to do is ask in faith, without doubt.
3. Asking for wisdom is easy because it is in accordance with His will.
4. Character defines who we are and what we value.
5. God is powerful and always in control.
6. God knows everything about you, your needs, and desires.
7. God is everywhere and always with you.
8. You can see God in all things that produce kindness, compassion, and love.
9. Being attentive to the needs of others pleases God.

STORM WATCH:
ADVERSITY DEFINES CHARACTER

Consider it all joy, my brethren, when you encounter various trials, knowing that the testing of your faith produces endurance.

—JAMES 1:2-3

Before our parents even considered having children, God was at work developing, testing, polishing, and refining their characters. Our parents' parents, and their parents' parents all, were blessed at birth by God for His good work. Regardless of where they lived, what they did for a living, or what church, if any, they attended, God was showing them His will and His way through those they worked with and encountered throughout the day.

Life and its struggles can be hard, even with today's comforts of indoor plumbing, instant electricity, and pre-stocked and shelf-ready food products on nearly every corner of America. Today we enjoy global reach and access to culture and family via the Internet. Cellular applications and 24-7 connectivity have forever changed our definition of social media and exchange. The old bricks-and-mortar infrastructure, hospitals, and emergency responders are within minutes of most our homes. This was not the case for some of our parents or for nearly all of our grandparents. Going even further back, folks not only had to forage for their own food, they had to invent and forge their own tools to work the land. Now that was a simpler life. Or was it?

While many yearn for simpler times (my wife and I certainly do), life back in the day was hard and taxing, and fraught with danger, struggle, and adversity. There was no shortage of ways to test one's resolve. Opportunities to refine one's character abounded.

To give birth to a child, let alone two children, biting down on an oak branch, back against a tree, is something difficult for me to imagine, on multiple levels. But the resolve and character also birthed through these life experiences are what this chapter is all about.

Simply stated, adversity and hardship define our characters more than any other form of learning. It doesn't matter how much teaching or how many words of wisdom your parents shared with you growing up, nor how many times your parole officer tried to warn you. When you ignore the counsel of the wise and step out in disobedience against the current, given time and opportunity, adversity and hardship will begin to affect you whether you like it or not.

> When pride comes, then comes dishonor, but with the humble is wisdom. The integrity of the upright will guide them . . .
>
> —PROVERBS 11:2-3

The younger, more affluent generation grew up enjoying the luxuries and conveniences described above. Many of them have never even seen a farm much less worked one. Our society has changed a great deal since the days of Christ and the apostles. It's important to keep that in mind when we read Scriptures and search text that is nearly 2,200 years old for understanding and application. What is most amazing to me is that these stories of lives lived and lessons learned, recorded so long ago, were specifically written and harshly on-point for the folks of that time, yet they are still relevant for us today.

By now we know that God seeds character, as we are all made in His image. We know that He has equipped each of us with different talents, gifts, and callings, and also has provided us with the same spirit of discernment to help us on our journeys. Our guide maps are identical; we reference the Bible for wisdom, discernment, and direction. It's the individual decisions and paths we take that determine if our journeys will be mountainous and challenging, or if traveling through meadows is more to our liking.

Either path, all paths, given time will produce opportunities that will challenge us and test our resolve. Because God wants us to continue to grow and learn until we have found Him, know Him and learn to abide in Him.

> O Lord, who may abide in Thy tent? He who walks with integrity, and works righteousness, and speaks truth in his heart.
> —PSALMS 15:1-2

So where do these opportunities for character building come from? They come from everyday life. Many happen through no fault of our own; we weren't disobedient, there were no open doors for Satan to sneak through, there was no sin at play. Sometimes, it simply rains on the just as well as the unjust. For whatever reason, one day you'll wake up ready to take on the day, but without warning, you will find drama, hardship, and adversity standing in your kitchen. When you went to bed, the skies were clear and bright. But somewhere in between pouring your first cup of coffee and answering the phone call that will test your resolve before your coffee even turns cold, storm clouds rolled in to darken your day.

When these storms of life roll in, they will either define you or consume you. Obviously, the less threatening or taxing the storm, the less the traits of your character will change. For example, your temperament and disposition might fluctuate dramatically if you were fired from your job without cause or reason and escorted out of the building. Your mind would flood with questions and fears. What will you tell your wife? How will you tell the kids? How will you pay the mortgage next month?

The longer this battle rages on, the more important it will be to trust in God, to have faith, and to stand firm.

On the other hand, your temperament may change little if your storm is nothing more serious than your teenage daughter getting into a mild fender-bender in your car. Sure, your own boyish charm or ladylike beauty might temporarily leave you while you restate to your daughter why she was grounded and why she shouldn't have been in the car in the first place. But there's no need to kick the car while you are having this chat with your lovely daughter. The car already has plenty of things in need of repair.

There are character traits that shouldn't change, regardless of the environment or circumstance we find ourselves in: moral fiber, integrity, and good reputation. These last two are the traits that I want us to think about as we examine character more closely. Your integrity and reputation should hold true no matter what comes your way.

Have you ever noticed that the most compelling, engaging, and inspiring stories or testimonies tend to have a lot of drama, conflict, and adversity in them? In the movies, if a character doesn't emerge stronger, victorious over whatever challenge he was facing, the story fails to inspire us.

In job interviews and in our resumes, what showcases our characters best are the challenges we faced, the problems we solved, the obstacles we overcame, and the improvements we made. These are the things of substance that interviewers find most compelling. What we did and how we handled it defines our added value; that resonates with interviewers.

So how does character mature? It is formed, fired, and molded by the traits and attributes we call into action, that are summoned into action by the grace of God: humility, forgiveness, faith, patience, perseverance, and vigilance.

Let's take a look at what God has to say about good character, integrity, and establishing a reputation worthy of honor, and worthy of emulating.

> He who walks in integrity walks securely, but he who perverts his ways will be found out.
> —PROVERBS 10:9

> Whatever is true, whatever is honorable, whatever is right, whatever is pure, whatever is lovely, whatever is of good repute, if there is any excellence and if anything worthy of praise, let your mind dwell on these things.
> —PHILIPPIANS 4:8

> A righteous man who walks in his integrity: how blessed are his sons after him.
> —PROVERBS 20:7

> It is by his deeds that a lad distinguishes himself, if his conduct is pure and right.
> —PROVERBS 20:11

> A good name is to be more desired than great riches. Favor is better than silver and gold.
> —PROVERBS 22:1

In the verse above we are advised that a good name (reputation) is to be more desired (sought after) than fame or fortune. Favor is better than either silver or gold. Secular favor means to have approval or to be preferred. It could manifest itself as a work promotion; there may be someone who is more qualified on paper, but because the boss sees something greater in you, approval is granted in your favor.

> He who diligently seeks good, seeks favor, but he who searches after evil, it will come to him.
> —PROVERBS 11:27

> A good man will obtain favor from the Lord, but He will condemn a man who devises evil.
> —PROVERBS 12:2

Why do we even need favor? We need it to endure future tough times and to showcase God's Grace to those watching us. A good name, strong reputation, our gifts and talents, make a way for us and brings us before great men. In today's vernacular: new clients; promotions; advancement and discovery of talent.

> "A man's gift makes room for him, and brings him before great men."
> —PROVERBS 18:16

> Anxiety in the heart of a man weighs it down, but a good word makes it glad. The righteous is a guide to his neighbor . . .
> —PROVERBS 12:25-26

> The wise in heart will be called discerning [prudent], and sweetness of speech increases persuasiveness.
> —PROVERBS 16:21

If you are in one of the fields of communications, marketing, or sales, you'll want to read the verse above again and again. Here's the formula: seek wisdom and find discernment. Season in a big lump of understanding and insight with a pinch of kindness and sweet words, and your persuasiveness increases. More wins, more sales, greater success.

> The backslider in heart will have his fill of his own ways, but a good man will be satisfied with his. The naïve believe everything, but the prudent man considers his steps. A wise man is cautious and turns away from evil.
> —PROVERBS 14:14-16

SIGNIFICANT OBSERVATIONS:

1. When you encounter trials, consider them to be joy.
2. Trials and tribulations build faith.
3. Faith generates endurance.
4. Storms will either define you or consume you. Chose the former.
5. He who walks with integrity walks securely.
6. Favor is of more value than gold or silver.
7. The wise will be called discerning.

PAYING IT FORWARD:
STRENGTHENING THE CHARACTER
OF OTHERS

Do nothing from selfishness or empty conceit, but with humility of mind let each of you regard one another as more important than himself; do not merely look out for your own personal interests, but also for the interests of others.

—PHILIPPIANS 2:3

God gives generously and without reproach to all men, and He knows that we strive to be good imitators, messengers, and followers of Christ. It should be a goal of ours to demonstrate His love, compassion, and understanding to those around us.

Besides the fact that the Bible strongly suggests we look after the interests of others instead of becoming consumed by our own, there are many benefits to taking the time and energy to pay good deeds forward. For those unfamiliar with this concept, the basic idea is that sometimes it's not possible to pay back someone who has done good deeds for us, so instead we should pay it forward by doing a good deed for another person. For example, someone holds the door open for you because your hands are full. You thank him, but you'd like to do more to return the favor. You can't follow him around all day waiting for him to need a door held open, so instead you simply share your good deed with a different person in need, paying it forward.

> The generous man will be prosperous, and he who waters
> will himself be watered.
> —PROVERBS 11:25

When it comes to sharing Christian beliefs with other people, especially strangers, many Christians choose to stay silent at the workplace to avoid confrontation or harassment. They prefer to save their vigilant enthusiasm for God for Sundays, or maybe for the confines of their homes.

My objective here is not to imply that we should all butch-up and start preaching and witnessing to everyone we meet, although the world would be a better place if we all did just that. But not all of us were blessed or anointed with the gifts of preaching, teaching, prophesying, or exhorting. Some of us have different gifts to do with helping, mercy, giving, intercession, or administration. Regardless of our own unique spiritual gift, we can all find simple ways to share God's love through a smile or a kind gesture.

To make these opportunities easier to spot throughout the day, we should take steps to strengthen our own characters, so that that character, God's character, becomes second nature, automatic. When we encounter a pay it forward moment, we probably won't even notice that our light has gone forth into the night and made a difference in someone else's life.

> Whatever is true, whatever is honorable, whatever is right,
> whatever is pure, whatever is lovely, whatever is of good
> repute, if there is any excellence and if anything worthy
> of praise, let your mind dwell on these things.
> —PHILIPPIANS 4:8

Very early in our marriage, my wife, Linda, and I had just moved to Hermosa Beach, California, after graduating from college. After settling into our humble little two-bedroom apartment just blocks away from the beach, we joined a Baptist community church in Manhattan Beach, California, primarily because they had an enormous Sunday school class of young married couples. It was called the Goldband class. The leader of the class was a guy by the name of Dennis. He and his wife, Karen, and all the other couples, were the nicest bunch of folks you'd ever want to meet. Since we were the new kids, Dennis and Karen took us under their wing and made sure we felt right at home and connected. This class was huge, so they formed smaller Bible study groups that took place at members' homes during the week. Even though Dennis and Karen's group technically had no vacancies at the time, they still made room for us and invited us to participate in their group.

As I recall, Dennis had strongly considered attending seminary school, but after much debate, opted to pursue law. I know what you must be thinking—but this aspiring attorney knew his Bible and also had a bent for Bible history, so attending his classes and preparing for his Bible study was a deep, thorough process that always offered multiple points of view.

During this season, I was the victim of a corporate downsizing that left me unemployed in a state where we had no family nearby to offer support; our only friends were those at church. This all took place during the early eighties, when unemployment hit 7.5 percent and our economy was suffering from the worst recession in forty years. This period of unemployment, which lasted over a year, was not only my first-ever such experience, it would not be my last bout of unemployment. The mental battle that rages in your mind when you can't even buy a job, any job, brings you to your knees. It was there, under a cloud of humility and self-worthlessness that I started to re-examine my priorities in life. While my wife was at work, I played B. J. Thomas's version of "In the Garden" over and over, broken and crying, reading my Bible through the tears. Back in those days, you typed up your resume and cover letters on a typewriter, and if you were lucky, you had an electric self-correcting typewriter, as we did. After typing your resume, cover letter, and envelope, you'd seal the envelope, affix the stamp, and drop it off at the post office. Then you would wait. No email technology of mass communication with the press of a button. No LinkedIn or Facebook accounts. No cell phones. Your social network was limited to people you had actually met in life or been introduced to by friends and family connections. Did I mention the waiting part? Nothing was instant about messaging back then.

I suppose I made an announcement or told someone that after over a year of searching for work, Linda and I had decided to pack it in and move back to the Midwest in search of new opportunities. To be honest, it's all very foggy to me, even today, after trying to refresh my memory for the details of this story for your edification. On the day we were to move, I parked the U-Haul truck out front, but we were far from ready to clear out our apartment. We were sitting on the couch, wondering how the two of us were going to move all our stuff into the truck (my wife is only five foot two and I can't lift much due to an injury I suffered in college), a knock came at the door.

It was Dennis. In his hands he held a pair of work gloves. I'll never forget that day, when God showed up to help us move, when no one else could help, or was aware that today was our moving day. Over the years we lost touch with Dennis and Karen, and for all I know they may still be leading the Goldband class. While I have no idea where they live or what they are up to, I have not forgotten the memory of this cherished moment. So Dennis, if you happen to stumble upon this book, thank you for taking the time to serve God during our time of need. I have paid your kindness forward numerous times.

> Anxiety in the heart of a man weighs it down, but a good word makes it glad. The righteous is a guide to his neighbor . . .
>
> —Proverbs 12:25-26

Fast-forward nineteen years to 2003. My daughters were now seventeen and thirteen. Throughout the nineties, I had held jobs in the high-tech Internet industry as director of marketing communications and business development for two of the largest professional consulting companies at the time. But post-911, everything had changed. The clients we were selling to were no longer interested. We found it difficult to ask folks to get on planes to travel to client work sites. Again, I found myself on the receiving end of a severance package. At first, it was a blessing in disguise. I was looking forward to spending more time with my girls. Traveling to the west coast every week for work wouldn't be necessary anymore, and I had managed to sock away some savings over the years. I refreshed my resume and posted it on CareerBuilder.com, along with a few other sites, dusted off my golf clubs and went to work on my handicap. Little did I know then that the Internet was about to crash and that my arrival to this party was a late one. For the last couple of years, I had enjoyed a mid-six-figure income at a very reputable consulting company. I had little doubt that it wouldn't be long before the phone started ringing with bigger offers from recruiters looking for my talents. Ticktock, ticktock.

Several months into this dry season of unemployment, Enron was exposed; Arthur Andersen fell, along with many other big names in the telecommunications Internet industries, where I played. By this time, by the grace of God, I had already decided to tighten the belt by downsizing our home. I had also unloaded our expensive toys several years in advance of the real estate market collapse. But I was still out of work and now a bit more anxious for interview requests to begin. Twelve months in, my clubs re-claimed their dusty covers, sitting in the garage unused, and I spent hours in my home office refreshing my resume, searching sites, and completing online job applications.

> When pride comes, then comes dishonor, but with the humble is wisdom. The integrity of the upright will guide them . . .
>
> —Proverbs 11:2-3

This time around, I was more seasoned; I had more online tools to help me network, more qualifications to boast about, and I was more able financially to weather this second bout of unemployment. More importantly though, I was attending a strong, Bible-based community church in Littleton, Colorado, and I was a very active Band of Brothers member. At the time, our Band of Brothers group of men, aged seventeen to over sixty, met every Tuesday morning at 6:30 a.m. for coffee, a brief devotional, testimonies, and support time. The group had swelled in numbers to over eighty guys showing up every Tuesday, rain or shine. If you needed encouragement, you couldn't afford to miss a session. If everything was just fine in your world, you didn't want to miss another guy's testimony. It was a powerful hour-and-a-half in the presence of God and your fellow brothers. Some twelve years hence, these brothers are still meeting.

Around my thirteenth month of unemployment, I received a book by Joel Osteen that my father had just finished reading. It sat next to my nightstand for a month or two before I decided to pick it up and start reading about what was wrong with me. A funny thing happened. The first page didn't say that anything was wrong with me. Even by the end of the third chapter there still hadn't been a major condemnation with my name on it. Nope, this book was uplifting, encouraging, motivating, and inspiring me to rise up and begin believing what God had been saying about me the whole time: *I am an Overcomer*! I got so inspired by this read that I had to share it with my Band of Brothers. After talking it over with Linda, because we really didn't have an extra dime to spend, we agreed that this would be good seed and an opportunity for God to bless not just us, but the Brothers as well. So we went to the Christian bookstore and bought thirty-four copies of Joel's book on my credit card, almost completely maxing it out. That following Tuesday, I handed out all thirty-four copies of the book and encouraged the Brothers to read it, and once they were done, to pass the copies on to other Brothers to read. This all happened before I became familiar with the popular phrase, pay it forward. I knew that if I merely told them about this neat book, they might never venture out to the store to buy it, so I removed that obstacle straight away.

While I had and continue to have wonderful tight relationships with many of the Brothers in this group, and have enjoyed a special moment with each one either through prayer, song, or testimony, there is one particular conversation I had with a Brother that I'll never forget as long as I live.

My bout with unemployment was now in its eighteenth month and my prospects were bleak. I had had hundreds of interviews, by phone and face-to-face. I had even been flown across the country for some of these interviews, but you still couldn't buy a job in the telecommunications business. Hundreds of thousands of seasoned Internet sales guys were clamoring for the same limited number of jobs. And just for the record, I was doing more than just waiting for the right job. I had secured my Colorado Real Estate and Brokers license, had sold a house or two and was doing some odd job consulting on the side.

This particular Tuesday morning, I really didn't want to crawl out of bed to talk to anyone about anything. I had grown rather frustrated and to be honest, was ticked off a bit that God had abandoned me. I was both mad and depressed. By now, surely even our kids were beginning to think their dad was crazy to keep praying to a God who couldn't even provide a job. All the neighbor's dads had jobs. To be honest, I don't know what was going through their minds during this time. Maybe they were so wrapped up with junior high and high school that thoughts about my troubles were confined to my head alone. And as those who have suffered being out of work for a long duration of time know all too well, the battle between hope and suicidal depression rages day and night in the dark recesses of our minds. A place our enemy loves to mess around in.

I thank God to this day for prodding me out of bed and into the shower, for getting me to the conversation awaiting me that Tuesday morning with a Brother named Steve. I hadn't scheduled a special meeting with

Steve that day, but God had. It was just a normal Tuesday morning for the Band of Brothers, but when Steve saw me drag myself in, he knew something was terribly wrong. Normally, I am a very enthusiastic and upbeat guy, Mr. Happy. Not today. Instead of joining the group, we grabbed a cup of coffee and took a table in the fellowship area. It didn't take long for me to break down. Sobbing like a little baby and wiping my eyes and nose on my sleeve, I told him about how I was afraid, scared to death, that my kids might turn away from God if things didn't change soon. You see, in my mind, everything my wife and I had taught our children over the years was at risk. The fear was enormous in my mind that after hearing Linda and I pray for interviews and favor during our dinner prayers, they might decide that this God guy was not coming through. It was then that Steve looked me in the eyes and said, "Dave, maybe God wants to teach your kids what faith looks like." I responded, "Then sign me up for another tour of duty!" Then it hit me. If Steve was right, and my kids could actually witness FAITH in action and learn from it, I would happily serve another tour. All of a sudden, there was nothing more important in life than to make sure my trial yielded them a faith benefit.

> A man has joy in an apt answer, and how delightful is a timely word.
>
> —PROVERBS 15:23

The battle raged on for another six months before I was gainfully employed again, but my faith study soared, and when I finally managed to stand up after coming out of my dark and dingy foxhole and heading back into the fray of battle, I stood upright and held my position.

> You will pray to Him, and He will hear you; and you will pay your vows. You will also decree a thing, and it will be established for you; and light will shine on your ways.
>
> —JOB 22:27-28

Friends, I'm sure you, too, have stories you can recall of a friend, sister, neighbor, or coworker helping you through a very tough time. Now it's our turn to pay it forward by seeking out someone who needs an encouraging word, or some cash to get by, or maybe just a free hot meal. If you know someone out of work, give him or her a copy of this book. It just might be the word of encouragement they need.

These are some tough and dark times for millions of Americans. Unemployment is nearing an all-time high and our budget deficit is north of 15 trillion dollars. Family homes are being foreclosed by the thousands. Congressional approval ratings are in the single digits and confidence in our leaders is at an all-time low. It's easy for us to remain in our personal foxholes and not come out to help those even worse off than we are—but we must.

Each of us can do something to share hope with others. A smile and an encouraging word don't cost a cent, but their value is priceless. It's time we became more vigilant and paid attention to those around us. Stay alert. Watch and be attentive. Listen and observe those around you. Learn to sense their need and ask God how you can help them, beyond prayer.

> The wise in heart will be called discerning [prudent], and sweetness of speech increases persuasiveness.
> —PROVERBS 16:21

We've all heard the saying, "You're an angel"; or, "It was like an angel was watching over me." Maybe we *are* angels—at least the sensitive folks like us, who keep an ear open and their eyes peeled for an opportunity to at least act like an angel and serve where they can.

> A faithful man will abound with blessings . . .
> —PROVERBS 28:20

My dearest friendship dates all the way back to early high school; that's over forty years of friendship with Mack. He is my Jonathan in the David and Jonathan story. Mack and I met in junior high school, attended high school together and went on to attend the same college. We joined the same fraternity, and were roommates for the first year. Then we both decided that it would be good to expand our horizons and experience rooming with other brothers within the house, not because we had grown tired of each other, but because we were both confident in the strength of our relationship. Neither of us was threatened or worried that our relationship would suffer if we ventured out to meet new brothers and make new friends. In doing this, we were both afforded the opportunity to hear different perspectives, and to meet guys who had different ambitions and likes, some parallel to ours and some not. Mack, who in high school was not interested in class politics or social leadership activities, found through a few fraternity brothers that he now had the leadership and social skills that had eluded him in high school. He soared in these new relationships and responsibilities and grew more social and outgoing, and discovered talents that he hadn't realized he had.

Over the course of the next thirty-something years, we stayed in touch and remained very close despite the fact that for many of these years, we didn't live in the same state. While there are many things that come into play in defining and establishing strong relationships and friendships, I find that two things are paramount: trust and true appreciation for each other. What I find most interesting about my friendship with Mack is that while we are both competitive, opinionated, and determined guys, we've never felt compelled to compete with one other. We have each always truly appreciated and been genuinely happy for the other's accomplishments and successes. There has never been resentment or jealousy. In fact, one of Mack's attributes that I admire most is his ability to encourage first, and critique second. No matter what is going on in my life, whatever the setback or frustration I share with him, he always first reminds me of my strengths *before* helping me explore or dissect the situation at hand. I'm sure there have been plenty of times when he could have said, "Dave, you fully deserve this. What did you think was going to happen?" And yet he has never approached our discussions with that tone.

> The heart of the wise teaches his mouth, and adds persuasiveness to his lips
>
> —PROVERBS 16:23

SIGNIFICANT OBSERVATIONS:

1. We are in God's will if we regard others more highly than ourselves.
2. He who helps (refreshes) another will himself be blessed.
3. Be alert and vigilant for opportunities to be a blessing in the lives of others.
4. Pay it forward, generously and without reproach.
5. Your acts of kindness do not go unnoticed.

ASSURANCE OF GUIDANCE

Trust in the Lord with all your heart and lean not on your own understanding; in all your ways acknowledge Him and He will make your paths straight.

—Proverbs 3:5-6

Before taking a trip, it's important that we be prepared. For most of us, that means having some idea of where we are going and how we expect to get there, and hopefully, having some guidance and assurance that the path we have chosen is wise.

The passage above gives us three statements and one promise. Statement number one: Trust in the Lord with all your heart. Statement two: Lean not on your own understanding. Statement three: In all your ways acknowledge Him. And finally, the big promise or reward for striving to honor the first three statements: He will make your paths straight.

To me, this sounds like a pretty good deal. I don't know about you, but I find life more enjoyable when all areas of my life are firing on all cylinders like a well-oiled machine. Breakdowns are inconvenient. Hasty decisions that take me off course can prove frustrating. Not listening to wise counsel, or overriding navigational directions could lead to dead ends meaning; I'd have to retrace my route back to start over again.

To the true roads-less-traveled enthusiasts, adventurers, and 4x4 off-roaders out there: being an outdoor enthusiast of Northern Colorado, I do enjoy leaving the safety of the pavement to explore old abandoned mining towns, splashing through streams in my Jeep Wrangler. Off-trail excursions that dare to push the limits of our vehicles and the resolve of those behind the wheel can be quite enjoyable. But I learned a few very important lessons one day, after surviving a testy afternoon on the Crystal Loop, a twenty-six-mile loop of everything one could want in an off-road experience. It would have been nice to have had a map with me, but more importantly, it would have been even better to have had someone with me who had actually been there and done that before. With Linda in the front seat and both my young daughters in the rear, we set off one morning for a fun day in the sun in search of ghost towns just outside of Buena Vista, Colorado.

On this particular day, with complete trust in the Lord and the assurance that my stock jeep was more than capable of handling all that my nerves could tolerate, I made the mistake of discounting statement two above. I made the mistake of leaning on my own understanding. You see, it was my understanding that I would not perform any risky maneuvers or take any side paths that might put my family at risk or my vehicle in jeopardy. The jeep was not outfitted with any gear that would help us if we should find ourselves in a pickle: no winch, no ropes, no shovel. We had only a backpack containing a first aid kit, a few bottles of water, some snacks, and our favorite Julie Andrews CD to confirm through the stereo that "the hills were alive." I know it sounds corny, but remember, I have girls. At least it wasn't a Disney tune.

Several hours into this trail, I had mastered the third statement in our verse above. With every boulder we put behind us, and every stream we forded, I was acknowledging God in all my ways. "Oh thank you, Jesus, the stream wasn't too deep." "Thank you, Lord, for not flooding the jeep." "Thank you, Jesus, I can see where we need to be. The trail is on that other range." I praise God to this day that my knee didn't pop out of joint (as it does on occasion without warning) during one forty-five-degree uphill ascent through a creek runoff pitch that offered no room for the weak of heart to turn around. As for those who might have tried, you could see how they finished up if you looked over the left side and down the seventy-five-foot drop-off. There were at least ten rusted out old jeeps that apparently didn't make it up this particular pitch. I made sure that no one in the car knew just how scared I really was until we saw pavement again, nearly four hours later. But I'm not kidding; I was thanking God so much during this adventure that my kids told me to chill out and quit acting like a dork. Little did they know just how dorky I felt inside, knowing too late that I shouldn't have put us all in this position in the first place. God did come through, and eventually we popped out of the trees and onto pavement that was straight as an arrow. No one was happier about that than yours truly.

With that little side story told, let's get back to understanding the passage from a spiritual point of view. The promise of having our paths "made straight" refers to an *assurance granted to us* that if we trust in Him, His word, His guidance, His Spirit, and His promises, our efforts will not be in vain; whatever we set our hearts, minds, and hands to accomplish will be done, according to His timing and His way, not ours.

But before we jump right to the benefits of this promise, let's examine the three steps or statements that must first occur before we reap the rewards.

First, we are to trust in the Lord with all our heart. This seems to me a fair enough request. We all have to trust or believe in something, and it only makes sense to me that we trust in the one thing that will never let us down: Christ. I'll be the first to admit that while I think I have all the answers most of the time, deep down I realize just how little I know in the grand scheme of things. While I've enjoyed a great deal of success in the business world over the past thirty-something years, and was even recognized as one of the "Top Ten Internet-savvy professionals" in the mid-nineties by one of the top five consulting companies, in hindsight, I can say that I didn't know squat. Sure, I had a pretty solid understanding of marketing strategies and positioning techniques to communicate our services in such a way that folks wanted to buy our stuff, but I didn't know beans about how to program computers or how to write code. There were younger and brighter folks who knew everything we needed to deliver to our clients.

I trusted kids who weren't old enough to shave to deliver website functionality and e-Commerce features that had never been written or coded before. Remember, this was in the early to mid-nineties, during the Internet surge, before she popped before our eyes, and years ahead of having mobile apps on every device known to man. Back in those days, we trusted engineers to build servers and define communications protocols between machines, and programmers to write scripts and code in machine language, to deliver what we promised our clients.

I'm sure from your own life experiences, you, too, can easily name things and people you placed your trust in to accomplish your job or your daily tasks. The whole concept of trusting in something is an easy step, at least on the surface, that most of us can accept.

Not leaning on our own understanding—that one might be a bit more challenging. Personally, after a few fits and starts (a nice way of describing years of stubbornness and impatience), I learned that my meddling in order to force predictable outcomes wasn't always the best thing to do; more often than not, it wasn't even close to what God had in mind. So if we agree that leaning on our own understanding may be a flawed action, and we know that leaning on others doesn't always turn out as expected, we can see that maybe it would be wise to test our theories and understanding of what God has to say. This can be done easily through a thing called prayer, but it does require an understanding of whom God is, how He operates, and what His promises are.

For most of my adult life, I have enjoyed acknowledging Him in all my ways. I find it rather easy to quickly acknowledge Him when things go my way, but to be completely honest, I find it difficult to defer to the standard unanswered prayer response, "It must not have been God's will," when things don't work out the way I thought or expected them to. After all, I thought I was in His will and doing the right thing, right up until things went south. Fortunately, if we learn to quickly and diligently reflect back on what we might have done differently, we can seriously consider, with an open mind, whether there was something we missed—or is this just a setback? Or, are we completely outside of God's will? And if so, where did we go wrong? If we ask these questions early and often, we might not have to travel too far back and risk missing God's prosperity when it arrives.

> Cursed is the man who trusts in mankind and makes flesh his strength, whose heart turns away from the Lord. For he will be like a bush in the desert, and will not see when prosperity comes . . .
>
> —JEREMIAH 17:5-6

By now, it should be clear that a life independent from God is senseless. But God works according to His own timetable, not ours. He does not hurry, nor does He delay.

> The Lord is not slow about His promise, as some count slowness, but is patient toward you, not wishing for any to perish but for all to come to repentance.
>
> —2 PETER 3:9

The passage above, within scriptural context, is referring to our repentance and salvation. But it can easily be applicable to our current discussion if we replace the word "repentance" with the phrase "the full knowledge of God." For it is His will that we all learn to trust in Him, lean on Him, and acknowledge Him, knowing full well that if we aspire to these things, we will indeed obtain the full knowledge of God.

> If any man is willing to do His will, he shall know of the teaching, whether it is of God, or whether I speak from Myself. He who speaks from himself seeks his own glory;

but He who is seeking the glory of the one who sent Him,
He is true, and there is no unrighteousness in Him.

—John 7:17-18

The key to knowing the will of God is our willingness to seek it. He has promised that when we ask for things that are in accordance with His will, He will give us what we ask for.

Trust in the Lord, and do good: Dwell in the land and cultivate faithfulness. Delight yourself in the Lord; And He will give you the desires of your heart. Commit your way to the Lord, Trust also in Him, and He will do it.

—Psalms 37:3-5

Trusting in God is scriptural, and obviously in accordance with His will, so in this act alone, we can have confidence that we are in good standing with the Lord when we approach Him in prayer. Those who are truly striving to do good by their fellow men, those who are dwelling in the land and are committed to cultivating faithfulness in those who cross our paths, are obviously in His will. Therefore, we should delight ourselves in the Lord. This simply means we should be happy and joyful. Why? Because we know He will grant us the desires of our hearts, and because we are praying for things that are also in God's heart.

Now may the God of hope fill you with all joy and peace in believing, that you may abound [have abundance] in hope by the power of the Holy Spirit.

—Romans 15:13

Beloved if our heart does not condemn us, we have confidence before God; and whatever we ask we receive

> from Him, because we keep His commandments and do
> the things that are pleasing in His sight.
>
> —1 John 3:21-22

We must learn to listen to our hearts. I'm not a doctor, nor have I ever played one on TV, but I believe that more often than we realize, our thoughts speak to our spiritual hearts, giving us both advice and instruction. Unfortunately, we don't listen as often as we should. If we learned to be more sensitive to the urgings of our hearts or the rumbling warnings of our guts, to check these feelings against our intentions and motives, to ensure there is no condemnation present, I believe we would experience less doubt and more joy in our decisions.

In the past, when I've experienced significant setbacks, or thought that maybe I was off track and was unsure of the path forward, I've found that it's not a bad idea to pause, check in with my heart, and even go back and review the guide map.

SIGNIFICANT OBSERVATIONS:

1. Assurance and guidance can be found in three statements and one promise.
2. Trust in the Lord with all your heart.
3. Lean not on your own understanding.
4. In everything, acknowledge Him and He will make your path straight.
5. Doing these three things puts us squarely and securely in God's will.
6. Life independent from God is senseless.
7. Knowing God offers assurance and guidance.

OPERATION OF THE KINGDOM
PART 1: KNOW YOUR RESOLVE

For this reason we must pay much closer attention to what we have heard; lest we drift away from it.
—HEBREWS 2:1

I'm sure that somewhere along the way, either early in your childhood or just prior to getting your first job, your parents or grandparents shared this bit of advice with you: "If it's worth doing, it's certainly worth doing right." Maybe at the time it sounded more like, "Hey! Show a little respect around here and finish raking the leaves. Pick up all the little pieces too. Drag the bags to the curb and stack'em neatly. Don't forget to put the rake away either. Hang it up this time, for a change."

I have to be completely honest here and quickly state that the nagging voice I describe above is not a voice from my past or some subconscious narrative from my father. Actually, my dad was and is a very level-headed and pleasant guy. I did have to rake leaves growing up in the hills of Tennessee, and my father probably did tell us to clean up after ourselves, but I was never yelled at or belittled by my parents while I was growing up.

When we find something in life that we are truly passionate about, that we love more than anything, we don't need a lot of encouragement or instruction to remind us to give it our best effort. But doing something that is not your number-one passion feels like a hindrance, a distraction, or a punishment. For example, if you are in your early to mid-twenties and love music and jamming with your band more than anything else, you may find it difficult to get up in time to make your 1:40 p.m. college chemistry midterm. You attend school because it's important (at least that's what they tell you), but right now, it's simply not your passion; making music is. Now, I'm not advocating you drop out of school because you think it's a distraction from your true passion. I'm simply making the point that you will excel and be most happy in the area where your passion lies. You won't need someone to remind you of band practice if you are already passionate and committed to what you are doing. So just to be clear: put the band on hold and finish school. Then, "go tell it on the mountain."

Likewise, if you have decided to seek wisdom, to get understanding and have a deeper, more productive, and fulfilling walk with God, you are going to have to make it a priority of passion and assign it cherished space in your day-planner, schedule, or iPhone. You can't expect to get anything of value from simply squeezing some Bible time or daily devotional reading into your already jam-packed schedule.

Remember, if it's worth doing, it is worth doing right. Sounds simple enough, right? But what happens after the honeymoon is over? You are now four weeks into your mission to visit the gym every day to lose those twenty pounds; now it's mid-February, and getting up in the morning to make that trek to the gym in the cold isn't so pleasant.

So, how do we avoid drifting away, losing interest, or abandoning our resolve?

The apostle Paul in the book of Romans takes on this question by presenting another: How does a man become righteous before God? To understand how the kingdom of God operates, it's important to understand what righteousness is, how to obtain it, and how to avoid drifting away from it.

Before I lose you on the whole righteousness thing, know this: righteousness in its simplest definition simply means, being in "right standing." All too often, when we hear bigger-than-life, lofty, or holier than thou terminology, we get discouraged and think, *I could never live up to that standard.* But the good news is this: as soon as you begin the quest to be in right standing with God, at that very moment, you *are* in right standing with Him. If you've been taught that only priests or ministers can enter the Holy of Holies, you need to start spending more time with the New Testament to learn more about how Christ's death, burial, and resurrection changed our ability to access God directly.

If you are like me, you probably don't feel righteous 24-7, or the moment your feet hit the floor in the morning. Like most revelations in the Bible, and what matters most is not how we feel; it's what we believe and profess. Just because we don't feel like mighty prayer warriors for God one day, it doesn't mean we've lost faith or drifted away from right standing.

How we feel, emotionally speaking, is often highly overrated. Let's say I'm hiking up a trail in the Rockies for hours. Darkness falls and I can no longer see the trail I'm on—that doesn't change the fact that I am still physically on the trail. I might not feel like continuing up when I can't see my route, but I am still on the trail. Similarly, if you've started a walk with Jesus and are seeking ways to improve your right standing in His sight, but you don't feel like you are making progress, or you can't see any change, remember this: you are still on the trail.

It may be helpful to examine what Paul was talking about in Romans 1:16-17, when he equates the gospel of God to the power of God.

> For I am not ashamed of the gospel for it *is* the power of God for salvation to everyone who believes, to the Jew first and also to the Greek. For in it [word of God] the

righteousness of God *is* revealed from faith to faith; as it is written, "but the righteous man shall live by faith."
—ROMANS 1:16-17

You'll notice I emphasized the word "is" to highlight another equal-to equation: the gospel, or Word of God, equals the power of God. It follows, then, that one cannot have the power of God working in one's life without also having the word of God operational in one's life.

Romans 1:17 makes it clear that one cannot be righteous (right-standing with God and one's fellow men) without also having faith working in one's life as well. Whether or not we feel righteous on any given day is irrelevant. What's important is that we continue to walk with faith, knowing that no matter what we may have done years ago or even yesterday that made us feel unworthy or less righteous, in the end we are in right standing with God as long as we continue to believe in Him; He is a forgiver and a healer of those who have gone astray or made a mistake.

Take care, brethren, lest there should be in any one of you an evil, unbelieving heart, in falling away from the living God.
—HEBREWS 3:12

This verse encourages us to take great care and caution *to protect what we allow into our hearts*. It seems to suggest that if we allow our hearts to engage in disbelief (we've all heard the phrase "Don't lose heart"), we run the risk of drifting away from the presence of God, which is where the power resides.

Another way to protect what goes into our hearts or spirit is to take an offensive position. When you are on defense, the play comes to you. As a defensemen you are forced to react as the play unfolds before you. But if you are on the offensive side of the ball, you are in control of the play call and responsible for executing the play to the best of your ability. Spiritually speaking, we can play offense whenever we choose by speaking the Word of God to our own hearts and to those around us.

Speaking the Word of God silently to yourself and reminding yourself of who you are in Christ builds up your spirit, strengthens your mind, and is a way of praising God. Openly sharing the knowledge of God and His words of encouragement as noted in many powerful Scriptures with others can tear down strongholds in their lives and penetrate their defenses in ways you and I can't even begin to imagine. Do you want to be in the ministry without quitting your job and moving to the Congo? Just share uplifting and encouraging words of faith with those you meet and speak with every day. No flu shot required.

The passage from Hebrews goes on to give us some insight into what we can do to keep our hearts from hardening.

> But encourage one another day after day, as long as it is still called "Today," lest any one of you be hardened by the deceitfulness of sin.
>
> —HEBREWS 3:13

If you are a living, breathing, human being like me, you will at some time be wronged or hurt by the words or actions of others, whether it be a family member, a coworker, a boss, or even a fellow believer. When this happens, and believe me, it happens more times than we would like, we are instructed to *encourage* others.

It's not exactly the natural response most folks would have. In situations like this, our natural tendency is to take offense and maybe even lash out against those who have misspoken on our behalf or hurt us in some other way. But there is a price for taking such action.

> And to whom did He swear that they should not enter His rest, but to those who were disobedient.
>
> —HEBREWS 3:18

In this passage, God promises that the disobedient shall have no rest. That's a bad thing. I don't know about you, but I find life can sometimes be a challenge even when everything is going well. The last thing we need is to engage in retaliation, to harbor ill feelings, or to feed thoughts or activities that promise less peace, no rest, and further frustration.

What's that you say? "That's a mouthful of hard work right there!" Yes, it is. Trust me on this one. We are walking this path together; I am far from close to understanding how to live in total forgiveness. But I am at least committed to walking the trail. I've come too far to turn back now.

While the debate rages on amongst scholars and theologians alike as to who actually wrote the book of Hebrews and for whom the book was written, most can agree the pronouns *them, they,* and *those,* in Hebrews refer to the general Christian body of believers who were at risk of apostasy. For a host of reasons, these weary Christians were on the verge of renouncing their faith. They were ready to defect and abandon their loyalty, faith, and belief in God.

Because of their lack of belief, they were unable to enter that place of rest and peace that only comes of knowing Him in a deep and personal way, and, to be more blunt, of sticking with Him through thick and thin, no matter how dark or bleak things appear.

> And so we see that they were not able to enter because of unbelief.
> —HEBREWS 3:19

So what separates today's believing Christians from the brothers and sisters in Christ who opted to abandon their former belief in God?

> For indeed we have had good news preached to us, just as they also; but the word they heard did not profit them, because it was not united by faith in those who heard.
> —HEBREWS 4:2

Apparently, the Word did not profit them because they did not ignite the Word through faith. It's like having great seeds to plant and excellent soil available in which to plant the seeds, but no water to unite the soil with the seed. Our faith and belief are the water that unites and ignites.

Without faith, the Word nets zip, zero, nothing. You can put water in a pot and drop noodles into the water, but until you fire up the burner, nothing is cooking. If you unite the Word of God with faith, then the power of God is released. Consider the woman whose faith, united with Gods power, made her whole.

> And a woman who had a hemorrhage *for twelve years*, and had *endured much* at the hands of many physicians, and had *spent all that she had* and was not helped at all, *but* rather had grown worse, *after hearing about Jesus*, came up in the crowd behind Him, and touched His cloak. For she *thought, If I just touch His garments, I shall get well.*
> —MARK 5:25-28

This story is a classic lesson in faith, hope, and valor. This woman probably didn't feel very righteous on that particular day. I doubt she had felt righteous for a very long time. Notice that in the course of her struggle, the woman had seen many physicians, to no avail. She had spent all the money she had in search of a cure. For twelve years, she experienced one failure after another. When one doctor failed, she regrouped and found another. When that doctor failed, she sought another. To keep carrying on for so long, after so many failures, she must have had deep determination, hope, and faith that life could, should, and would be different for her if she just pressed on.

Now reread the verse above, but this time, read only the italicized words. "For twelve years, enduring much and spending all that she had . . . but . . . after hearing about Jesus . . . thought, if I, could just touch His garments, I will be well.'

The woman was determined, committed, not a quitter. What's even more amazing to me about this valiant woman is that we don't even know whether she was a converted follower of Christ, or attended synagogue, or was a church-goer. The Bible doesn't give us these details, I think for good reason. Because we don't know those details, we are free to extract deeper meaning and value from the account. Perhaps merely hearing about Jesus from conversations in the street, spoken words of encouragement, and the testimonies of everyday folks in the crowd that day were all the hope she needed to spark her faith into action.

> And immediately Jesus, perceiving in Himself that the power proceeding from Him had gone forth, turned around in the crowd and said, "Who touched My garments?"
> —MARK 5:30

Notice that in this verse, the power in this case to heal left Jesus the moment her faith touched His cloak. There were a lot of folks crowding in on Jesus and the disciples. Probably many of them were brushing up against His clothing, but only one was touched in a special way. Why weren't there more accounts of people being healed, delivered, and set free from whatever ailed them during this release of power? The Bible doesn't say, but I like to think that it's because the relationship between faith and power, or power and faith, is relational and very personal. It was *her faith* that pushed her through the crowd, and when she was close enough, made her reach, believing that if she could just touch His cloak, she would be made well.

Considering the times back then, we can assume that others were also in need of a special touch from God. But this single account of faith demonstrated shows us that God not only notices our faith, he also feels it when our faith unites with His power and ignites.

> And His disciples said to Him, "You see the multitude pressing in on you, and you say, "Who touched Me?"
>
> —MARK 5:31

In other words, the disciples said, "Are you serious? Everyone is touching us!" Imagine how silly Jesus' question would have been in today's world of celebrities and rock stars. Surrounded by the paparazzi, bulbs flashing left and right, no elbow room to speak of, Jesus says, "Who touched me?"

> And when the woman saw that she had not escaped notice, she came trembling and fell down before Him, and declared in the presence of all the people the reason why she had touched Him, and how she had been immediately healed. And He said to her, "Daughter, your faith has made you well; go in peace."
>
> LUKE 8:47-48

The Bible is chock full of healings, miracles, and acts of God initiated by faith, God's sovereign power, and even by man's lack of faith. Typically, in the Old Testament, when God takes action because of lack of faith or disobedience, folks find themselves wandering around aimlessly in the desert or swallowed up by big fish. Personally, I would prefer that when God acts on my behalf, it's because my faith has touched His heart and released His power in my favor. I know hundreds of believers who have attested and will attest to amazing things happening in their lives, to prayers being answered, to huge, unmovable obstacles being removed, to promotions being granted, and to new opportunities arriving just in time, exceeding all they could have imagined or asked of God.

> For the word of God is living and active and sharper than any two-edged sword, and piercing as far as the division of soul and spirit, of both joints and marrow, and able to judge the thoughts and intentions of the heart.
>
> —HEBREWS 4:12

To avoid drifting away and losing interest, to continue to rest in right standing (righteousness) before God and man, we must acknowledge that the Word of God is living and active every day, even during the dark days when we think that we are walking alone and that God has abandoned us. This journey is, in a word, faith.

It is during this part of the journey when we desperately seek God's wisdom, healing, and favor, that we should judge our thoughts and the intentions of our hearts to see if there is anything we need to correct in our lives. It could be something minor, a tweak or adjustment needed to bring our right standing back into balance. Or, after much soul-searching, we might realize that we have seriously misled or mistreated someone, and until that is made right, forward progress might take the shape of a circle. But here's some good news.

> For we do not have a high priest who cannot sympathize with our weaknesses, but one who has been tempted in all things as we are, yet without sin.
> —HEBREWS 4:15

Notice that the word "weaknesses" is plural. The writer of Hebrews knew we might suffer from more than one weakness. We are only human after all, but our God can still sympathize; He fully understands how we feel when we've been hurt, falsely accused, or are just plain weary from the battles of the day.

> Let us therefore draw near with confidence to the throne of grace, that we may receive mercy and may find grace to help in time of need.
> —HEBREWS 4:16

This verse gives us a way out, an action we can take to ensure we rebalance and remain in right standing with God, even if we want to retaliate or defend ourselves. We are to turn to the throne of grace to receive mercy. However, notice what must happen first. We have to draw near—but with what? Are we to draw near with a spirit of fear, begging like a dog for mercy? Whining like a three-year-old child revving her engines before the tantrum? Are we supposed to draw near, doubting and guilt-ridden? Say it ain't so! It ain't so. We are to draw near, with *confidence,* to the throne of grace.

How awesome that is! Think about this verse for a minute. There's a lot going on here. In the midst of the storm, when our weaknesses are fully exposed, our hearts broken, when, like the woman in Mark, we don't feel all that great about ourselves, and are far from being on top of a mountain of unshakable faith, when we most need help and mercy, we are instructed to *approach the throne with confidence.*

While many of these emotions run counter to confidence, we must possess confidence *before* we can receive mercy and find grace in times of need. What can we do to make sure we don't grow weary and fall prey to the same demise as the fallen who have gone before us? We can examine our hearts, humble ourselves, search the Word of God for understanding, stir up our faith—and then approach the throne. In doing this, we are acting in accordance with God's will, and that alone should provide all the confidence we need.

SIGNIFICANT OBSERVATIONS:

1. To avoid drifting away, we must remain humble, yet confident in God.
2. Continually strive to remain in right standing before God.
3. Faith comes by hearing (reading, studying, and speaking) the Word of God.
4. The power of God is *in* the Word of God.
5. Unite the Word of God with faith to release the power of God.
6. While you wait for better circumstances, examine your heart and stand in faith.

7. Protect your heart from hardening or falling into disobedience.
8. Learn, trust, and never doubt that God's Word is living and active.

OPERATION OF THE KINGDOM
PART 2: MATURITY BREEDS DISCERNMENT

But solid food is for the mature, who because of practice have their senses trained to discern good and evil.

—HEBREWS 5:14

In the previous chapter, we learned a few lessons about righteousness, what it is to be in right standing with God, how to find righteousness, and the perils of losing righteousness due to unbelief. We learned that faith comes from reading, studying, and speaking the word of God to others and over our own lives. We learned that the power of God is actually in the spoken Word of God. We learned that it is our faith that ignites and releases the power of God into our lives, as was the case for the woman with the hemorrhage. We also learned that while we wait for better circumstances, such as an upcoming promotion or a new relationship to take off, we need to stand firm in faith and be patient.

This protects our hearts from hardening. Staying fervent for hope protects us from falling into disbelief and disobedience.

And thus, having patiently waited, he obtained the promise.

—HEBREWS 6:15

But what are we to do while we are patiently waiting and standing firm on the promises of hope? Dig deeper. Take the time to dig deeper into the things of God. For example, if you have a pretty good grasp of faith, spend some time learning more about prayer. Or you might challenge yourself to commit more time to prayer. Instead of spending five minutes a day praying for your family and friends, practice devoting thirty minutes to prayer; pray for other countries, ministries, or our government officials. Invest the time to jot down some prayer requests you've made to God and the Scriptures you are studying for those requests. Revisit your journal prayerfully from time to time to see if your requests have already been answered or if your request is no longer a pressing concern. In this way, you will begin to see God moving and acting on your behalf. Things that were weighing heavy on your mind thirty days ago may no longer be a challenge or an issue. When you push into new territory, there are always new things to see and experiences to learn from.

Let's face facts. We live in a time that seems to move at the speed of light: instant messaging, text messaging, e-mail alerts, a cell phone in every pocket. We are both connected and distracted, 24-7, 365 days a year. Being an Internet junkie, I certainly appreciate the value of technology and the ease with which we can stay connected with our friends, family, and social networks. More than ever before, we need to remain vigilant and protect our downtime for reflection and regeneration of our spirits.

Just because we've decided to stand on God's promises and wait patiently for Him to answer, it doesn't mean we can stop moving forward.

Just as our physical bodies require food and nourishment, our spiritual and mental beings require refreshment and recharging. If we don't take charge of making sure that we eat and think right, who will assume those tasks for us? The answer is obvious: no one. Sure, your parents will nag you to eat food besides junk food, and our pastors will urge us to ponder the Scriptures and consider our ways, but no one in the natural world other than you can actually take steps to improve your situation. Until we take responsibility for our own growth and begin taking actions on our own behalf, all the advice and encouragement we receive from others serve only as guilty reminders of what we should've, could've, or would've been.

I've matured a lot since my last bout of unemployment. This last time around, I saw the writing on the wall. The company I was working for was up for sale and we had a very interested buyer. While I was hopeful that they would want to keep me on and retain all our business units, I decided to start framing out a Plan B in the event that things didn't work out as promised. I should point out that I purposefully took the high road. I decided to stick it out and on company time, I worked diligently at my job. But at night, I worked on a business plan to start my own marketing communications company. I designed a logo and built a website. All I had to do was post it live. Linda and I prayed for God's direction. When the axe finally fell in April of 2011, we had already decided that in this event, we were going to trust God for the opportunity to move back to Colorado and be closer to our girls. After all, if God is indeed our source and supply, He can perform His duties regardless of where we are living. We put the house on the market and traveled back to Northern Colorado in search of a new beginning. In late May, we were in Estes Park looking at properties to buy or rent when we received an offer on our house. We accepted the offer and closing was set for July 20. We now had just over sixty days to pack the house, schedule a mover, find a job, and find a place to move into. "Don't worry, be happy." No pressure.

So we focused on what we could accomplish, packing up the house, and trusted God to handle the harder obstacles on our behalf. In late June, we were back in Estes, looking for apartments or a home to rent, as the banks weren't looking to finance mortgages, especially if you were an entrepreneur (read: unemployed). God led us to a property that was more than we had hoped for. And it was a rental. We signed the rental agreement, gave them the deposit and prayed God would grant us favor. That was a Friday. On Monday, I received a call from a company back in Missouri that wanted to talk with me about a job opportunity. I told them that I was moving to Northern Colorado and that I'd be happy to discuss the position as long as I could stick with my plan. They agreed, and asked me to come in and meet some of the officers. Two days later, we had to start driving back to Missouri for the interview meeting. We still hadn't heard from the property manager if we had been approved to rent the house. But as we got onto the freeway ramp to Missouri, our agent called to tell us we had been approved and that we could move in on July 22. How awesome is God? Within a seventy-two hour period, God had provided us with a beautiful home facing the snow-capped Rocky Mountains and a six-month consulting gig, The house in Missouri was packed and sold and our closing date and move-in dates were two days apart. There was no need for temporary storage, or for a temporary apartment; it was a smooth transition during what could have been a potentially stressful situation.

So why did I share this personal account with you? I wanted you to see the difference between this last experience of unemployment and my previous ones. This time around, I was much more mature in Christ. Linda and I had already been talking for months about what we would like to do should the company be sold. We had already established a plan of attack. We had been praying about what we would do, how we would do it, and we were more than ready to execute our plan when the opportunity arose. We had already prayed through the issues of whether it was God's will. When we finally put the house on the market and stuck the sign in the yard, it was as if the sign read, "This is our statement of faith. God is in charge of our lives. We are heading west, without a job or a home. Know this: God has gone before us and He is preparing a way for us."

We've been here now for almost six months. During this short time, we have found a great Bible-teaching church, gone white-water rafting and hiking, and have reconnected with our girls and all of their friends. I've launched the new company, finished a project for one client, gotten ready to start another for a new client, and have written this book. God *is* indeed a rewarder of those who diligently seek Him.

The secret to finding happiness and fulfillment in life isn't really a secret to those who have learned the principle reason for and value of life. It's not what you acquire that's important; it's what you share with others that defines your character and purpose in life.

> Instruct those who are rich in this present world not to be conceited or to fix their hope on the uncertainty of riches, but on God, who richly supplies us with all things to enjoy. Instruct them to do good, to be rich in good works, to be generous and ready to share.
>
> —1 TIMOTHY 6:17-18

At some point on our Christian walk, we must show growth, maturity, and wisdom in both what we share with others, as well as how we treat others. While we might not all be cut out to teach a Bible study or a Sunday school class, we all can teach and share our faith, our trials, and our successes with others.

> For though by this time you ought to be teachers, you have need again for someone to teach you the elementary principles of the oracles of God, and you have come to need milk and not solid food.
>
> —HEBREWS 5:12

Herein lie the insights of this chapter. As we mature in Christ and begin to share our stories and teach others, we must feed more on solid food and less on milk. Simply stated, as teachers, we need to have deeper insight so that when the questions come (and they will come), we have solid answers, references, and experiences to pull from.

Solid food is for the mature who are able to learn and grow. Do we learn because we have a steady diet of teaching? Do we grow because we have a stellar church attendance record? No. We mature from practice; we train our senses to discern good and evil.

> For everyone who partakes only of milk is not accustomed
> to the word of righteousness, for he is a babe. But solid
> food is for the mature, who because of practice have their
> senses trained to discern good and evil.
> —HEBREWS 5:13-14

So, now we are exploring ways to put what we've learned into practice. "Actions speak louder than words," as they say. Practicing what we preach is not an easy task. Nothing worth doing or achieving ever is. A marathon runner will never enjoy crossing the finish line if he doesn't first put in the miles and hours of training required to be able to endure the race to the end. A hiker will never personally appreciate panoramic views from atop a "fourteener" if he doesn't first condition his body to be able to ascend 14,000-foot peaks.

> That you may not be sluggish, but imitators of those who
> through faith and patience inherit the promises.
> —HEBREWS 6:12

If your objective is to become a marathon runner, you might want to start hanging around other long distance runners or previous marathon participants. Learn from their experiences. Find out what they changed or added to their diets to begin their conditioning. Maybe the longest distance you've ever run is two miles. Start then by setting a goal to run a mini-marathon first, and begin training so that your body knows what is expected of it in order to complete a 5k or a 10k run. If your desire is to be a big giver but your current financial position doesn't support your vision, think of different ways to accomplish the same goal. When our finances got tight and we were not in a position to continue financing the establishment of freshwater wells and churches through the Hand of Hope Ministries of Joyce Meyers, Linda and I looked for other ways to make a difference. We enjoy antiquing very much, and often our road trips into the mountains and visits to old ghost towns lead us past yard sales. Certain items always seem to be available for nickels and dimes: maternity clothes and baby outfits no longer needed. Linda and I have no need for these items, but there are local ministries and shelters for single moms that would love to have them. So now we keep an eye out for items like these and make sure we get them to our local shelters and to mothers with babies, of course at no cost to them. Our investment to acquire the needed clothing and toys is minimal, but it is more than some struggling moms have to spend. In the end, the results are the same. We are giving where there is a need, and our lives, as well as theirs, are deeply enriched.

Instead of complaining that we didn't have the same charitable budget that we used to have, and that we were unable to continue funding a Hand of Hope village in need, we looked for other ways to make a difference in someone's life. While we still remain hopeful that we will again be able to help fund additional wells and churches in the not-too-distant future, we understand that while we wait upon the Lord for our finances to improve, we can do other things to keep our faith and purpose moving forward.

In this way, we are training and exercising our senses to know how to discern good from evil. By keeping our minds and spirits active around ways to help and give rather than sitting idly by waiting for our situation to change, we are growing and maturing. We are discovering new ways to be of service to others, and in the process, we are meeting new folks with different challenges and unique needs that we weren't aware of before. Now we are.

Notice I did not suggest that we should give up hope on own previous dreams, ambitions, or desires. I simply suggest that while we wait, we continue to grow by being open to new adventures and opportunities.

> For whatever was written in earlier times were written for our instruction, that through perseverance and the encouragement of the Scriptures we might have hope.
> —ROMANS 15:4

> Now may the God of hope fill you with all joy and peace
> in believing, that you may abound in hope by the power
> of the Holy Spirit.
>
> —ROMANS 15:13

Hope is a wonderful thing. It's more than just a nice word that implies that things are going to be better soon. Hope fills us with two other powerful character traits worthy of acquiring: joy and peace.

Unfortunately, when you drive around town these days and look at the other drivers on the road, or when you people-watch at the mall, you notice that a lot of folks have lost their happy faces. In the movie *Hook*, poor Peter Pan can't fly because he's lost his happy thoughts. Unfortunately, I think many people have lost sight of their purpose and passion in life.

Without hope, people perish.

> In the same way God, desiring even more to show to the
> heirs of the promise the unchangeableness of His purpose,
> interposed with an oath, in order that by two unchangeable
> things, in which it is impossible for God to lie, we may
> have strong encouragement, we who have fled for refuge
> in laying hold of the hope set before us.
>
> —HEBREWS 6:17-18

When your hope subsides, so will your joy. And when your joy subsides, so does your strength. Thus, it follows that as our strength wanes and we become weary and tired, whether from battle (fighting the fight of faith) or boredom (waiting on the Lord), we need to seek ways to recapture our joy, to rest in His peace, and to reignite our hope.

If any man is willing to do His will, he shall know of the teaching, whether it is of God, or whether I speak from myself.

—JOHN 7:17

SIGNIFICANT OBSERVATIONS:

1. Deep calleth unto deep.
2. Maturity in Christ breeds deeper understanding and discernment.
3. Practice, practice, practice; train your senses to discern His purpose for you.
4. Associate and imitate those of faith who have insight and knowledge.
5. Seed hope; grow faith; reap joy and peace.

FAVOR IN GODS SIGHT:
A LIFE OF PRAYER

*If you abide in me, and My Word abides in you, ask whatever
you wish, and it shall be done for you.*

—John 15:7

To gain favor in anything or anywhere we need to be seen. At the office,
you need the boss to look your way and notice that you exist and are
making a contribution. The same holds true if you're in school. Raise
your hand. Get noticed. Submit a well-thought midterm essay and the
professor will appreciate it. It's no different with God.

To access God's favor you need Him to look your way. Prayer not only
brings strength and refreshment to your soul, it also yields power and
grants insight. Prayer is the means by which we approach God.

> And He came to the disciples and found them sleeping,
> and said to Peter, "so you men could not keep watch with
> Me for one hour?"
>
> —Matthew 26:40

Jesus was in the garden praying and had asked His disciples to join Him.
According to the account in Matthew, Jesus had gone just a ways ahead

of the disciples to pray. When He returned, He found them sleeping. He asked, "Could you not keep watch with Me for one hour?" Some point to this Scripture as a minimum requirement for prayer. Pray an hour, then you are done, just as we might tell our kids, "Practice your violin for forty minutes and then you can go out and play." While I firmly promote a habit of prayer, I think here Jesus was simply saying, "Guys, seriously, can't you stay awake and pray with me a while?"

The Lord's Prayer gives some insight into how we should pray. Many believe it is the only prayer acceptable or that it's an example of what to say in a prayer. Actually, I think it's a framework or a process for prayer. Let's take a closer look.

> Our Father who art in Heaven, hallowed be they name. Thy kingdom come, thy will be done, on earth as it is in heaven.Give us this day our daily bread.And forgive us our debts, as we also have forgiven our debtors.And lead us not into temptation, but deliver us from evil.For Thine is the kingdom, and the power, and the glory, forever. Amen.
> —MATTHEW 6:9-13

The first two lines (verses) above are acknowledging God and praying for His will first and foremost. The next three verses provide a framework for praying for our needs second. The last verse calls it all into action.

If you want to experience a deeper prayer life, one that transforms and transcends anything you may have experienced in the past, learn to pray by engaging your spiritual mind into the eyes and voice of God. The Lord's Prayer is an excellent example of how to get started down this path to an enriched and enchanted prayer life. To begin, think of this prayer as a process or framework instead of as Holy Writ that if not recited or spoken holy enough, might yield lightning bolts from above.

But before I walk all over your traditions, which is not really my intent, let me share a comment made by a preacher who was introducing his congregation to different ways of interpreting Scriptures. His advice was simple: "If what we are studying becomes too much for you to process or accept straight away, don't spit it out and discard it completely. Instead, set it aside, place it on the shelf, and revisit it later when your heart is more receptive." I think that's some pretty good advice, especially as we venture into areas where you may be hearing a perspective or viewpoint different from what you have been taught. That said, let's consider each section of the Lord's Prayer.

> Our Father who art in heaven, hallowed be Thy name.
> —MATTHEW 6:9

This first verse is about "hallowing," or showing and declaring reverence for His name. This is acknowledging, praising, pondering, and professing the awesomeness of God. It is an affirmation that He is the only God, the Alpha and the Omega. This acknowledgment and pronouncement establishes God as our source and supply. He has omnipresent and omniscient power as not only our Creator, but also the Creator of all things, above and beneath. As wide as the east from the west is His presence, which is available to all mankind who will humble themselves and acknowledge and admire both the hand and handiwork of Almighty God. One could spend thirty minutes just enumerating the beauties of God and the powers that rest in His holy name.

> Thy kingdom come, thy will be done, on earth as it is in heaven.
> —MATTHEW 6:10

Likewise, with time and practice, one could spend a significant amount of time praying specifically for God's kingdom to come, that His will be done, both within the lives of immediate family, then extended families, then within the lives of our neighbor's family, their children's families, our church family, our nation, etc. For example:

"God, I thank you for the privilege to come before you in prayer. We need your help. Grant our nation a spirit of justice and balance in accordance to Your will. Help us identify how to inspire justice again in this world. Bring forth those who can lead us back to righteousness before you. Show us how to restore trust and leadership to other nations. Begin nurturing and maturing the silent voices of our youth, that they may one day rise up and speak Your truths to all nations. Help us to know Your will when it appears; to hear Your voice when it speaks, and to praise Your name for all to hear. Strengthen the resolve of the mighty in Christ to stand and deliver. Strengthen the hopes of the weary that they may once again stand and rejoin the good fight of faith. Lead us all to cross paths daily with those You wish to speak to, and do so through us as often as You desire, that the lost may be found and the broken restored.'

Give us this day our daily bread.
—Matthew 6:11

"Thank you, Lord, for the food on this table, the staples in our cabinets, and the cubes of ice in the fridge. Thank you, Lord, for the opportunity to provide for my family. Thank you for my health and for the job you have given me which pays for the food we enjoy. Thank you, Lord, that our church has a Food Pantry, from which those who are struggling may have food and supplies. Thank you, Lord, for our abundance, so that we are able to share with those less fortunate. Thank you, Lord, that we are able to participate in funding the development of freshwater wells, gathering places, shelters, and houses of worship that don't leak during the rainy season by supporting ministries called to this purpose. Thank you for your gracious provision and continual favor, that those in whom we are able to invest and bless will in turn help those less fortunate who are within their reach. Continue to bless this home and our efforts. Abundantly continue to supply all our needs, so that we can share more with others."

> And forgive us our debts, as we also have forgiven our debtors.
> —MATTHEW 6:9-12

"And Lord, here I need much help. Forgive me where I have offended others unknowingly. Show me how to make things right where it is possible to do so. Help me to forgive those who have mistreated or misguided me, knowing that some may never know how much they have damaged my heart and messed with my mind. Help me to heal inside and throughout. Help us, Lord, to let go of the things we thought were due and expected. Search us, Lord, and show us how to avoid putting our faith in man, ahead of You. Help me to heal stronger than I was. In You alone I find rest and comfort."

> And do not lead us into temptation, but deliver us from evil.
> —MATTHEW 6:9-13A

"Keep me safe in all my ways, Lord. Talk to me, show me, light a bush on fire if needed, so that I shall know Your will and not turn to the left when I should go right. Wake me from a dead sleep in the middle of the night to show me something or speak with me. Guide me and show me Your plan through visions and dreams. Grant me ability to not only recall them, but to correctly interpret them. Keep my family safe, encamp round about my children and my wife at all times, but especially when I trek off in faith to expose the devil or share the wisdom of God. I know when we get close to winning a soul or enlightening a brother that the enemy isn't happy about it. Protect us when we venture outside the walls to expose evil and stand for good. Thank you, Lord, for wisdom to know that greater is He who dwells in me than he who is in the world. For the same spirit that raised Christ

Jesus from the grave dwells in me. If God is for me, who possibly could come against me? You are my rock, my refuge, and deliverance. By Your hand I am led away from temptation and into the light. You alone understand the sequence of events that will occur leading up to Your return. You know what things we need to accomplish here on earth to help pave a way for others to find Your kingdom. In You, and in You alone, is the power to create, restore, heal, and save. Let Your glory, honor, and name be declared and magnified, both in heaven and earth, forever and ever."

> For Thine is the kingdom, and the power, and the glory, forever. Amen.
> —MATTHEW 6:13B

Hopefully, now you can see and appreciate that the Lord's Prayer is more than just an example of prayer. We can structure our prayer time to be deeper and richer, more specific, more complete and effective.

> Prepare a war; rouse the mighty men! Let all the soldiers draw near, let them come up! Beat your plowshares into swords, and your pruning hooks into spears; Let the weak say, "I am a mighty man!
> —JOEL 3:9-11

Strive to become a mighty man or woman of prayer. Resolve to become a mighty prayer warrior for the King. If not you, then who? We can't sit back and rely solely on our pastors to pray, nor our neighbors to stand in the gap on behalf of our community, our nation, or on our behalf. Will they speak on our behalf when it's our turn to knock on the pearly gates and have a chat with Peter? Make no mistake. We are all called to be His disciples. By definition, that makes each of us followers. Who are we following? We are soldiers and warriors for the King of Kings and Lord of Lords. Make no mistake:. we are at war against all things contrary to the kingdom of God. We are encouraged to draw near and come up to a deeper understanding of our calling and purpose in life, that is, to make a positive impact and a difference in the lives of others. We are encouraged to make the best of whatever we have been given, to further the cause of righteousness and of freedom in Christ.

I think Joel was pretty wise to include the line, "Let the weak say, I am a mighty man!" I think he knew that some people would sound off with statements like, "Well, I'm not feeling up to it right now; I'm weak and not a leader." It's not how you feel that's important, it's what God says about you and how He sees you that should move your soul to action. In God's eyes, we are more than conquerors. God says we are mighty, despite how we might feel.

On 9/11, do you think that Todd Morgan Beamer and the rest of the passengers on United Airlines flight 93 felt like taking back that plane from the terrorists? After reciting the Lord's Prayer with an operator on the ground over the air phone, Todd Beamer called his fellow soldiers into battle that day with only two words: "Let's roll!"

SIGNIFICANT OBSERVATIONS:

1. Securing and maintaining God's favor requires a life of prayer.
2. Abide in Him and whatever you ask, it shall be granted.
3. The Lord's Prayer is more than just an example of prayer.
4. It is a framework or a process that prioritizes His will first, ours second.
5. It's time to rouse the mighty soldier within you. There's work to be done.
6. Draw near and come up; it's time to fight for the kingdom.

PRAYER—CAN WE TALK?
PART 1: CHATTING WITH THE CREATOR

Rejoice always; pray without ceasing; in everything give thanks; for this is God's will for you in Christ Jesus.
— 1 THESSALONIANS 5:16-18

Having a habit of prayer *is* God's will for each of us. More important than tradition, ritual, or religious legalization is God's desire to hear and communicate with His people. Altars, sacrifices and self-induced bondage, as was showcased in the movie *The Da Vinci Code*, are not what God requests of us today. In the Old Testament, God used many kings, rulers, prophets, and priests to both serve and communicate with His people. And because that didn't work out so well, He gave us His only Son to be the final sacrifice and salvation for all mankind. Enter the New Testament, the new and improved covenant between God and man. Under this new covenant, God made a way for every man and woman to know Him personally: through the life, death, and resurrection of Jesus Christ.

> For we do not have a high priest who cannot sympathize with our weaknesses, but one who has been tempted in all things as we are, yet without sin. Let us therefore draw

> near with confidence to the throne of grace, that we may
> receive mercy and may find grace to help in time of need.
> —HEBREWS 4:15-16

> The sacrifice of the wicked is an abomination to the lord,
> but the prayer of the upright is His delight.
> —PROVERBS 15:8

> The Lord is not slow about His promise, as some count
> slowness, but is patient toward you, not wishing for any
> to perish but for all to come to repentance.
> —2 PETER 3:9

Praying to God is not only His will for each of us, it is also His delight that we do so; he wishes all to come to know Him and to come to repentance. Talking with God is like talking with a friend. I heard this a long time ago, and to be honest, I can't remember who said it, but I found it rather profound. Growing up Baptist, I was pretty reverent of the whole prayer thing. When the preacher started to pray, I always bowed my head and closed my eyes before taking advantage of a minute or two of snooze-time. Just kidding, but that's probably not too far off base.

Anyway, as I matured, I made the same mistakes many people do when they first start to experience public prayer. For some reason, we seem to think that the bigger the words are, the deeper we make our voices, and the holier our thous sound, the more effective our prayers.

> And when you are praying, do not use meaningless
> repetition, as the Gentiles do, for they suppose that they
> will be heard for their many words. Therefore do not be
> like them; for your Father knows what you need, before
> you ask Him.
> —MATTHEW 6:7-8

I don't know about you, but I stopped trying to pull the wool over my father's eyes a long time ago, because it wasn't working. He, like my heavenly Father, knows who I am, so I gave up trying to spin tales with fancy words or use lame rationalizations to promote my cause sometime during college. Now I just talk to both of them and treat them as what they are: my friend and greatest ally.

In the last chapter we learned how to follow the Lord's Prayer as both an example of prayer, and a framework to prayer. We also learned that it is to God that we pray, and that we approach His throne in reverence, respect, honor, and awe. Sometimes our prayers may remain serious in delivery; maybe that approach is necessary in certain circumstances.

But in my personal, daily prayers, I try to maintain a more casual, conversational dialogue. I try to avoid using holy chatter in an effort to impress Him or to get His attention. We know just how well that works. Rather, I keep the dialogue simple, as though we are chatting with one another—kind of like the tone in which I've written this book. Please understand that I do remain respectful and reverent, as I do know with whom I'm speaking, but I also realize that He is more than my Creator. He is also my friend and Father. And that makes me His child.

> "Lord, I am fully aware that some of the concepts shared in this book may be new to some. I'm counting on You to show me how to write in such a way as not to offend anyone. I pray our approach doesn't mislead."

I realize that some readers who have never heard that it is completely acceptable, even commanded, dare I say, for we common folk to pray on our own behalves. So let's address those questions straight away and possibly re-learn some fundamentals on which to build our prayer foundation as we go forward.

So, who can pray? Those who belong to Christ can pray:

But as many as received Him, to them He gave the right to become children of God, even to those who believe in His name.

—JOHN 1:12

Behold, I stand at the door and knock; if anyone hears My voice and opens the door, I will come in to him, and will dine with him, and he with Me.

—REVELATION 3:20

The unfolding of Thy words gives light; it gives understanding to the simple.

—PSALM 119:130

That's right. Even we simple folk are encouraged to open His Word, consider His instructions, receive insight to light our paths, and obtain understanding.

Those who have a forgiving spirit can pray:

And whenever you stand praying, forgive, if you have anything against anyone; so that your Father also who is in heaven may forgive you your transgressions.

—MARK 11:25

Those who come in Faith can pray:

And the prayer offered in faith will restore the one who is sick, and the Lord will raise him up, and if he has committed sins, they will be forgiven him.

—JAMES 5: 15-16

And all things you ask in prayer, believing, you shall receive.

—MATTHEW 21:22

If you ask anything in My name, I will do it.

—JOHN 14:14

Those who have a clean heart can pray:

Therefore confess your sins to one another, and pray for one another, so that you may be healed. The effective prayer of a righteous man can accomplish much.

—JAMES 5:16

If I regard wickedness in my heart, the Lord will not hear.

—PSALM 66:18

So it should be well established by now, that *anyone* who calls upon the name of the Lord can humble himself and pray. But what if you don't currently feel clean, or struggle with having a forgiving spirit, or still are unclear about what God's will is?

It is the will of God that we trust Him:

Trust in the Lord with all your heart, lean not on your own understanding. In all your ways acknowledge Him, and He will make your paths straight.

—PROVERBS 3:5-6

It is the will of God that believers are filled with His Spirit:

> And do not get drunk with wine, for that is dissipation, but be filled with the Spirit, speaking to one another in psalms and hymns and spiritual songs, singing and making melody with your heart to the Lord; always giving thanks for all things in the name of our Lord Jesus Christ.
> —EPHESIANS 5:18-20

When things we desire accord with the Word of God, God will give you peace in prayer concerning them. When godly counsel agrees with your desire or request, when you find the circumstances favorable, and your heart is not condemning you, then you can be assured that what you are seeking or asking is most probably God's will for you.

There is an analogy that might help those still wrestling with knowing whether or not they are asking according to His will. The analogy is a simple phone number.

When you know the number of the person you are calling, you know who will answer and what to expect from them. Knowing the number is like knowing the will of God. There's no need to doubt or second-guess. You already know what He has to say about a certain topic or subject, so you *already know* His will, or opinion, on the matter.

When you don't know the number, or are unsure if the number you are dialing is the correct one, that's like *not knowing* God's will. In this case, you simply need to inquire further to make sure you have the right number. If you're not sure whether what you are asking for is His will, pray for insight, knowledge, and discernment on the topic, and don't give up until you find your answer. Warning: you might not like the answer you get, but if you're willing to listen and adjust to His instruction, at least you won't be confused or clueless for long. He will show you the way, and He will answer the door. Oh, and if it seems like the number you are dialing is busy, keep calling.

It might be interesting to note these facts about God: He will do only what He intends; He will not do anything against His own character. He is not limited by circumstances. His plans for our lives will never be frustrated or pitched aside because of the mistakes of others or the obstacles they have placed in our paths.

Many of us have heard the story of Joseph and his multicolored coat. Joseph was the youngest son of Jacob. He had ten half-brothers, yet young Joseph was his daddy's favorite. Jacob had a beautiful multicolored coat made for his favorite son. The brothers probably didn't appreciate that very much. To make matters worse for the brothers, Joseph was also a dreamer. He not only had the gift of dreaming, but could interpret dreams as well. One day, Joseph shared one of his crazy dreams with his brothers; it pushed them over the edge. "You'll bow down to me someday," was the essence of the dream, and the brothers didn't appreciate it one bit. So they conspired to remove young Joe from the fold. They threw him in a pit, and then decided to sell young Joe into slavery to some travelers on their way to Egypt. The brothers covered their story by dipping Joseph's coat in goat's blood. They told their father Jacob that a wild animal had killed poor little Joe.

Joseph was sold as a slave to the household of Potiphar, Pharaoh's captain of the guard. Potiphar's wife found young Joseph quite attractive and attempted several times to seduce him, but he was faithful and repelled her advances. Frustrated and ashamed, she decided to falsely accuse Joseph of wrongdoing; this earned him a pass to go immediately to prison. Joseph, despite being imprisoned, continued to make friends and gain favor with both his cellmates and the guards. The word got out that he had the gift of being able to interpret dreams. This eventually came to the attention of Pharaoh, who was having some disturbing dreams of his own.

So Joseph was summoned. He interpreted Pharaoh's dream as a warning that a famine was soon coming to Egypt. Joseph suggested to the Pharaoh that he plan ahead and begin gathering and storing food so they would be prepared for the lean years ahead. Finding favor in young

Joseph, Pharaoh appointed him head Czar of this campaign. For seven years they collected and stored the country's grain. When the famine came, it affected all the nations; people flocked to Egypt to buy grain. Among them were Joseph's half-brothers. When they arrived, they did not recognize their brother, but Joseph recognized them. After having some fun with his brothers in an effort to show them the error of their ways, Joseph finally gave them provisions and revealed himself to them. Joseph's brothers had acted to harm him and benefit themselves, but God had had other plans.

> And as for you, you meant evil against me, but God meant it for good in order to bring about this present result, to preserve many people alive.
>
> —GENESIS 50:20

None of us know what tomorrow may bring. Nonetheless, we make plans, book appointments, keep schedules, and move forward towards our goals and objectives. But when our plans change and our dreams are dashed away through no fault of our own, we need to remind ourselves that God is still in control. He may have another plan. Maybe the detour you are on is not a detour or a setback at all. Maybe it's the exact path God wants you on at this particular time.

> Do not boast about tomorrow, for you do not know what a day may bring forth.
>
> —PROVERBS 27:1

SIGNIFICANT OBSERVATIONS:

1. All of us are called to pray, not just the church leaders.
2. It is God's will, desire, and delight that we come to Him in prayer.
3. Rejoice always, knowing that we, with all our faults, can talk to God.

4. For everything, we are to give thanks: the good, the bad and the ugly.
5. Our high priest is Jesus Christ, who sympathizes with all our weaknesses.
6. Talk to God as you would to a friend; just be yourself.
7. When your luck parallels that of poor Joseph's, hold on to your dream.

PRAYER—CAN WE TALK?
PART 2: CHATTING WITH YOUR SAVIOR

*Be anxious for nothing, but in everything by prayer and
supplication with thanksgiving let your requests be made
known to God.*

—Philippians 4:6

Non-believers have often asked me why I pray. Normally, I don't
answer that question by telling them that God commands us to pray, or
that prayer is a form of serving God. I think it's because these responses,
as true as they are, may turn some people off, and their listening ears
and open hearts may close before they hear the really good news as to
why I pray.

I pray because there is great benefit in it for me. It keeps my spiritual
life in balance and keeps me humble before God. I pray knowing that
if I am sincere in my prayers and truly attempt to forgive others and do
the right thing, God is delighted with me, warts and all. I know that
it's the practice of prayer and not the perfection of it that God wants
me to pursue. And that's great news, because practice is achievable;
perfection is not.

Draw near to God and He will draw near to you . . .

—James 4:8

> Now to Him who is able to do exceeding abundantly beyond all that we ask or think, according to the power that works within us.
>
> —Ephesians 3:20

> Therefore confess your sins to one another, and pray for one another, so that you may be healed. The effective prayer of a righteous man can accomplish much.
>
> —James 5:16

There are a host of Scriptures in the Bible that give us insight into why we should pray. If you want to be closer to God and have Him draw near to you, prayer is the means with which to achieve this. If you wish to accomplish much and be effective in everything you do, prayer enables it. There is an equal number of Scriptures that speak to the question of when we should pray. In short, prayer is the means by which we gain insight and obtain solutions to the problems and challenges of the day.

When Jesus was trying to pick his cabinet of disciples out of the lot who were following him, he separated himself from the crowd and went into the hills to pray. There, he prayed for insight, discretion, and wisdom. This was a very big decision, one that deserved thought, reflection, and advice.

> And it was at this time that He went off to the mountain to pray, and He spent the whole night in prayer to God. And when day came, He called His disciples to Him; and chose twelve of them, whom He also named as apostles.
>
> —Luke 6:12-13

A habit of prayer helps us keep temptations at bay, strengthens our character, and solidifies our resolve to the cause of faith. With the Roman soldiers en route and Jesus' final triumph nearing, Jesus prayed with Peter and the two sons of Zebedee in the garden of Gethsemane.

Even at that late hour, Jesus encouraged his sleepy wingmen to stay alert and pray.

> Keep watching and praying, that you may not enter into temptation; the spirit is willing, but the flesh is weak.
> —MATTHEW 26:41

We should pray when we know our fellow brothers and sisters in Christ are struggling with or preparing for a big meeting, a long-awaited wedding, or an ailing parent. Don't be afraid to ask someone to pray for you; it just might make his or her day that you would even ask.

I'm both humbled and honored when I get calls and e-mails from friends and even business associates asking me to pray for them or for someone they know. When my kids tell me about one of their friends getting hurt and they ask me to pray for them, I'm touched. I know people wouldn't ask if they didn't know that I am a believer, nor would they ask if I were a hypocrite. Over time, the more people see you walking in faith, the more prayer requests you'll receive. When it happens, consider it God's way of acknowledging that you are maturing in Him.

> With all prayer and petition pray at all times in the Spirit, and with this in view, be on the alert, with all perseverance and petition for all the saints.
> —EPHESIANS 6:18-19

We've already learned that another good time for us to pray is whenever we need wisdom or peace regarding an issue, or when we need our joy restored.

> If any of you lack wisdom let him ask God, who gives to all men generously and without reproach, and it will be given to him.
> —JAMES 1: 5

> Until now you have asked for nothing in my name; ask and
> you will receive, that your joy may be made full.
>   —JOHN 16:24

Let me close this chapter by sharing with you a very personal story about how I started taking this prayer thing to a whole new level.

Remember my earlier account of when my friend Dennis showed up at our apartment in California to help Linda and I pack up the U-Haul? Well, we moved back to St. Louis to live with my parents until I could find new employment. We started attending a non-denominational Bible-teaching church that opened my eyes to Scripture interpretations that I had never heard before. Many of them are captured in this book.

Before finding this church, I had started using the basement of my dad's house as my personal Bible study and prayer room. I preferred the basement to the kitchen table because I could be free from distractions and have plenty of room to walk around while I prayed.

It wasn't long before I found work and we moved out of my parents' place and into another apartment while our very first house was being built. The Bible-based church we were attending was a teaching church on steroids. The pastor was a simple man, a man who had simply decided to take God and His Word for granted. The church was nothing more than a metal-frame building; there was no fancy stonework or masonry on the outside to boast about. Inside, there was an office, a kiddie room for infants and toddlers, and the main room that held about 500 plastic orange chairs. Oh and just next to the kiddie room was the prayer room.

Now this room, the prayer room, was highly anointed. Folks came early for church so they could go into this room and pray. They prayed for nations and people they didn't even know. There were pictures and prayer requests tacked up on a board for you to read and pray over. There was a globe for those who wanted to pray for the world and have a reference point with which to connect. There were always candles burning around the room and folks were free to pray silently, to speak in tongues, to sing, cry, weep; however the spirit moved them, they were welcome to act. When I finally found the courage to enter this room, I found a chair against the wall and prayed silently to myself, while also watching how God was moving other people in prayer. It was probably the most reverent room I had ever encountered. At first, I was a bit uncomfortable with the host of different ways people prayed, but over time, I came to appreciate that God probably liked every form of these prayers, praises, and pleas. After all, these people were truly on fire and serious about talking with God, praying through problems, and quoting Scriptures aloud without referring to an open Bible. These prayer warriors had learned to hide the Word of God in their hearts, and when they needed a strong word to remind the devil that he was defeated, they could rattle off Scriptures like nobody's business.

Because the pastor highly revered this room and the power of prayer, it was never used as a breakroom, lunchroom, or anything other than a prayer room.

On Sunday mornings, just before church began, the pastor had a habit of using the prayer room to pray and prepare his heart for the service. On a couple of occasions, as he made his way around the room, he had tapped my shoulder to give me a wink or a thumbs-up. I recall that one day, he leaned over and said, "David. God loves to hear you pray, keep it up." That made my month! It was a bump of confidence, an encouraging word that inspired me to think that maybe, just maybe, I was beginning to understand this prayer thing. It wasn't long after that I summoned up the courage to ask the pastor for a favor. Linda and I were still living in the apartment, waiting for our house to be built. In that small apartment, I was having a hard time praying and walking around as I like to do. I didn't want to wake up Linda at 5:00 a.m. with all my whining—I mean, praying.

So I asked the pastor one Sunday morning if I could have access to the church building and the prayer room in order to begin a daily, two-hour prayer session before going off to work. He gladly got a key made for me and gave me only one rule to follow. It was something like this: "This key gives you, and only you, access to this building and to the prayer room. You may invite no others. Understand?"

For the next thirteen months, every morning without fail, seven days a week, week after week, month after month, I got to experience God all alone in this room, the Holy of Holies. I was there every morning by 5:00 a.m. and I tried to be finished by 7:00 a.m. so that I could get to work just before 8:00. I became a prayer Warrior for the King in this room.

I memorized Scriptures, read the Bible, praised the Lord, rested in the Lord, paced the room, laid hands on photos of people I didn't even know, and prayed for nations mentioned on the news that I couldn't even find on the globe provided. I praised God, thanked God, and even raised my voice a few times. I felt Him in the room and I found His voice in many things. I also had bouts with darker spirits, and I recall, as though it happened three minutes ago, a lengthy battle with darkness one morning. The hair on the back of my neck was standing straight up, fear surrounded me and pressed in so close that I could feel its breath on my face, but I stood my ground and confessed, quite loudly I might add, that where I stood was holy ground, (even this piece of ground), that the Word of God was light, and that darkness could not exist *in* the light. The spirit left immediately.

I had many such encounters in this humble little prayer room. Some were standoffs, and some were battles of victory. All were real. None forgotten.

Today, some twenty-five years later, I don't pray as fervently as I did back then. That was a special time of training and conditioning, like joining the Navy Seals or Delta Force. Those thirteen months were my boot camp; God worked with me, molded me, taught me, and tested me. To this day, I think that the pastor knew this would be the case, which is why he made it quite clear that I was to invite no other. Today,

I chat with God pretty regularly throughout the day. Sometimes, when my wife's not around and my kids aren't visiting, I'll have an hour or so with God, or with my adversary; my prayers heat up and I know I'm being challenged by the spirit of fear, lack, resentment, or some other spirit, not of God. But these demons don't scare me as they did before; not since that day that the Holy Spirit spoke through me and told the Prince of Darkness he could not exist in the light of God's Word. That was my burning bush.

If your current environment doesn't lend itself to effective prayer, ask your pastor if he has a prayer room you can use. If he doesn't have one, you might be in the wrong church, or maybe it's an opportunity from God for you to start one.

> And in the morning, while it was still dark, He arose and went out and departed to a lonely place, and was praying there.
>
> —MARK 1:35

> But you, when you pray, go into your inner room, and when you have shut your door, pray to your Father who is in secret, and your Father who sees in secret will repay you.
>
> —MATTHEW 6:6

SIGNIFICANT OBSERVATIONS:

1. Be anxious for nothing, but in prayer make your request known.
2. Practice prayer is achievable; perfection is not.
3. God delights in our prayers.
4. The effective prayers of the righteous can accomplish much.
5. Hide God's Word within your heart; you'll never know when you'll need it.
6. The best time of day to pray is all day.

PRAYER—CAN WE TALK?
PART 3: HINDRANCES TO PRAYER

Likewise, ye husbands dwell with them according to knowledge, giving honor unto the wife, as unto the weaker vessel, and as being heirs together of the grace of life; that your prayers be not hindered.

—1 Peter 3:1-7

As important as it is to approach the throne of God in search of wisdom, guidance, favor, and answers to our prayers, and as important as it is to fully explore and know the character of God, what pleases Him, and what our purpose in this world is, it is equally important, if not more so, to know what hinders prayers.

The information in this chapter might be familiar to most readers. There probably aren't any pearls of wisdom that you haven't heard before. These are the don'ts of life that our parents taught us or that we know by our own internal wisdom. Quite possibly, we have seen the traits discussed here in other people, and found them to be suspect, leading us to deduce that these behaviors aren't ones we would like to emulate.

If we want our prayers both heard and answered, as promised throughout God's Word, we need to acknowledge and be on the alert for things that will hinder our prayers.

Hindrances to prayer include, but are not limited to the following: selfishness, unforgivingness, unbelief, living in known sin, disobedience, poor self-image of who we are in Christ, and listening to the lies of the enemy over what God has to say about us.

> To one who knows the right thing to do, and does not do it, to him it is sin.
>
> —James 4:17

> If I regard iniquity in my heart, the Lord will not hear me.
>
> —Psalm 66:18

> Then they will cry out to the Lord, but He will not answer them. Instead, He will hide His face from them at that time, because they have practiced evil deeds.
>
> —Micah 3:4

> He that turns away his ear from hearing the law, even his prayer is an abomination.
>
> —Proverbs 28:9

Ouch! These are very harsh realities. They are promises just like the nice promises we've already read about, but these tough love warnings aren't easy pills to swallow. It hardly makes you want to turn the page to find out what else we might be guilty of or doing wrong. But let's not get too down on ourselves too quickly and lose hope. I suggest we step back out of ourselves for a moment while we examine and consider these Scriptures. Later, in individual prayer time, we can each begin to ask God to reveal the areas of our lives and characters that He wants us to work on. In doing so, He will be faithful and hear our prayers because as we've already learned, it is His will that we approach Him, ask of Him and trust Him to help us grow in Him.

First, let's call them as we see them. If it looks like a duck, walks like a duck, and quacks like a duck, then it probably is a duck. The same is true of sin. If it feels like sin, looks like sin, and acts like sin, it *is* sin. Let's not sugarcoat it. It's bad behavior, undesirable in God's sight, and probably also in the eyes of those around us. Now that we've admitted the sin exists, and we acknowledge that all have fallen prey to it, we can ask for forgiveness and erase it from our slate. If we pray sincerely, and we make an effort to keep the sin out of our lives, we have assurance that it has been removed and paid for in full.

> As far as the east is from the west, so far has He removed our transgressions from us, just as a father has compassion on his children, so the Lord has compassion on those who fear Him.
>
> —PSALM 103:12

> Christ died for our sins . . .
>
> —1 CORINTHIANS 15:3

> If we confess our sins, He is faithful and righteous to forgive us our sins and to cleanse us from all unrighteousness.
>
> —1 JOHN 1:9

> I am writing these things, to you that you may not sin. And if anyone sins, we have an Advocate with the Father, Jesus Christ the righteous.
>
> —1 JOHN 2:1

Neither do I condemn you; go your way. From now on sin no more.

—JOHN 8:11

Evil comes in all shapes and sizes. The most obvious and heinous evil floods the news media now more than ever before. Most of us don't cross over into the abyss, but nonetheless, we have committed lesser evil deeds at different times in our lives. Some people behave this way as a matter of course at the places they work. It's who they are, and oddly enough, they know it and actually feed off of it. They actually enjoy being talked about by their subordinates. These power-hungry overlords, and folks like them, really need our prayers.

God is opposed to the proud, but gives grace to the humble.

—JAMES 4:6

There they cry out, but He does not answer because of the pride of evil men. Surely God will not listen to an empty cry, nor will the Almighty regard it.

—JOB 35:12-13

Arrogance and hypocrisy are also ungodly behaviors that can hinder our prayers.

Beware of the scribes who like to walk around in long robes, and like respectful greetings in the market places, and chief seats in the synagogues, and places of honor at banquets, who devour widows houses, and for appearance's sake offer long prayers; these will receive greater condemnation.

—MARK 12:38-40

Refusal to hear the cries of others or to help those in need can also hinder our prayers. As they say, "Actions speak louder than words." If we profess to be followers of Christ, yet we don't go out of our way to help those less fortunate who are within our paths and within our means to assist, nor do we offer comfort and support, then how can we expect to receive anything when we are in need?

> He who shuts his ear to the cry of the poor will also cry himself and not be answered.
> —Proverbs 21:13

> Let love be without hypocrisy. Abhor what is evil; cling to what is good. Be devoted to one another in brotherly love; *give preference to one another* in honor; not lagging behind in diligence; fervent in spirit, *serving the Lord; rejoicing in hope, persevering in tribulation, devoted to prayer.*
> —Romans 12:9 12

Finally, here is a Scripture that brings us back full circle to the purpose of prayer and the meaning of a fulfilled and happy life. "Serving the Lord" means that we should be devoted to others, honor and respect one another, be quick and diligent in service, rejoice in spreading hope, and be devoted to prayer.

That's a mouthful and a mighty high bar to clear, for sure. To accomplish this assignment we need to renew our minds. This transformation is unlike the way the world works; it is separate and apart. A dedication to service and sacrifice is necessary.

> And do not be conformed to this world, but be transformed by the renewing of your mind, *that you may prove what the will of God is*; that which is good and acceptable and perfect.
> —Romans 12:2

Apparently, this renewing of our minds brings with it some responsibility or duty that we are called into action to perform. In renewing our minds, we are tasked with proving what the will of God is. This requires us all to live lives that are good, acceptable, and to the best of our abilities, above reproach. We are going to need some help with this. Fortunately, the Bible, in addition to telling us the hindrances to prayer, also offers us some accelerators to prayer. These accelerators, or enablers, of prayer include but are not limited to the following: doing selfless service, being humble, having a forgiving spirit, believing in Him who made us, trusting in Him who strengthens us, diligently striving to have compassionate and clean hearts, standing in hope, not wavering in faith, and having confidence in whom Christ is and acting upon what He says about us.

> No matter how deep the stains of your sins, I can take it out and make you as clean as freshly fallen snow. Even if you are stained as red as crimson, I can make you white as wool.
>
> —ISAIAH 1:18

> You are already clean because of the word which I have spoken to you.
>
> —JOHN 15:3

> Therefore if any man is in Christ, he is a new creature; the old things passed away; behold, new things have come.
>
> —2 CORINTHIANS 5:17

> You are from God, little children, and have overcome them; because greater is He who is in you than he who is in the world.
>
> —1 JOHN 4:4

For I can do all things through Him who strengthens me.

—PHILIPPIANS 4:13

For God has not given you a spirit of timidity [fear], but of power and love and of sound mind.

—2 TIMOTHY 1:7

No weapon formed against you shall prosper . . .

—ISAIAH 54:17

The same Spirit that rose Christ Jesus from the dead, dwells in you.

—ROMANS 8:11

For all who are being led by the Spirit of God, these are the sons of God.

—ROMANS 8:14

If God is for us, who can stand against us?

—ROMANS 8:31

These are but a few of the Scriptures I had hidden in my heart and ready on my tongue when that dark spirit of fear swooped into the prayer room and breathed down my neck. These are the verses I summoned up in the heat of battle. They were my rock, my fortress, and *my right as an heir* to the kingdom. They are the Word of God. Spoken and believed, they are the power of God. They were my sword when darkness came—it gave way to the light.

SIGNIFICANT OBSERVATIONS:

1. All have sinned and have fallen short of the kingdom of God.
2. Forgiveness is but an admission away.
3. Your sins are removed as far as the east is from the west.
4. Practice avoiding acts that hinder prayer until they no longer are hindrances.
5. Fire up the prayer accelerators.
6. Know who you are *in* Christ and what He has promised to His heirs.
7. When our adversary shows up, remind him how the story ends.
8. Stand and deliver. Unleash the Word of God in battle with a vengeance.

FAITH—THE FINAL FRONTIER:
WHEN ALL IS DONE—STAND

*Now faith is the assurance of things hoped for, the conviction
of things not seen.*

—HEBREWS 11:1

Do you remember those crazy mathematical word problems in school
that required you to break down every sentence and analyze every word
to find the components necessary to calculate the distance you would
need to travel and the fuel you would expend to get to a place you had
no interest in going to? I strongly disliked those word problems, but I
like this one a lot.

Take another look at the Scripture reference above. Do you see the
mathematical equation? Remember, the word "is" equates to an equals
sign.

(Warning: this is a word problem. Some knowledge of mathematical
symbols is required.)

So, Faith = Assurance.

But assurance of what? Things hoped for. These things hoped for are
a mix of things such as desires, dreams, and ambitions which together

form a substance. This substance is therefore the essence of all you hope for. According to the Scripture, we have assurances *in advance* of these hopes, a promise that our things hoped for will indeed come to pass. Furthermore, we have strong conviction in knowing that our substances will manifest *even before* we actually see anything happen. Our evidence of this being the case is in our conviction.

Faith = Assurance of things hoped for + Conviction of things not seen

Faith occurs in the *now*. Once something happens—let's say a package is delivered to your house or you learn that a prayer request has been fulfilled—there is no longer a need for faith, as what you were standing in faith for has already come to pass. So faith happens first, and it happens before we receive physical evidence or confirmation. This faith carries over and sustains us through the hope stage. Hope is that time period of anticipation, like Christmas Eve for the little ones. Hope *is* that confident expectation of an upcoming good coming to pass.

The Scripture below is one of my most favorite Scriptures on prayer. This is another one of those formula verses that tell us if we do this, then that will happen. It's a Lego verse; you add another piece to the design and something deeper emerges and begins to take shape.

> And this is the confidence that we have before him, that, if we ask anything according to His will, He hears us. And if we know that He hears us in whatever we ask, we know that we have the requests, which we have asked from Him.
>
> —1 JOHN 5: 14-15

The verse starts out by assuring us that we should have great confidence in what we are about to hear.

Step 1: "If we ask . . ." The first thing that we must do is to ask.

Step 2: "Ask anything in accordance to His will . . ." Did you know that it is His will for you to be blessed, healthy, strong both physically and mentally, full of joy, full of faith, bondage-free, happy, and an example to others? The list goes on and on, so know that God wants the very best of all He has provided for us. Don't get too lost in trying to find God's will like it's a secret. It's laid out for us on nearly every page of the Bible.

Step 3: "He hears us!" That's a great start.

Step 4: "If we know that He hears us in whatever we ask . . ."

Step 5: "We know that we have the requests . . ."

This is faith in action with a twist. Because you have this confidence in your prayer requests, you actually have a faith-accelerating advantage; you know in advance that your requests will be granted.

> If you abide in Me, and My words abide in you, ask whatever you wish, and it shall be done for you.
> —JOHN 15:7

> Ask and it shall be given to you; seek and you shall find; knock and it shall be opened to you. For everyone who asks receives; and he who seeks finds, and to him who knocks it shall be opened.
> —MATTHEW 7:7-8

Ask, seek, and knock. Receive, find, and enter. We initiate the three actions and God promises the three results. Notice again that this passage is for everyone, not just for the elders of the church; nor is it reserved for any favored religion or body of believers. These are universal promises to all who will call upon the name of the Lord with a sincere, humble heart in search of God's perfect will.

> For truly I say to you, if you have faith as a mustard seed, you shall say to this mountain, 'move from here to there,' and it shall move; and nothing shall be impossible to you.
>
> —MATTHEW 17:20

How many of you have actually walked up to a mountain, said, "Move from here to there," and have actually seen the mountain move? Don't answer too quickly, because I'm betting you have. I know I have! That said, my mountains were not literal mountains, but they may as well have been. They were huge, insurmountable obstacles that stood before me, taunting me, and they had to be removed before I could move forward. God parted the Red Sea, Moses tapped a rock and water poured out of it. Jesus raised Lazarus from the dead, and for a few short steps, Peter actually walked on water. Anything is possible with God. However, I believe this passage is speaking more of the spiritual heart than of the physical mind. I believe it is summoning up our faith more than anything else.

In the words of Elvis, "Lord, you gave me a mountain this time." Like Elvis, I've cried out to God about my mountains. I've actually had several mountains that seemed totally unchangeable and impenetrable; through prayer, patience, and faith, these seemingly insurmountable obstacles were indeed moved, torn down, shattered, or resolved to my satisfaction. Some of them stood in my way at the work place. Others erupted at home. Looking back, I'm convinced that without God's supernatural intervention, passage forward would not have been possible.

> Have Faith in God. "Truly I say to you, *whoever says* to this mountain, "be taken up and cast into the sea," *and* does not doubt in his heart, but *believes that what he says is going to happen*, it shall be granted him. Therefore I say to you, *all things for which you pray and ask, believe that you have received them* and they shall be granted you. And

whenever you stand praying, forgive; if you have anything against anyone, so that your Father also who is in heaven may forgive you your transgressions.

—MARK 11:22-25

Note the italicized text above. We have to say and believe in advance of something happening. Notice the words, "going to happen." This is future, not past, tense. Also, note that we are to believe we've received them. The word "received" is also in past tense, yet what we requested hasn't yet occurred.

It may appear as though I'm dicing words here like a master chef chops garlic, but I'm convinced that God is in the details, and that once we see how Faith works, we will find both rest and peace within the essence of faith. No longer will our thoughts be tossed to and fro. Doubt will no longer take precedence. For a moment, look at faith from God's perspective. From His point of view, all things are possible. When He decided to separate the heavens from the land, He simply spoke this into existence. When the ancient world stopped appreciating and observing His signs and wonders, and few gave heed to His voice through miracles, He offered His Son, knowing full well that through Christ's life, death, burial, and resurrection, His voice would be heard throughout time. God's faith in His creation, man, has been demonstrated time and time again since the very beginning. He has never stopped believing in us, or hoping the best for us; He has been faithful and stands ready to help us.

I tell you that He will bring about justice for them speedily. However, when the Son of Man comes, will He find faith on the earth?

—LUKE 18:8

Because of God's actions and through the life of His Son, He does find faith on this earth. He sees it in our actions. He hears it in our prayers. He found hope and faith in Noah, and because of Noah's prayers, God saved Noah's family, granting us all a second chance. There was faith on the earth when the woman with the hemorrhage reached out and touched the hem of Jesus' cloak, giving us an example of faith in action. There was faith in the land when both Caleb and Joshua went into Canaan to spy out the land for Moses and the people of Israel, giving us an example of how to see and report things through the eyes of faith. Faith was found in a young shepherd boy named David, a young boy, not a warrior, who slayed Goliath with nothing more than a sling shot; he is an example of knowing without question who we are in Christ and who will win the battle. Jesus honored the Roman Centurion who approached him on the road and asked that his servant be healed with just a word from Jesus, no house visit required. God found faithfulness in wicked King Ahab's son, Hezekiah. And today, there is much faith to be found across the globe.

> Therefore having been justified by faith, we have peace with God through our Lord Jesus Christ, through whom also we have obtained our introduction by faith into this grace in which we stand; and we exult in hope of the glory of God. And not only this, but we also exult in our tribulations, knowing that tribulation brings about perseverance; and perseverance, proven character; and proven character, hope.
> —ROMANS 5:1-4

Perseverance is the bridge to proving our character. According to the dictionary, perseverance means persistence, determination, grit, stubbornness, tenacity, steadfastness, and resolve. These character traits, when processed and pressed into one product, shrink-wrapped and ready for distribution, form a character who has proven his ability to stand, endure, and be a beacon of hope whom others can rely on.

We've all heard the phrase, "If it were easy, anyone could do it." It may be more accurate to say, "If it were easy, no one would value it." If everything that came to us was delivered on a silver platter, we would not appreciate the effort that was required to provide it.

Imagine you are the ruler of a mighty and fruitful land called Prosperity Kingdom. You have servants in your court who bring you whatever your heart desires. In your kingdom, you have farmers and workers who plant seeds, till the land, water the plants, trim the fruit trees, pick the fruit, and prepare it in advance of you requesting it. Furthermore, imagine that the soil best suited for these fruit trees, which are your favorite, only exists on the other side of your kingdom some twenty days away by foot; it lies on the other side of a mighty, dangerous river, and beyond a mountain pass. The farmers make this journey at great risk to themselves.

Unless your Lordship ventures outside the palace walls to learn how to plant your own seed, till your own soil, make the long trek, ford the river, and ascend the mountain to trim your trees and pick your own fruit, you'll never truly appreciate the full flavor of what went into the blessing that you enjoy.

Today in America, the land of opportunity, many feel entitled; affluent silver-spoon young adults have had little experience testing their faith. They run the risk of not learning what is required to gain the position and stature of one lacking in nothing, as described in our next verse. Generally speaking, they have been spoiled to the point that when money runs out, when their iPhone apps no longer work, when their employers are too demanding, insensitive, or unfair, and they are forced to turn to God for answers, their earned foundation of perseverance will be rather thin if it even exists.

> Consider it all joy, my brethren, when you encounter various trials, knowing that the testing of your faith produces endurance. And let endurance have its perfect result, that you may be perfect and complete, lacking in nothing.
>
> —JAMES 1:3

Trust me on this one: I'm not down on the wealthy or the privileged. Rather, I am up on building character traits that will not only sustain us, but propel us forward to become a kinder people and a nation that truly is a beacon of light and a city on the hill.

> Do you not know that those who run in a race all run, but only one receives the prize? Run in such a way that you may win. And everyone who competes in the games exercises self-control in all things. Therefore, I run in such a way, as not without aim . . .
>
> —1 CORINTHIANS 9:24-26

Learning what faith is, why we need it, how to call it up, and how to stand in it ensures that we are running our race with a vision to win, with a hope that is fixed, focused, and not without aim.

> Let us hold fast the confessions of our Hope without wavering, for He who promised is Faithful.
>
> —HEBREWS 10:23

> And without faith it is impossible to please Him, for he who comes to God must believe that He is, and that He is a rewarder of those who seek him.
>
> —HEBREWS 11:6

As we discussed already, Faith honors God, and God always honors Faith. These are two excellent reasons why we need faith in our lives. Being a beacon of hope to others honors God. When your neighbors see your faith in action, how you continue to smile through the loss of a loved one, or how you never waver under the heat of difficulty, their hope and faith will be strengthened. It is the shield of faith that protects us when trials come, one after another. Having a thick shield, one that has been proven strong and reliable in battle, is a great comfort.

In addition to all, taking up the shield of faith with which you will be able to extinguish all the flaming missiles of the evil one.

—Ephesians 6:16

Humble yourselves, therefore, under the mighty hand of God, that He may exalt you at the proper time, casting all your anxiety upon Him, because He cares for you. Be of sober spirit; be on the alert. Your adversary, the devil, prowls about like a roaring lion, seeking someone to devour. But resist him, firm in your faith.

—1 Peter 5:6-9

But our battles are not all about raising kids, school assignments, challenges at work, or ailing grandparents. The two passages above seem to indicate that our battles, trials, and bouts in faith will come into play more in the spiritual realm than in the natural one. As we mature, our battles between yes or no, right and wrong, good and evil, become crystal clear; the difference is easy to discern.

Once you've practiced prayer and have witnessed His power firsthand, both in the small things and in the greater battles, everything begins to fall into place. Knowing His will regarding certain decisions becomes easier. Whether you should do or not do something (Should I go there or stay here?) becomes clearer. Life's decisions become easier to process. The gray area between right and wrong becomes black. It either is or it isn't. Distinguishing between good and evil (for example, integrity and ethics vs. gray areas to advancement at work) even comes into greater focus the longer you walk with God.

Here's a live-fire example of trying to make a decision on the borders of those gray areas.

Late in 2005, I accepted a job that was located in the Midwest, even though we were living just south of Denver, Colorado, at the time. My oldest daughter had already started college and was now part of the Disney college program; she played Minnie and Mickey Mouse plus a host of other zoo characters, as they referred to them, at Disneyworld in Orlando. My younger daughter was just beginning her sophomore year of high school at Columbine High School. Yes, that Columbine. She was very active in sports, wrote for the school yearbook, took photos for the yearbook, enjoyed great grades, had more friends than Linda and I could keep track of, and was fully engaged and loved everything about high school. So what do you do? Pull her from school right when she's firing on all cylinders so that Dad can pursue his dreams, even though it means dashing hers? This was a tough spot to be in. We devoted much prayer towards the decision. A bit more background might be of interest in further complicating the situation. Linda and I were very fortunate and blessed in that we actually had the means to afford our home in Colorado and an apartment for me to live in while working in Missouri. We were also quite blessed that our marriage was strong enough to endure time apart from each other for weeks on end. It was not outside of our reach to avoid disrupting our daughter's high school experience and fulfill her wish and desire to graduate from Columbine with all her friends. Not everyone would have been able to make the decision we did, but I thank God we were given that opportunity.

I share this story to simply point out that even though we were able to afford two places, we still had to wrestle with the issues surrounding the situation, such as whether or not it was advisable to be away from my youngest daughter during her impressionable high school years. We had to seek God's wisdom as to whether we were doing the right thing or not. We knew it was God's will for me to have a job and continue to be the provider for my family. We knew that conventional wisdom suggested we should all stay together. But we also knew that this job opportunity would be short-lived, as the objective was to prepare the company to be acquired by another one. Many of our service men and women when called up for duty, have to say goodbye to their families for a season; we figured if they could make such a sacrifice, so could we. Yet unlike our service men and women, I could easily fly home in two hours to attend an important softball game or to be there for her prom and other special occasions. We asked our youngest daughter about her thoughts on the matter. We consulted with family and friends to get their opinions. Some thought we were nuts to put such strain on the family, and suggested that we all move back together. Others appreciated and admired what we were willing to do to ensure our daughter had the best high school experience possible. After much prayer and consideration, I packed up my little jeep and headed to Missouri to begin my new job, knowing that we had sought God, had included Him in our plans, and trusted Him to bless and honor our decision.

Sometimes, it's easy to know the will of God and make decisions. Other times, a decision requires additional insight, counsel, and trust in what you are able to deduce and conclude. Just because you can afford to do certain things, like own multiple homes, or live a certain lifestyle, doesn't necessarily mean you should. What's important is to include God in your planning, rely on Him for insight and guidance, and listen for His voice.

If, after consulting God through prayers and conversations, you have complete confidence and peace about a topic, then you have heard God's voice. The prayer room Pastor I mentioned earlier once said, "Hearing from God is five percent human spirit, five percent Holy Ghost, and ninety percent that inner witness or knowing deep inside that you have God's peace." Linda and I have found that sometimes, when things fall into place painlessly, without anything being forced, this is God's way of speaking to us; He favors our plan and is blessing our efforts. Conversely, when things feel forced and do not go smoothly, when things break down time after time, again and again, maybe this is God's way of telling us we are rushing His timing or taking the wrong path, and that we should reconsider our motives.

Here are four additional things to remember when you really need to hear from God. First, you must be free of pressure to hear from the Holy Ghost. Second, never make a decision if fear is around. Third, if you permit your mind or flesh to override and drive your decision-making, you will not be able to hear God's voice.

Last, Faith is not passive or wishful thinking; it is *an active practice or discipline of thinking.* Worry, on the other hand, is undisciplined thought. Remain focused and think about God's promises and what He has to say about you; this will help silence fear, doubt, and worry.

As we mature and dive deeper into the spiritual things of God, which will border if not downright cross over into enemy territory, this is where our true colors of faith will be tested and proven.

> For though we walk in the flesh, we do not war according to the flesh, for the weapons of our warfare are not of the flesh, but divinely powerful for the destruction of fortresses. We are destroying speculations and every lofty thing [thought], raised up against the knowledge of God, and we are to take every thought captive to the obedience of Christ.
>
> —2 CORINTHIANS 10:3-5

This passage has practical instructions as well as deep spiritual instructions for us. It suggests that many battles occur in our minds and that we need to be diligent in bringing every thought and speculation that is contrary to the knowledge of God to its knees. Just because you were born poor or came from a family that has struggled and scratched out a living, it doesn't mean you have to continue to settle, or to listen to the thoughts in your mind that say, "It's always been this way, and you'll never be able to change your situation." These thoughts are not in line with what God has to say about you, or about your situation. You are an overcomer. God says He is a rewarder of those who diligently seek Him. So seek Him with everything you have, do not waver, and watch Him begin to change your circumstances and make you the head, and not the tail.

However, to fully obtain everything God has promised us, and to effectively and successfully pursue the things worth fighting for, we will need more than just our shield of faith. We will need the full armor of God.

SIGNIFICANT OBSERVATIONS:

1. Faith is the assurance of things hoped for.
2. Faith occurs in the *now*.
3. Perseverance is the bridge to proving our character.
4. If it were easy, no one would value it.
5. Make no mistake, we do have an adversary.
6. We must be free of pressure to hear from the Holy Ghost.
7. Never make decisions when fear is around.
8. Worry is undisciplined thought.
9. Faith is the active practice of disciplining thought.

BIRTH OF A WARRIOR
PART 1: SALVATION TO SOLDIER

Therefore, take up the full armor of God, that you may be able to resist in the evil day, having done everything, to stand firm.

—EPHESIANS 6:13

With a solid foundation now under our belts of what God's will is, what His character is all about, where to find wisdom, why establishing a habit of prayer is important, and why faith is critical to everyday life, let's take the next two chapters to explore how all that we've learned matures into a purposeful life that is pleasing to God.

To do this, we will quickly walk through the life stages of maturity towards becoming a Warrior for the King. We will reaffirm God's pre-existing love for each of us, and what that means, review some Scriptures that talk about the rearing years of young adults, visit the teenage years, and finally, step into the age of accountability.

There's an old saying: "If you don't believe in something, you will fall for anything." I believe this saying is also captured in song, and rightfully so, as it is a very deserving and true statement. Obviously, if you don't have a solid inner understanding of your personal morals, ethics, and integrity, when you are faced with a decision between two gray options, you may forget that there could be another option or a higher road to take besides what is being offered at the time. It also follows that if you don't believe in God, don't accept what He has done or what He says about each of us, then you will probably fall for other, less favorable belief systems that will lead you to empty purpose and little fulfillment. For those who have yet to fully accept and receive what God has done for them and what He has enabled them to accomplish, I pray that you take in this chapter slowly and fully absorb all the Scriptures have to say about how much God loves you, and what He promises for those who have accepted His grace. For all others, let this chapter serve as a reminder of God's love for you, and of His call for rededication.

Let's start with God's pre-existing love for each and every one of us; this love existed even before we were introduced to His goodness. It existed before we decided to receive it, before we accepted the call to be born again by the renewing of our minds. This love continues even when we misbehave, or lose our way, or try to outrun Him.

> But God demonstrates His own love towards us, in that while we were yet sinners, Christ died for us.
> —ROMANS 5:8

> For God so loved the world that He gave His only begotten Son, that whoever believes in Him should not perish, but have eternal life.
> —JOHN 3:16

I love this verse, especially the word "whoever." Are you a whoever? Notice it doesn't say, "Only the holy and worthy who believe in Him," or, "God so loved the rich folks that He provided His only Son for these chosen few." No sir, it clearly states that *whoever* believes in Him shall not perish, but have eternal life. I am a whoever, and you are a whoever too.

That if you confess with your mouth Jesus as Lord, and believe in your heart that God raised Him from the dead, you shall be saved; for with the heart man believes, resulting in righteousness, and with the mouth he confesses, resulting in salvation.

—ROMANS 10:9

So then, my beloved, just as you have always obeyed, not as in my presence only, but now much more in my absence, work out your salvation with fear and trembling.

—PHILIPPIANS 2:12

To restate these verses, now that we have accepted and believed, thus making an effort to secure and maintain right standing (righteousness in Him), we simply need to work out (practice, practice, practice) our own salvation with reverence and purpose in Christ.

Therefore be imitators of God, as beloved children; and walk in love, just as Christ also loved you, and gave Himself up for us, an offering and a sacrifice to God as a fragrant aroma.

—EPHESIANS 5:1-2

He made Him who knew no sin to be sin on our behalf, that we might become the righteousness of God in Him.

—2 CORINTHIANS 5:21

Blessed are those who hunger and thirst for righteousness, for they shall be satisfied.

—MATTHEW 5:6

And for what purpose or calling did Christ give up His life for us? What was God thinking when He gave His only Son, to die on the cross for me, even before I was born?

> Nevertheless He saved them for the sake of His name, that He might make His power known.
>
> —PSALM 106:8

> Who has saved us, and called us with a holy calling, not according to our works, but according to His own purpose and grace which was granted us in Christ Jesus from all eternity.
>
> —2 TIMOTHY 1:9

> And we know that God causes all things to work together for good to those who love God, to those who are called according to His purpose.
>
> —ROMANS 8:28

It has been said, that the only ability God lacks is availability. Our purpose here on earth is to be available and to let His purpose and His will play out through our lives so that "He might make His power known." What this means is really rather simple. When your coworkers, neighbors, kids, and other family members see that you are no longer the old dirtbag of a person you once were (selfish, greedy, drunk all the time, you name it) and they begin to witness a new person shaping up and out of that old heathen of your old self, they will have witnessed the power of God in action. His power will be known.

> And do not participate in the unfruitful deeds of darkness, but instead, even expose them.
>
> —EPHESIANS 5:11

For our struggle is not against flesh and blood, but against the rulers, against the powers, against the world forces of this darkness, against the spiritual forces of wickedness, in the heavenly places.

—EPHESIANS 6:12

Behold, I send you out as sheep in the midst of wolves; therefore be shrewd as serpents, and innocent as doves.

—MATTHEW 10:16

Stand firm therefore, having girded your loins with truth, and having put on the breastplate of righteousness.

—EPHESIANS 6:14

And take the helmet of salvation, and the sword of the Spirit, which is the word of God.

—EPHESIANS 6:17

And for this reason I remind you to kindle afresh the gift of God which is in you through the laying on of hands. For God has not given us a spirit of timidity [fear], but of power, and love and discipline [sound judgment].

—2 TIMOTHY 1:6-7

With this knowledge and with these tools, we are promised his protection; just as our children are promised our protection as they approach their teens and young adulthood. As they mature, we share deeper insight with them into how to survive in the real world, just as God instructs us.

I can do all things through Him who strengthens me.

—PHILIPPIANS 4:13

For no weapon formed against you shall prosper . . .

—Isaiah 54:17

No evil will befall you, nor will any plague come near your tent. For He will give His angels charge concerning you, to guard you in all your ways.

—Psalms 91:10-11

The eyes of the Lord are toward [upon] the righteous, and His ears are open [attentive to] their cry.

—Psalm 34:15

Hence, also, He is able to save forever those who draw near to God through Him [Jesus], since He always loves to make intercession (praying) for them.

—Hebrews 7:25

It's always comforting to hear from friends and family that they are praying for you, especially during difficult times. Often when we experience tough times, whether they are financial struggles due to being let go from a job, or separation in a long-term relationship, feelings of loneliness and depression can be overwhelming. But when we understand and recognize that Christ Himself is making intercession (praying) on our behalf, the journey takes on a whole new meaning. For example, instead of simply trying to find a new job to replace the income we have lost, the quest becomes deeper as we begin to ask God for insight and direction, not just for replacement income. Perhaps He will provide additional insight into new opportunities that align more closely with the destiny He has planned for our lives.

When I was going through the valley of unemployment for the second or third time, I learned lessons I didn't even know I needed to learn, and I learned a few that I seriously didn't want to learn.

Of all the lessons I have had the joy of learning (either the hard way or the easy way), I recall two stories that even today remain paramount in my mind, as though they happened only yesterday.

Remember my story of the meltdown discussion that I had with my Brother, Steve? After being out of work for just over a year, I had reached my boiling point, or in this case, meltdown mountain. As you'll recall, I was quite upset with God for not answering my prayers for employment. Worse yet, I had now recruited my young daughters to help pray for daddy to get a job, and I was afraid that they might begin to think God was a joke if He didn't start answering *their* prayers soon. The thought of their mustard seed faith being messed with was unthinkable, unacceptable. You can mess with me all you want, but mess with my kids? Not going to happen, not without hearing from momma or me. Not on my watch. But then Brother Steve looked me square in the eye and said, "David, maybe God wants them to learn about the fight of Faith by watching you."

It was like getting whacked in the back of the head with a two-by-four . . . And as quickly as he said it, I said, "Well, if that's His plan, then sign me up for another tour of duty."

Now how stupid that was! Who would want another twelve months or even twelve hours of hopelessness, feelings of worthlessness, and every other low feeling that comes from being out of work for so long? No one! But in hindsight, I believe that God judged my heart and words that day, and found me humbled to the core, ready to butch up, to pull up my big boy pants, and to stand and deliver.

If continuing the battle would help my girls learn how to stand in Faith, I would do it, even if I didn't have the strength to hold my head high or stick out my chin. I was ready to re-engage, because now I had a purpose worth fighting for.

> And in the same way the Spirit also helps our weakness;
> for we do not know how to pray as we should, but the

> Spirit Himself intercedes for us with groaning too deep
> for words; and He who searches the hearts knows what the
> mind of the Spirit is, because He intercedes for the saints
> according to the will of God.
>
> —ROMANS 8:26

The second lesson came just a few months later. My wife had cut an ad out of the paper and placed it in my briefcase. They were hiring at Dillard's in the men's department. It sat in my briefcase for at least a week, maybe longer.

On my way to a local interview, I told myself that if I didn't get the job, I would stop by Dillard's and apply for the job in the men's department. Let me put this in perspective for you. Before being downsized from one of the top five consulting companies in the country just after 9/11, where I managed their Internet and e-Commerce business, traveled abroad, and had even been a keynote speaker in Geneva, Switzerland, I had been earning a mid-six-figure income. I think Dillard's was paying ten dollars an hour.

Suffice it to say, I didn't think I did a good job answering the hiring kids' questions during the interview, so I drove straight to Dillard's, rode the elevator to the management floor, and asked to speak with the hiring manager, who took one look at me and asked if I needed a job. It must have been obvious to the hiring manager that I was playing my last card. Later that day, I found myself sitting in a cluttered stock room with four other new hires, watching videos on how to fold clothes and straighten tables.

I'm not kidding. This is a true story. For some reason, God thought I needed another serving of humble pie; yes, again I sat down at the table, swallowed my pride, and finished my plate. About sixty days later, the kids at the company where I'd interviewed called and offered me a job as their boss. I humbly accepted, and today, a photocopy of my first Dillard's paycheck and my little name tag are framed in a shadow box that hangs above my nightstand at about head height. Every day when

I wake up, this plaque serves as a constant reminder that humility is painful, but that God will always see me through it.

> Rejoicing in hope, persevering in tribulation, devoted to prayer.
>
> —ROMANS 12:12

As we gain more understanding of how principles work within the kingdom, and of what components are at work in the kingdom, we learn more about the Helper, the Holy Spirit, who dwells within each of us and is there to offer instruction and guidance. Think of the Helper as the inner voice of reason that we hope our teenagers carry with them and defer to every time they leave the house without us around to guide them. As we wave goodbye to them, we pray they will recall and listen to the voice of wisdom we've shared with them over the years.

> But the Helper, the Holy Spirit, whom the Father will send in My name, He will teach you all things, and bring to your remembrance all that I said to you.
>
> —JOHN 14:26

> As for me, I baptize you with water for repentance, but He who is coming after me is mightier than I, and I am not fit to remove His sandals; He will baptize you with the Holy Spirit and fire.
>
> —MATTHEW 3:11

> Do you not know that you are a temple of God, and that the Spirit of God dwells in you?
>
> —1 CORINTHIANS 3:16

But if the Spirit of Him who raised Jesus from the dead dwells in you, He who raised Christ Jesus from the dead will also give life to your mortal bodies, through His Spirit who indwells you.

—ROMANS 8:11

And do not get drunk with wine, for that is dissipation, but be filled with the Spirit, speaking to one another in psalms and hymns and spiritual songs, singing and making melody with your heart to the Lord; always giving thanks for all things in the name of our Lord Jesus Christ to God, even the Father.

—EPHESIANS 5:18-19

Do not become anxious about how or what you should speak in your defense, or what you should say; for the Holy Spirit will teach you in that very hour what you ought to say.

—LUKE 12:11-12

And Peter said to them, repent, and let each of you be baptized in the name of Jesus Christ for the forgiveness of your sins; and you shall receive the gift of the Holy Spirit.

—ACTS 2:38

He who believes in Me, the works that I do shall he do also; and greater works than these shall he do; because I go to the Father.

—JOHN 14:12

As we grow from baby Christians feeding on milk to more established and tested Christians feeding on solid food (the deeper things of God), and then to full-fledged, responsible soldiers with accountability for the spiritual welfare of others as well as ourselves, it becomes necessary to have a solid, firm, and even bold opinion and voice with which to speak out against the things of darkness that confuse the weak.

> In whom we have boldness and confident access through faith in Him.
>
> —EPHESIANS 3:12

> For He was teaching them as one having authority, and not as their scribes.
>
> —MATTHEW 7:29

Not only do we have a higher sense of accountability, also God gives us authority, through His Son, to perform His will, to fight the good fight, and to overcome.

> And having summoned His twelve disciples, He gave them authority over unclean spirits, to cast them out, and to heal every kind of disease and every kind of sickness.
>
> —MATTHEW 10:1

> And Jesus came up and spoke to them, saying, "all authority has been given to Me in heaven and on earth. Go therefore and make disciples of all the nations, baptizing them in the name of the Father, and the Son and the Holy Spirit, teaching them to observe all that I commanded you; and lo, I am with you always, even to the end of the age."
>
> —MATTHEW 28:18-20

The passage above is known as the Great Commission. This commission is not only the call and purpose of every born-again Christian; it is also the purpose and call to the Church, the united body of believers who call Jesus their Lord and Savior. There are Churches (bricks-and-mortar institutions) as well as bodies of believers who disagree or are split on the practice of some religious rites, traditions, and principles. But on this, the Great Commission, we should all be of one accord.

SIGNIFICANT OBSERVATIONS:

1. God loved us before we even knew of Him.
2. There are life stages each Christian passes through along his journey.
3. From birth through the rearing years; youthful defiance to adulthood.
4. Through each phase, Christ intercedes for us.
5. Our Helper, the Holy Spirit, dwells in those who believe.
6. We may discern God's will in the deeper things of God.
7. We may claim authority through His Son to expose darkness and injustice.
8. That He might make His power known through us.

BIRTH OF A WARRIOR
PART 2: SOLDIERS AND WARRIORS

Prepare a war rouse the mighty men! Let all the soldiers draw near; let them come up! Beat your plowshares into swords, and your pruning hooks into spears; let the weak say, I am a mighty man!

—Joel 3:9-10

In this day and age of political correctness and making sure folks keep things said or printed in context, I am not advocating or calling for a revolution to rise up and overthrow any establishment in the physical sense. Rather, I am calling the mighty men and women of prayer to humble themselves and rededicate themselves to vigilant prayer on behalf of our nation and of all nations of the world.

If we, who profess to be Christians, will not be the moral backbone and voice of a nation, soldiers for Christ and warriors for the King, then who will?

The word "rouse" means encourage, inspire, and motivate. In the verse above it means to stir up, revive, and awaken via remembrance what God has done for us; to galvanize and renew afresh what He has called us to do in this world.

We are to make the best of what we have. It's way past time for us to beat our plowshares into swords, and our pruning hooks into spears. It's high time we reclaimed our voice and said, "We are mighty in the Lord."

In the Old Testament, which contains the book of Joel, there are more references to warring tribes and nations than anyone would like to count. It's unfortunate and sad to think that so much bloodshed and destruction occurred in days gone by. Why tribes and nations couldn't just settle on a piece of land and live in harmony with one another is a mystery to me, one better left to factual interpretation from those more capable than I. Maybe if they had had better musical instruments or a visitation from John Lennon singing "Imagine" the music that soothes the savage beast would have prevailed.

It was this constant theme of war, land grabs, rebellion against oppression, injustice, and over taxation that led prophets, teachers, and writers of both the Old and New Testaments to write and speak with prose that were commonly understood and practiced in those days. Today, we are far from done with war or even rumors of war, but we do live in a more balanced society than our forefathers. So while we aren't perfect by any stretch of the imagination, we are capable of applying contemporary interpretations to the Scriptures of old to help us uncover wisdom we can use today.

So while Joel was literally calling for folks to postpone farming activities and beat their plowshares into swords, today we could define this same call to arms as a spiritual revival, a call to sharpen our gifts and individual talents into instruments that will rouse folks to get back in the game, back to God. If you possess the gift of teaching, then dust off your Bible, bone up on the word and sign up to teach a Bible study at your church or in your neighborhood. If you have the gift of helping, but are no longer applying that gift for the benefit of the kingdom, ask yourself why. When you are in the workplace and you have an opportunity to encourage, uplift, and inspire others to be more sensitive to and mindful of their coworkers, diligently do so. When you see "stinkin' thinkin'" call it out. When you see injustice, just as Nehemiah did, find a way to bring it to the attention of someone who can make a difference. Each of these suggestions might cause discomfort or put your position at risk, but if we know there are things that God would like addressed, yet we don't do anything about them out of fear of the consequences, we are in the wrong.

Throughout my careers as management executives or officers in companies, I've had countless encounters with stupidity and egotopia (I made this word up but I'm sure you know what I mean), and in the boardroom, I have witnessed dysfunctional behavior beyond description. In fact, after months of listening and participating with a group of officers at one of my employs, I actually got fed up one day and told them all that we (myself included) were the most dysfunctional group of decision-makers and supposed leaders I had ever seen.

It wasn't a particularly smooth career move if you know what I mean, especially in light of the fact that I was the newest member of the team. For months, I had struggled with how to approach or even avoid sharing my assessment of our situation. Someone needed to say something to help us learn to be better collaborators and leaders. In this particular case, no one was fired, not even yours truly. However, the CEO did concur with my assessment, and hence he fired "the board from the board." What did that mean in the scheme of things? Not much. Instead of trying to work as a group, we then had to work individually towards our shared initiatives without meeting in a formal boardroom setting. I'm sure if I had made that same decision in different boardrooms across our country, I would have been fired on the spot at some companies, but promoted at others.

> You therefore, my son, be strong in the grace that is in Christ Jesus, and the things which you have heard from me in the presence of many witnesses, these entrust to faithful

men, who will be able to teach others also. Suffer hardship
with me, as a good soldier of Christ Jesus.

—2 TIMOTHY 2:1-3

Behold, I have given you authority to tread upon serpents
and scorpions, and over all the power of the enemy, and
nothing shall injure you.

—LUKE 10:19

Personally, I don't like creepy crawly things, serpents, or reptiles, so you
won't find me out in the backyard charming snakes out of a basket to
demonstrate my comprehension of Scripture. To me, these Scriptures
refer to having faith, confidence, and assurance that when we take on
evil, and stand for those things that honor God and are pleasing in His
sight, we will have the favor of God on our side.

Truly I say unto you, whatever you shall bind on earth
shall be bound in heaven; and whatever you loose on earth
shall be loosed in heaven.

—MATTHEW 18:18

For the weapons of our warfare are not of the flesh, but
divinely powerful for the destruction of fortresses.

—2 CORINTHIANS 10:4

And the devil who deceived them was thrown into the
lake of fire and brimstone, where the beast and the false
prophet are also; and they will be tormented day and night
forever and ever.

—REVELATION 20:10

This is one Scripture you will want to memorize and have at the ready
as you enter into the realm of prayer warfare, for without doubt the

enemy will come to discourage you as he did that day I was in the prayer room. Be quick to remind him and his minions, that you've finished the Good Book and know how the story ends; they have already lost the contest, and they are destined a never-ending swim in the lake of fire. This is a very powerful statement in the heat of spiritual warfare.

> And these signs shall accompany those who have believed in My name, they will cast out demons, they will speak with new tongues; they will pick up serpents, and if they drink any deadly poison, it shall not hurt them; they will lay hands on the sick, and they will recover.
>
> —MARK 16: 17-18

> And from the Gadites there came over to David in the stronghold in the wilderness, mighty men of valor, men trained for war, who could handle shield and spear, and whose faces were like the faces of lions, and they were as swift as the gazelles on the mountains.
>
> —1 CHRONICLES 12:8

In the verse above there are many metaphors for the talent of David's warriors that might help us adapt this verse into something quite meaningful today. In the Bible, the shield is also compared with faith, the spear and sword, the Word of God. The phrase "swift as gazelles" refers back to "their quickness and agility to maneuver in tough spots."

So those mighty men of valor, who have trained their senses to know God's will, who have practiced and exercised their faith, who have hidden God's Word in their hearts, who have sharpened their tongues to be effective, whose faces are seasoned with wisdom like the lion's, are well able to assess a need and quickly respond to it, even in very tough spots.

The militant historians reading this book might enjoy reading about the origin of King David's mighty men. I refer them to 1 Chronicles 11:10 and 12:38.

While I certainly respect and honor the men and women who serve our country and volunteer to defend our freedoms, the reality and horror of war are truly nightmarish and far from being worthy of being romanticized. All one has to do to get a weak glimpse of the horrors that our modern day warriors have faced is watch the first two minutes of the film *Saving Private Ryan, Full Metal Jacket, Hamburger Hill,* or *The Hurt Locker;* there is a host of movies out there that attempt to bring the painful realities of modern warfare into our living rooms. For those seeking stronger visuals of the horrors of war in biblical times, "The Spartans," *300,* or *Gladiator* will make you thank God you were born when you were. Without question, war is an ugly evil; it is always bloody and seems quite senseless. But because evil does exist and by its nature will not rest until it prevails or is defeated, good must rise up against evil to make a stand.

Likewise, when evil raises its ugly head in the spiritual world where spiritual warfare in prayer takes place, taking a stand is also called for. When things are tougher than tough, stay in faith and persevere. When your back is against the wall and the forces of darkness are in your face, stand and deliver the Word. Remind the forces of darkness what the Word of God says. Remind them that you serve the living God, the only God, the Alpha and Omega, who is the Light of the World. Tell them who you are in Christ, that you are an heir according to the promise, washed in and covered by the blood of Jesus. Declare that the ground you are standing on is holy ground. Remind them that they are destined for the lake of fire. And when you're done giving fear, doubt, and the voices of darkness a piece of God's mind, dismiss them. Remember that they are not able to reside in the presence of the light!

SIGNIFICANT OBSERVATIONS:

1. Mighty men and women of prayer: revive your vigilance for prayer.
2. Entrust the things you've heard to the faithful.
3. We have been given authority and power over the enemy.
4. What we bind on earth shall be bound in heaven.
5. The weapons of our warfare are not carnal, but divinely powerful.
6. The mighty in valor are trained and practiced.
7. Be bold, be vigilant, and above all else, stand.

NOAH:
LAST MAN STANDING

Thus Noah did; according to all that God commanded him, so he did.

—GENESIS 6:22

Not long after God created humankind, His forbearance ran out, and He decided to bring a cataclysm upon the earth. He selected a man named Noah to undertake the world's first shipbuilding project. First, He told Noah what He planned to do.

Noah was a descendant of Seth, the third child of Adam and Eve. At first, the children of this line were faithful followers of God. One of them was a man called Enoch, the very same Enoch whom God translated alive into heaven. Noah was Enoch's great-grandson. Cain's descendants were not faithful to God; over time, they aided greatly in corrupting the line of Seth to the point that God had had enough. You don't have to dig very deep or dive too far into the Scriptures to quickly discern that in the society of biblical times things were ugly, corrupt, and violent. Crime, greed, deceit, murder, abuse, and a host of other sins and transgressions against humankind ran rampant.

> The Nephilim were on the earth in those days, and also afterward, when the sons of God [Seth's line] came in to

the daughters of men [Cain's line], and they bore children to them. Then the Lord saw that the wickedness of man was great on the earth, and that every intent of the thoughts of his heart was only evil continually.

—Genesis 6:4-5

So the Lord said, "I will destroy man whom I have created from the face of the earth, both man and beast, creeping things and birds of the air, for I am sorry that I have made them."

—Genesis 6:7

Noah faced a crisis of belief where he had to decide what he believed about God. Could he believe in a God whose purpose was to destroy all creation? Human reason suggested it was time to run and hide. Faith said, *Listen and obey.* All the characters you learn about in the Scriptures were just plain ordinary people. It was their relationships with God that made each of them extraordinary.

Besides being tasked by God to build the ark that would save his family and one of every species that roamed the earth, Noah's faithfulness bought mankind a second chance at life. Noah was a righteous man who found favor in God's sight.

But Noah found favor in the eyes of the Lord. These are the records of the generations of Noah. Noah was a righteous man, blameless in his time; Noah walked with God.

—Genesis 6:8-9

Then the Lord said to Noah, "Enter the ark, you and all your household; for you alone I have seen to be righteous before Me in this time."

—Genesis 7:1

Can only one man, one family, one devoted church or village, one community, or one nation really make a difference today? You bet they can! Noah was the one righteous man remaining in a dark and desolate time. Because God saw righteousness and faith in the land amongst the sin of the people, He made a covenant with Noah to save his family and all the inhabitants of the ark.

Given all that was happening at this time in history, Noah must have had an enormously deep relationship with God to be able to tolerate living in the company of sin gone wild. He must also have been strong in the Lord to endure the ridicule and harassment the local people must have showered on both him and his family. Despite the abuse, Noah was obedient to God's call. Not only did he start building the ark as instructed, he kept building it when there were no rain clouds in sight. It's conceivable that Noah tried desperately to warn extended family members and neighbors of the looming judgment; this would not have strengthened his position within the community.

When the time came for all the creatures of the earth to leave their habitat, and they filed into the ark, two-by-two, the entire cast of local nay-Sayers must have had puzzled looks on their faces. For seven days, the ridicule, taunting, and jokes prevailed. But on the eighth day, it began to rain.

> For after seven more days, I will send rain on the earth forty days and forty nights; and I will blot out from the face of the land every living thing that I have made.
> —GENESIS 7:4

> And God blessed Noah and his sons and said to them, "Be fruitful and multiply, and fill the earth. And the fear of you and the terror of you shall be on every beast of the earth and on every bird of the sky; with everything that creeps

on the ground, and all the fish of the sea, into your hands they are given."

—Genesis 9:1-2

When God reveals Himself, it is our cue and invitation to examine and adjust our lives to His desires. Once we've done that, we are in position to obey—but obedience does not promise the easy life. You can expect ridicule and rejection by those who don't understand your relationship with God.

Like Noah, we need to be willing to stand, to endure, and to defend our faithfulness to things we hold true and honorable, including the Word of God. We can learn from Noah that despite how things may appear, regardless of the nay-Sayers in our lives, God has a plan. We need to trust Him to carry it out it in His perfect time.

SIGNIFICANT OBSERVATIONS:

1. Through all the noise, God can find and speak with you.
2. One righteous person can make a difference.
3. Your obedience to God's calling could affect many.
4. Whether others follow your lead or not, God honors your obedience.
5. Walking with God isn't easy; more often than not it can be downright painful.

GIDEON:
O VALIANT WARRIOR

The Lord is with you, O valiant warrior!
—JUDGES 6:12

The book of Judges spans a period of about two hundred years following the entry of Israel into the land of Canaan. During the time of Judges, God Himself was considered Israel's King, as there was no designated king or ruler in charge at the time. External pressures from neighboring invaders eventually led the people to cry out for a king to judge the acts of others and bring harmony to the land. The generation of people who had entered Canaan under Joshua accomplished a great deal in establishing and assigning territories to the tribes. But not all of the territories were assigned. There remained some strongholds that had not been assigned by Joshua, and these unclaimed territories were what the individual tribes were constantly fighting over.

As we will soon learn through the accounts of Hezekiah, Nehemiah, and David, the Philistines were pushing in from the Mediterranean Coast, and they had a pretty tight stranglehold on the land and the people of Israel. The Midianites, a tribe from the desert region, applied pressure to Israel from the east. This turbulent time of land grabs and oppression marks the period between the conquest of Canaan under Joshua and the rise of the great prophet and judge Samuel, who at the request of the people anointed Saul as their king elect in the 11th century BC.

With this historical backdrop, we meet Gideon, God's man of the hour, chosen and called out to deliver His people from despair and oppression. In this story we are introduced to the notion and theme that God often raises up the weak to confound the strong. It is in Gideon's story that we learn that faith in God is stronger and mightier than a thousand armies. It is here we learn that sometimes smaller is better.

In Gideon's days, all of Israel was besieged by the raiding parties of Midianites and Amalekites, who would cross the Jordon River to plunder for food and whatever else they could get their hands on. Because of these constant raids from Midian, the sons of Israel made their homes in the dens and caves of the mountains. They were places of refuge and strength.

> And the power of Midian prevailed against Israel. Because of Midian, the sons of Israel made for themselves the dens, which were in the mountains and the caves and the strongholds. For it was when Israel had sown, that the Midianites would come up with the Amalekites and the sons of the east and go against them.
>
> —JUDGES 6:2-3

This oppression continues for seven years until the people of Israel are humbled to the point of calling out to God, again, for relief, assistance, and forgiveness. One day, Gideon is beating out wheat in the wine press to save it from being taken by the Midianites. Here, he has a heavenly encounter.

> And the angel of the Lord appeared to him and said to him, "The Lord is with you, O Valiant Warrior."
>
> —JUDGES 6:12

I'm not sure how I would have react upon seeing an angel sitting under an oak tree watching me sweat my brains out, wheat particles and wheat dust flying everywhere. I think my first thought would be, "I need some water, I think I'm starting to have hallucinations." But Gideon, without missing a beat, began to lay into the angel and accuse him of abandoning the people of Israel. Not my reaction, for sure.

> Then Gideon said to him, "O my lord, if the Lord is with us, why then has all this happened to us? And where are all His miracles, which our fathers told us about, saying 'Did not the Lord bring us up from Egypt?' But now the Lord has abandoned us and given us into the hand of Midian."
> —JUDGES 6:13

Talk about a holy boldness with an attitude! I think it's safe to say that Gideon was a powder keg just waiting for the opportunity to blow. My interpretation is confirmed in the angel's response to Gideon.

> "Go in this your strength and deliver Israel from the hand of Midian. Have I not sent you?"
> —JUDGES 6:14

To me, this sounds like, "Take up your anger, leverage this attitude, and do something about it!" I may be taking some interpretive liberties here, but only in an attempt to decipher the code and find the wisdom. You see, in that one-line response, the angel silenced any further discussion about why Gideon felt abandoned or why his people were still suffering under the hand of their oppressors. In that straightforward one-liner, the discussion changed direction. They no longer talked about past troubles or past expectations. The discussion clearly turned and was now squarely focused on Gideon.

"O Lord, how shall I deliver Israel? My family is the least in Manasseh, and I am the youngest in my father's house."
—JUDGES 6:15

To this, the angel of the Lord responded "Surely I will be with you, and you shall defeat Midian as one man," to which Gideon replies, "If now I have found favor in Thy sight, then show me a sign that it is Thou who speaks with me."

Finally, this sounds like something I might say. "If I'm not talking to myself out here in the sun, if this isn't a hallucination, then show me a sign that I'm not just talking to myself." Today, some 3,000 years later, can you relate at all to any of the events described thus far? Were there times in your life that you felt betrayed, abandoned, or forgotten? Have you ever been so bottled up over something that when good people entered your world and gave you a compliment out of nowhere, your first response was to bite off their heads and explode on them, like Gideon did to the angel of the Lord? Sure you have; so have I. That's what makes us human. That's also why we need God in our lives: because we aren't God.

Here, we find ourselves through Gideon acting completely logical in the presence of the Lord. *Show me a sign*, he says. Gideon asked the angel of the Lord to not move. *Stay right there, until I prepare you an offering.* The angel of the Lord agrees. So Gideon goes into the kitchen and makes a meal. He prepares a kid goat and unleavened bread, then puts the meat in a basket and the broth in a pot and brings them out to the angel of Lord, who is still sitting under the old oak tree.

> And the angel of God said to him, "Take the meat and the unleavened bread and lay them on this rock, and pour out the broth." Then the angel of the Lord put out the end of the staff that was in his hand and touched the meat and the unleavened bread; and fire sprang up from the rock and

consumed the meat and the unleavened bread. Then the angel vanished from his sight.

—JUDGES 6:20-21

And with that, Gideon was convinced he had seen an angel face-to-face. He built an altar there in honor of the Lord. Later that same night, the Lord spoke to Gideon and told him to go into town and tear down the altar of Baal (an ancient Semitic false god worshiped by the Semites) and cut down the Asherah, which stood next to the altar of Baal.

Then Gideon took ten men of his servants and did as the Lord had spoken to him; and it came about, because he was too afraid of his father's household and the men of the city to do it by day, that he did it by night.

—JUDGES 6:27

When morning broke, the men of the city were angry, to say the least, and they began questioning everyone about who had done this terrible thing. As is often the case, someone nearby was willing to serve as the accuser of the brethren. Words were exchanged between the men of the city and Gideon's father Joash, but from my study of this passage nothing else ever came of this act. Personally, I think God used this little act as a test to see if Gideon would listen to His voice and carry out His instructions to the letter, because a day was coming when Gideon would have to trust in God's plan and His instructions to overcome the Midianites.

The Midianites and the Amalekites grew restless or maybe hungry, and as was their custom, they gathered together in the valley of Jezreel. Trouble was once again brewing, but the Spirit of the Lord came upon Gideon. Gideon blew the trumpet and gathered the tribesmen of his region together in anticipation of an invasion.

Then Gideon said to God, "If Thou wilt deliver Israel through me, as Thou hast spoken, behold, I will put a fleece of wool on the threshing floor. If there is dew on the fleece only, and it is dry on all the ground, then I will know that Thou wilt deliver Israel through me."

—JUDGES 6:36-37

And on the next day, when he arose, it had been done as he had asked. The fleece was saturated with water—a bowlful—yet the ground was dry.

Then Gideon said to God, "Do not let Thine anger burn against me that I may speak once more; please let me make a test once more with the fleece, let it now be dry only on the fleece, and let there be dew on all the ground."

—JUDGES 6:39

And then it was as Gideon had asked. The fleece was dry, but the ground was wet. While I can certainly relate to Gideon wanting to make sure he was getting his instructions from God, these little fleeces are starting to make it sound like we're attending a heavenly magic show, and if we'll just stick around, a rabbit will appear from inside a hat, and then that man over there is going to be shot out of a cannon. Seriously though, let's take inventory.

Gideon, the youngest of his household, is working in the fields one day when out of nowhere an angel appears to him, sitting under a tree with a staff in his hand. The angel starts up a conversation, calling Gideon, a valiant warrior. Gideon, showing little surprise about conversing with an angel, snaps back at him with a bit of attitude. The angel replies with a challenge for the young lad, who now wishes to confirm that he's not hearing things; he prepares a meal to present to the angel. The food is consumed by fire and the angel disappears, but the voice remains. He has several enemy tribes assembling in the valley to fight against him and his friendly neighboring tribesmen assemble to stand with him against the invaders. Okay, when you put it like that, maybe

I *would* want a few more fleece-assurances that God was for me and not against me.

So there they were, the 33,000 followers of Gideon, atop Mount Gilead just south of the Midian camp in the valley. The Lord said to Gideon, "The people you have with you are too many, lest Israel become boastful, saying, our own power has delivered us." So God told Gideon to inform those gathered that if any of them were afraid they should depart and return to their homes. Given the first opportunity to bail out, 22,000 left Mount Gilead that morning. That was just over two-thirds of the army dismissed; no harm, no foul. Then the Lord said to Gideon, "There are still too many. Bring the remaining 10,000 down to the water's edge, and I'll test them. Those who lap up water with their tongues like dogs, we'll dismiss; those who kneel and take water by putting their hands to their mouths, we'll keep." This revealed the people who stayed on the alert while drinking. They were the warriors He sought. The number was only 300.

> So he brought the people down to the water. And the Lord said to Gideon, "You shall separate everyone who laps the water with his tongue, as a dog laps, as well as everyone who kneels to drink." Now the number of those who lapped, putting their hand to their mouth, was 300 men; but the rest of the people kneeled to drink water.
>
> —JUDGES 7:5-6

> And the Lord said to Gideon, "I will deliver you with the 300 men who lapped and will give the Midianites into your hands; so let all the other people go, each man to his home."
>
> —JUDGES 7:7

So the 300 men who remained took up the provisions left by those who had been dismissed, and their trumpets, and they camped just above the Midian camp down in the valley. That same night, God spoke to Gideon and told him to go down and fight against the camp, *for they are there for your taking.* Instead of waiting for Gideon to throw out another fleece, God said that if he was still afraid and needed reassurance, he should sneak down to the Midian camp and listen to what they were saying, and he would be strengthened by what he heard. Gideon, being the valiant, yet cautious warrior that he was, decided to take his servant down to hear what the enemy was talking about. As they approached the outpost of the camp, Gideon and his servant Purah overheard two Midianites talking. One was sharing a dream he'd had with his friend.

> "Behold, I had a dream; a loaf of barley bread was tumbling into the camp of Midian, and it came to the tent and struck it so that it fell, and turned it upside down so the tent lay flat." And his friend answered and said, "This is nothing less than the sword of Gideon the son of Joash, a man of Israel; God has given Midian and all the camp into his hand."
>
> —JUDGES 7:13-14

Having heard this man's dream and its interpretation, Gideon returned to the camp and called for his men to "Arise, for the Lord has given the camp of Midian into your hands." He divides the 300 into three separate companies. Each man had a trumpet in one hand and a torch inside an earthen pitcher in the other. They encircled the encampment where the Midianites were and waited for Gideon's signal.

> When the three companies blew the trumpets and broke the pitchers, they held the torches in their left hands and the trumpets in their right hands blowing, and cried, "A sword for the Lord and for Gideon!"
>
> —JUDGES 7:20

And when they blew 300 trumpets, the Lord set the sword
of one against another even throughout the whole army;
and the army fled . . .

—JUDGES 7:22

So Midian was subdued before the sons of Israel, and they
did not lift up their heads anymore. And the land was
undisturbed for forty years in the days of Gideon.

—JUDGES 8:28

There are many things we can learn from our young warrior, Gideon,
and his story. Often, young people and even folks my age don't take the
time to test out ideas before they act. Gideon was not impulsive. Even
in the presence of an angel from the Lord, he wanted confirmation that
what he was hearing and seeing was of the Lord. That's not to say that
Gideon was short on faith. On the contrary, Gideon was a great man
of faith. Once he had assurances that the Lord was speaking to him, he
was quick to follow the Lord's instructions. When the Lord told him
he had too many men to win this battle God's way, he didn't complain
or argue. He trusted God completely. Armed with only a trumpet and
a torch hidden within a pitcher, would you have encircled an army that
was said to be in the numbers of locusts? Would you have held the line
and continued screaming into the night, "A sword for the Lord and for
Gideon!" Or would you have decided that the strategy was nuts?

SIGNIFICANT OBSERVATIONS:

1. Don't be afraid to talk to God, even if you find Him sitting
   under a tree.
2. It's okay to speak your mind with God; He already knows
   your heart.
3. Ponder, consider, even test what you hear to ensure you've
   heard from Him.

4. Our battles are the Lord's; His ways are most certainly not our ways.
5. Be obedient to do things God's way.
6. Sometimes, less is better.
7. God can use even our enemies to reveal His will, His purpose, and His plan.

JOSHUA:
WHOLEHEARTEDLY COMMITTED

Moses said to Joshua, "Choose some of our men and go out to fight the Amalekites. Tomorrow I will stand on top of the hill with the staff of God in my hands."

— EXODUS 17:9

Joshua fought the battle of Jericho, Jericho, Jericho, / Joshua fought the battle of Jericho, / and the walls came tumbling down. Did you just sing that last line? If you did, you probably grew up Southern Baptist, or maybe other denominations also teach kids the Bible stories through music. Maybe if this were an audio book, my little musical ditty would have had a better impact. Or not.

If you thought Gideon's battle orders were a bit bizarre, wait until you hear what God instructed Joshua to do. In his youth, Joshua was a servant to Moses. As he grew, he became Moses's right-hand man. Joshua accompanied Moses to Mount Sinai and was there to witness the receipt of the Ten Commandments. But Joshua, along with Caleb, may be more commonly noted as one of the people Moses sent into the land of Canaan with orders to spy out the land and then report back.

But before Joshua's acts of courage at Jericho became a nice little song for Sunday school classes, Joshua led the Israelites in battle against the

Amalekites. Victory was gained, not due to a brilliant battle plan or to the superiority of his soldiers, but rather on the arms of Moses.

> So it came about when Moses held his hands up, that Israel prevailed, and when he let his hands down, Amalek prevailed.
>
> —EXODUS 17:11

How funny that must have looked to anyone watching. Moses held his arms high and the Israelites advanced over the battlefield. When his arms grew tired, the advancement turned to retreat, and the Amalekites moved forward. I'll bet that before Aaron and Hur helped to hold up Moses's arms late in the day, the battle must have looked like a two-hour singles matchpoint rally between Roger Federer and Rafael Nadal. Back and forth, back and forth.

> But Moses' hands were heavy. Then they took a stone and put it under him, and he sat on it; and Aaron and Hur supported his hands, one on one side and one on the other. Thus his hands were steady until the sun set.
>
> —EXODUS 17:12

While I have little doubt that God was able to direct His power through the aerobic exercise of Moses, I am also convinced that this story has a deeper application for us today. Through prayer, we can lift up other people, like Aaron and Hur did, as they fight through their own battles. As a body of believers, we need to hold up and lift up the hands and ministries of the mighty who are on the front lines providing humanitarian aid to sick and hungry nations. We need to remember and pray for our service men and women, who every day put themselves in harm's way to protect and defend the helpless and oppressed.

Watch an hour of news on any given day and you'll have more than enough to pray about when you head off to your prayer room. While the Bible stories are packed with crazy heroics and noble acts of courage, if we study the Bible more deeply, there is much there for us to learn and apply to our lives today.

Of the twelve people sent forth by Moses to spy out the land of Canaan, only two came back with a report based on faith instead of fear: Joshua and Caleb. It's an interesting point that some forty years later, only these two men entered the Promised Land.

> Then the Lord spoke to Moses saying, "Send out for yourself men so that they may spy out the land of Canaan, which I am going to give to the sons of Israel."
>
> —NUMBERS 13:1-2

Even before Moses named the men to go on this mission, before they were commissioned as spies, and long before they returned to report what they observed, God had promised to give Moses the land. So why did he need spies in the first place?

Well let's not forget that back then, and even today, God was trying to teach His people the fundamental principles of walking by faith and not by sight. So twelve spies were sent out, and at the end of forty days they returned to Moses and the entire congregation, and showed them the fruits of the land.

> Thus they told him, "We went in to the land where you sent us; and it certainly does flow with milk and honey, and this is its fruit. Nevertheless, the people who live in the land are strong, and the cities are fortified and very large; and moreover, we saw the descendants of Anak there."
>
> —NUMBERS 13:27-28

I have no problem with this story, not even with this account, which I believe was an honest assessment of the situation. I believe God wants us to be honest in our assessments, be they of the heart, or of the physical and mental challenges we face in everyday life. It's in the second part of this story that all the spies save Caleb and Joshua miss the mark. They proclaim before the congregation, "We are not able to go up against the people, for they are too strong for us." Their honest assessment turns from an acceptable report to a bad one. Because of their faithless and negative last statement, fear is birthed in the hearts of the people, and they become defeated before they have even started.

> Then all the congregation lifted up their voices and cried, and the people wept that night. "Would that we had died in the land of Egypt! Or would that we had died in this wilderness . . . and why is the Lord bringing us into this land, to fall by the sword?"
> —Numbers 14:1-3

Can you hear these people screaming out? Men shouting about the leadership of Moses and Aaron, and women crying uncontrollably in their midst, mourning and weeping as though everyone in their family had died and wasted away to dust. So while the ten spies gave what might have been an accurate account of the actual conditions, they went beyond their authority when they proceeded to plant doubt, fear, and heartache in the hearts and minds of the people. Fear breeds paranoia, confusion, and hysteria. What these ten spies failed to understand is that they had a responsibility, not only to report to Moses as instructed, but also for the welfare of others. They should have been more sensitive and careful with their words, knowing the congregation of people would be hanging on their every word. These men were chosen because they were the leaders of their fathers' tribes. All leaders, people of influence, mentors, and parents alike, need to acknowledge that because of their positions, they have an obligation to be accountable for every word that proceeds from their mouths, as well as for their actions.

Then Joshua and Caleb chimed in.

"The land which we passed through to spy out is an exceedingly good land. If the Lord is pleased with us, then He will bring us into this land, and give it to us—a land which flows with milk and honey. Only do not rebel against the Lord; and do not fear the people of the land, for they shall be our prey. Their protection has been removed from them, and the Lord is with us; do not fear them."

—NUMBERS 14:8-9

Obviously, this second, more optimistic report was very different than the first report given to the congregation. Which report generated hope and faith in the listeners? Which report relied on and restated what God had already promised Moses at the beginning of this mission? This second report called on the people to check their faith and trust in the Lord. The men said, "If the Lord is pleased with us," which afforded everyone an opportunity to check their hearts and reconnect with God. This is the report the people should have given deeper consideration. Instead, the congregation set out to stone these two men; they were suspicious of their disparate account. However, before the people could act, the glory of the Lord appeared, and their plans were thwarted.

And then there was the battle of Jericho. I promise I won't quote that little ditty again, although, I'll bet those of you who know the tune are having a hard time getting it out of your heads. Sorry about that.

Now Jericho was tightly shut because of the sons of Israel; no one went out and no one came in. And the Lord said to Joshua, "See, I have given Jericho into your hands, with its king and the valiant warriors."

—JOSHUA 6:1-22

God told Joshua to march around the city, circling the city once every day for six days. This battle would prove to be one of the strangest in history. For six days, soldiers and priests were to march around the city without saying a word. And on the seventh day, they would repeat the march, but this time, circle the city seven times.

> "Then on the seventh day you shall march around the city seven times, and the priests shall blow the trumpets. And it shall be that when they make a long blast with the ram's horn, and when you hear the sound of the trumpet, all the people shall shout with a great shout; and the wall of the city will fall down flat . . ."
>
> —JOSHUA 6:4-5

Unlike Gideon's bizarre nighttime raid with trumpets, torches, and shouting, this battle plan was executed in broad daylight. No one fled the battle scene out of fear, wondering how many soldiers were out there in the night. The battle of Jericho was a live-fire Memorex event. Remember those old commercials for Memorex? "Is it live or is it Memorex?" Maybe the trumpets blasting, the shouting of the people, and the heavy marching caused the ground to shake and the walls to collapse. Maybe there was an earthquake. These are all logical questions for those who seek rational explanations for the ways of God. Unfortunately, these folks will be frustrated in their quest for understanding, because the Bible mentions nothing about the earth moving or the ground shaking. This is a simple story of God demonstrating His unwavering promise and ability to bring down every stronghold before us with His own might and power, if we simply trust in Him.

This story isn't Joshua's childlike faith being called into action, like David's was as he ran toward Goliath. It's not about Joshua's resolve to test God with fleeces, to confirm his instructions were divine, like Gideon did. This account is about Joshua's complete trust in God; no matter how bizarre the request, Joshua listened and carried out what God told him to do. I find it interesting that there is no mention of any of the seven priests calling Joshua's plan into question, nor of any of the battle commanders tapping on Joshua's tent flap to inquire if he had thought his plan through. This strengthens my belief that Joshua was a confident and trusted leader, one dedicated to the people, and whose character was never questioned by those who followed him. One thing Joshua learned from listening to and following God over the years was that when you obey God's instructions, you will succeed, but when you sin, you will fail.

While I pray our lives will not always be under attack nor in a state of continual conflict, there is much strength to be found in Joshua's war of faith, and in ours as well. At his death, Moses commissioned Joshua to be his successor and finish what Moses started by bringing the Israelites to the Promised Land.

> "But as for me and my house, we will serve the Lord."
> —JOSHUA 24:15

SIGNIFICANT OBSERVATIONS:

1. Joshua was a faithful servant of Moses and was content with this role.
2. Moses trusted Joshua; Joshua's faithfulness allowed him to see great things.
3. Joshua was a leader of few words; his character was defined by his faith.
4. In his two most famous battles, Joshua never questioned God's tactics.
5. Joshua executed God's instructions to the letter and was rewarded every time.
6. Joshua's valor is defined by his unwavering trust in what God asks him to do.
7. Joshua was an accountable, confident leader trusted by those in his care.

DAVID:
SON OF JESSE A MIGHTY MAN OF VALOR

But the Lord said to Samuel, "Do not look at his appearance or at the height of his stature, because I have rejected him; for God sees not as man sees, for man looks at the outward appearance, but the Lord looks at the heart.

—Samuel 16:7

Who hasn't heard the story of David and Goliath? David: shepherd boy turned giant-slayer. Before he became known throughout Judea, all of Israel, and around the world as a mighty man of valor for his most courageous and noble battle in the valley of Elah, he was a just a boy, the youngest of eight sons, and the least important in his father's eyes.

Yet in the eyes of His heavenly Father, David was a man after God's own heart.

The year was 1020 BC, and Saul, Israel's king elect at the time, had lost favor with God due to his disobedience. Samuel was God's prophet for Saul and the people of Israel. He was given instructions by God to have Saul deal harshly with the tribe of the Amalekites in response to the way they had treated the people of God. But instead, Saul, like many of us who opt not to listen fully to God's instructions, only partially carried out what he was supposed to do.

The Lord spoke to Samuel regarding this; He regretted having made Saul king. Samuel confronted Saul about the matter, hoping to make things right in the eyes of God, but stubborn king Saul ended up lying to Samuel about the event.

In chapter 16 of Samuel, God has grown weary of Samuel's grief over Saul's demise. The Lord instructed Samuel to go to Bethlehem, where God would show him His next choice for king.

> Now the Lord said to Samuel, "How long will you grieve over Saul, since I have rejected him from being king over Israel? Fill your horn with oil, and go; I will send you to Jesse the Bethlehemite, for I have selected a king for Myself among his sons."
>
> —1 SAMUEL 16:1

To have a prophet visit your town, much less your home, was a very big deal. Most folks were afraid that the prophet was in town to judge or carry out some harsh punishment for something they did or didn't do.

But Samuel was actually on a peace mission, and was simply there to observe the sons of Jesse, as instructed, so that he could anoint the one God had chosen to be the next king of Israel. Samuel explained the purpose of his visit to Jesse, who immediately called for his sons to come before the great prophet.

But Jesse called only seven of his sons before Samuel, completely overlooking or forgetting about his youngest son David, who was out tending to the family sheep. Jesse thought his eldest would be chosen, as Eliab was big in stature, and maybe, in Jesse's eyes, kingly-looking. But why wouldn't Jesse call David in from the field, at least to see the mighty prophet of God? Why would Jesse deprive David of meeting the most influential and important person ever to visit their home, if for no other reason than to afford David the opportunity to witness the most exciting event in their family's lifetime, that is, the anointing of one of his brothers as the next king of Israel. What was Jesse thinking? More importantly, what did David think about being left out?

Have you ever felt you were the last to know something? Were you the youngest sibling in your family, like David was? Were you maybe not treated as fairly, or respected less than your older siblings? Or were you the eldest, but nonetheless overlooked by your parents? If so, take heart. You and David have much in common. As parents, we must be very careful not to show preference for one child over another. We need to acknowledge that every child has unique, God-given gifts and talents that we should strive to highlight, nurture, and bring to the forefront. While the other sons were bigger in stature, and looked more kingly by outward appearances, God told Samuel that He judged a man by looking at his heart.

> "Do not look at his appearance or at the height of his stature, because I have rejected him; for God sees not as man sees, for man looks at the outward appearance, but the Lord looks at the heart."
>
> —1 SAMUEL 16:7

God told Samuel that the eldest son, Eliab, was not the one, so Samuel pressed on and asked if there were more sons. Jesse made all seven of his sons pass before Samuel, yet not one spoke to the heart of Samuel as being the one God had chosen. So again, Samuel asked Jesse, "Are these all the children?" Then, and only then, did Jesse acknowledge that he had yet one more: the youngest, who was out tending sheep.

> So he sent and brought him in. Now he was ruddy, with beautiful eyes and a handsome appearance. And the Lord said, "Arise, anoint him; for this is he."
>
> —1 SAMUEL 16:12

> And Samuel took the horn of oil and anointed him in
> the midst of his brothers; and the Spirit of the Lord came
> mightily upon David from that day forward.
>
> —1 SAMUEL 16:13

The story goes on to tell us that the Spirit of the Lord departed from
Saul, and that he was greatly tormented by an evil spirit. Maybe he
was tormented by guilt, knowing he had lost God's favor due to his
disobedience and his deaf ear to God's instruction. Music has a way of
soothing the savage beast within; it brings peace and comfort to the
listening heart. So in an effort to silence the tormenting voice within
him, Saul called for a musician, a skillful player of the harp.

> So Saul said to his servants, "Provide for me now a man
> who can play well, and bring him to me." Then one of
> the young men answered and said, "Behold, I have seen a
> son of Jesse the Bethlehemite who is a skillful musician, a
> mighty man of valor, a warrior, one prudent in speech, and
> a handsome man; and the Lord is with him."
>
> —1 SAMUEL 16:17-18

Now we get our first glimpse into who David was at this early stage
in his life. A young man gives an account of an encounter with David.
It's important to note that even though Samuel had already anointed
David, there was no decree throughout the land announcing the event;
it had been done on the down-low. Instead, life went on as though
nothing had changed. David tended sheep the following day and every
day thereafter, until such time that his reputation preceded him, via the
account of the young man mentioned above. This account caused Saul
to summon David to the palace.

> Then David came to Saul and attended him, and Saul loved
> him greatly; and he became his armor bearer. And Saul

sent to Jesse, saying, "Let David now stand before me; for
he has found favor in my sight."

—1 SAMUEL 16:21-22

Before David gained Saul's favor, he had a reputation that preceded him.
While the Bible doesn't tell us how the young lad who recommended
David to Saul came to know of David in the first place, it's safe to assume
that it wasn't from watching a YouTube video of David playing his harp
to the sheep or through David's Facebook account. Back then, word
about people and events traveled through the eye-witness accounts and
the testimony of others. Folks shared with each other the experiences
and events they encountered on their travels. More important than
knowing how that young lad came to know of David is realizing that
for David to have a reputation in the first place, he must have shared his
gifts and talents so freely and openly with others that he made a great
impression. David must have led a life that allowed him to let his light
shine before others.

Now let's find out how David came to be near the front lines of battle,
engaging in conversation with some soldiers of Israel, including his elder
brother Eliab. According to 1 Samuel 17, the armies of Israel were in
the valley of Elah, fighting with the Philistines. Three of David's older
brothers had enlisted in Saul's army and were serving there. One day,
Jesse instructed David to take his brothers a care package of food. So
off young David went with a backpack of roasted grains, ten loaves of
bread, and ten cuts of cheese, along with instructions to look into their
welfare and bring back news of their condition to Jesse.

So, before David came on the scene as a mighty man of valor, he was
simply an errand boy sent by his father to check up and report back
about the welfare of his three elder siblings.

> So David arose early in the morning and left the flock
> with a keeper and took the supplies and went as Jesse had
> commanded him. And he came to the circle of the camp

while the army was going out in battle array shouting the
war cry.

—1 SAMUEL 17:20

When David arrived on the scene, he heard about the boast of the
Philistine warrior, Goliath of Gath, who would come to the hillside
day and night to taunt the army of Israel. "Bring me someone to fight
with," he would yell out.

"If he is able to fight with me and kill me, then we will
become your servants; but if I prevail against him and kill
him, then you shall become our servants and serve us."

—1 SAMUEL 17:9

But when David heard these boasts and noticed how afraid the soldiers
around him were of this loud-mouthed Philistine, he turned to the
soldiers next to him and asked:

"What will be done for the man who kills this Philistine,
and takes away the reproach from Israel? For who is this
uncircumcised Philistine, that he should taunt the armies
of the living God?"

—1 SAMUEL 17:26

David's first question shows us that David was a mere man before he
became a superhero and giant-slayer. His first inquiry was all about
"me." "What will be done for the man who kills this Philistine?" he
asked. Like most of us, he thought first about his own status and personal
gain. The soldiers told him the king had promised to make the one
who killed Goliath very rich, and to give him his daughter, and make
his father's house free in Israel (1 Samuel 17:25). Back in those days,
that would have been a pretty compelling incentive package. It was an
offer that should have been compelling and achievable to many of the
seasoned warriors who had not only experience to draw from, but also

confidence in their skillful use of weaponry. What these soldiers lacked was the heart of God and a deep knowledge of who the God of Israel was in their personal lives. These two insights were all David needed to stand apart. Hearing his question to the soldiers, David's brother Eliab became angry and harassed David, accusing him of leaving the sheep unattended so that he could come and see the battle. But David responded to his brother with, "It's just a question," and then continued to question the soldiers. "So what is to be done unto the man who kills the Philistine?"

David's second question struck a chord with the soldiers and eventually reached the tent of Saul. "For who is this uncircumcised Philistine, that he should taunt the armies of the living God?" I can imagine that, just from the way he said this, his tone of voice and in his eyes, those who heard the question recognized a holy boldness of confidence that only comes from spending time with God. This kid had attitude with altitude. The question spread across the ranks until it reached Saul's tent. Upon hearing about it, Saul called for this man to come forward. When David arrived, he said to Saul (translated to today's slang), "Chill out dude, I got this."

> And David said to Saul, "Let no man's heart fail on account of him; your servant will go and fight with this Philistine."
>
> —1 SAMUEL 17:32

> Then Saul said to David, "You are not able to go against this Philistine to fight with him; for you are but a youth while he has been a warrior from his youth."
>
> —1 SAMUEL 17:33

This is proof that Saul had long forgotten how to walk by faith and not by sight. He quickly judged that David was too small, unworthy, and unable. He judged David by his outward appearances and not by the size of his heart.

So David started to sell Saul on his abilities. By some standards, these accomplishments might have seemed trite or at least incomparable to such a task as taking on Goliath. Nonetheless, David had previous accounts to reference. In short, he recited his resume of qualifications. "Put me in coach, I'm ready to play!"

> And David said, "the Lord who delivered me from the paw of the lion and from the paw of the bear, He will deliver me from the hand of this Philistine." And Saul said to David, "Go, and may the Lord be with you."
>
> —1 SAMUEL 17:37

Significantly, David didn't boast or take credit for killing either the lion or the bear. Nor did he presume to take credit for killing the mighty Philistine. David attributed all the glory and credit to the Lord, who delivered and will deliver him from all battles. David understood that the battles were the Lord's and that his role in the conflict was to simply be willing to trust God with the outcome.

So Saul finally gave in to David's argument, which must have lasted more than a question or two. After all, if David failed this assignment, Saul and his entire army would become the servants of the Philistines. I've heard some argue that Saul just got tired of listening to David, that he just decided to let him go and give it his best shot, and that Saul had no intention of surrendering to Philistines if David had failed. Regardless of his intentions, Saul decided to let David go forth. I happen to believe that Saul conceded in his own mind that if David failed, he and his armies would surrender to the Philistines. Why else would Saul offer up his own armor and sword to David? If he intended to fight the Philistines after David failed, wouldn't he need his armor to lead his soldiers into battle? Either way, Saul offered David his armor, his helmet, and his sword. But David realized he wouldn't even be able to walk in this garb. He removed Saul's armor, took up his slingshot, and gathered five smooth stones from the brook.

> And he took his stick in his hand and chose for himself
> five smooth stones from the brook, and put them in the
> shepherd's bag which he had, even in his pouch, and his
> sling was in his hand; and he approached the Philistine.
> —1 SAMUEL 17:40

David opted not to wear Saul's armor, but instead relied on God's favor and protection. He was so confident in who God was and confident in his relationship with God that he didn't even feel the need to pray up or seek God's will in advance of making his vow, nor did he pause at the brook to pray over the stones he had chosen, or second-guess himself as he approached the mighty warrior of Gath.

On this day, the Philistines had gathered against Israel for battle. On one side of the mountain stood the Philistines; on the other, camped in the valley of Elah, was the army of Israel, Saul, and a ruddy looking kid with a slingshot in his hand.

The mighty Philistine warrior, Goliath of Gath, had been taunting the armies of Israel day and night for forty days. He stood six cubits and a span high; that's nearly nine feet tall! Tall even by NBA standards. His helmet was made of bronze with scale-armor weighting 5,000 shekels, or 125 pounds. His neck must have been enormous to hold that much weight on his head. He had bronze leg armor and a bronze javelin slung between his shoulders.

> And the Philistine came forward morning and evening for
> forty days, and took his stand.
> —1 SAMUEL 17:16

Like Goliath of Gath, our adversary, Satan, taunts us day and night if we listen to him. Like Goliath, he appears to be bigger than life, indestructible, and heavily reliant on fear tactics, always telling us how insurmountable our situations are.

Some mornings, as soon as you wake up, fear and doubt find their way into your frontal lobe and start barking disbelief to your still sleepy head. These thoughts of disbelief are the very speculations and thoughts that we must bring down and gain control over.

Like David, we need to speak to our own Goliaths and remind them that we are children of the Most-High God, and that we stand in and upon His name.

> "You come to me with a sword, a spear, and a javelin, but I come to you in the name of the Lord of hosts, the God of the armies of Israel, whom you have taunted."
>
> —1 SAMUEL 17:45

David spoke by faith about how this day would proceed and how this day would end. He spoke with confidence and boldness before all the armies present that day, regardless of which side of the valley they stood on. He knew not only that the Lord would deliver him, but that he would remove Goliath's head, even though all he had was a bag full of stones and a slingshot in his hand.

> "This day the Lord will deliver you up into my hands, and I will strike you down and remove your head from you. And I will give the dead bodies of the army of the Philistines this day to the birds of the sky and the wild beasts of the earth, that all the earth may know that there is a God in Israel."
>
> —1 SAMUEL 17:46

Militarily speaking, there is a good reason why no one wanted to initiate the attack on the other army. Whoever attacked first would lose the advantage of being above the enemy on top of the fortified hill. The attacker would have to charge *up* the opponent's hill, and thus be at a significant disadvantage.

But David, not a trained soldier or even schooled in the tactics of warfare, again stepped out in Faith and attacked Goliath. He ran towards his oppressor, demonstrating how he operated in the supernatural realm.

> Then it happened when the Philistine rose and came and drew near to meet David, that David ran quickly toward the battle line to meet the Philistine.
>
> —1 SAMUEL 17:48

David didn't try to sneak up on his enemy under the cover of darkness, but ran towards his challenger, demonstrating that one should trust God explicitly, that we should attack our challenges head on, confident that God will make a way. As one Bible teacher put it, "We should attack our lack" and trust that God will reward our faithful efforts to press on in spite of the circumstances in our lives that taunt us and try to hold us back.

What I find most interesting about this part of the story is that when David took off running towards Goliath, his slingshot wasn't even loaded. His bullets (the five smooth stones) were still in his pouch when he started his attack. I don't know about you, but if it were me, I would have had one in the sling already, spinning around my head as fast as possible, and I would have had two more in hand at the ready should the first one miss its mark. But not David. Prior to this noble day, David the giant-slayer obviously spent much time with God, tending his father's sheep, talking and praying, learning to trust in his Lord and his God.

> And David put his hand into his bag and took from it a stone and slung it, and struck the Philistine on his forehead. And the stone sank into his forehead, so that he fell on his face to the ground.
>
> —1 SAMUEL 17:49

But this story is far from over. With Goliath down but not dead, David fulfilled his promise and declaration to both armies and proceeded to remove Goliath's head with his own sword.

> Then David ran and stood over the Philistine and took his sword and drew it out of its sheath and killed him, and cut off his head with it. When the Philistines saw that their champion was dead, they fled.
>
> —1 SAMUEL 17:51

This day was a mighty day of victory for David and the armies of Israel, and was a great victory for Saul as well. Saul made David head over all the men of war; after all, David had kept his word and promise to Saul, and Israel was far better off with Goliath out of the way. However, as grateful and proud of what David had accomplished as Saul was, he became angry about David's rise in popularity. The people sang, "Saul has slain his thousands, and David his ten thousands."

> Then Saul became very angry, for this saying displeased him; and he said, "They have ascribed to David ten thousand, but to me they have ascribed thousands. Now what more can he have but the kingdom?" And Saul looked at David with suspicion from that day on.
>
> —1 SAMUEL 18:8-9

Over the next several years, Saul made multiple attempts to end David's life. Jealousy and resentment had raised their ugly, twisted heads. Twice Saul attempted to kill David with his spear while David played the harp in service to him. After several blatant attempts and failures, Saul decided to appoint David as his commander of the armies, thinking that he would surely die at the hands of the Philistines, and then Saul's troubles would be over. But David prospered in all his ways, for the Lord was with him.

Saul's anger and hatred for David burned on. One day, Saul sent men to kill David at his home, while he was with his wife Michal, Saul's daughter. But when she learned of her father's plan, she warned David, and he escapes into the night to a place called Naioth in Ramah. There, David took refuge with Samuel the prophet, the same prophet who had anointed him in his father's house. Receiving word of David's whereabouts, three times Saul sent messengers to take David's life in the presence of Samuel; three times did they fail to do so in Samuel's presence and under the power of God.

Despite Saul's hatred for him, David attempted to understand why Saul's heart burned so intently against him. The bond between David and Saul's son Jonathan, heir apparent, was strong. Their friendship is an excellent example of what true and sincere friendship between two people can be. Jonathan loved his father and respected him as such, but Jonathan also loved David, and knew that David had done nothing to deserve his father's hatred. At his own risk and peril, he defended David in the presence of his father and tried to reason with him several times. But Saul would have nothing to do with it. Saul was convinced that as long as David lived, his son's kingdom would not be established.

> "For as long as the son of Jesse lives on the earth, neither you nor your kingdom will be established. Therefore now, send and bring him to me, for he must surely die."
> —1 SAMUEL 20:31

After questioning his father about what David had done to offend him, Jonathan, too, had a spear thrown at him by his father. He decided to advise David that things weren't looking good. The odds of Jonathan persuading his father to change his position about David lay somewhere between slim to none.

So Saul's pursuit continued, and David, who was once a mighty man of valor, became a man paranoid and fearful—rightfully so—of a man who three times proved he couldn't throw a spear to save his life (or more accurately, take a life), and who had made four failed attempts to send messengers out to kill him. It makes you wonder why David feared Saul so much. I think it was due to respect. He sincerely could not see where or how he had offended Saul. Surly he heard the chants of the people saying he had done greater things than Saul, but in David's heart, he didn't see himself as greater. He simply saw himself as a devoted servant.

David's mighty encounter with Goliath of Gath in the valley of Elah, is the part of the story most well-known. Fortunately, the story does not end there. The remainder of his life was fraught with fears, failures, bad decisions, adultery, and even murder.

These less notable traits of character that further defined David in his later years remind us that God is still faithful and forgives us if we repent and continue to return, failure after failure, unto Him with a repentant heart.

I find it reassuring that I can find courage and faith in my own life, through the story of David the giant-slayer and also through David the mere man, failures and all. I think we all have moments of greatness within us which could emerge if we are bold enough to trust in the One who planted these seeds of greatness and accomplishment within us. We may not see the moment coming or even realize it when we are standing in its midst, but if we do stand in it, whatever it may be, trusting that God indeed has a purpose and a plan, we will experience more great moments of victory in what God brings our way. Perhaps this book is one of my great moments for the kingdom. Maybe, just maybe, hundreds of people, if not thousands, dare I believe, even tens of thousands could be encouraged by the stories and insights within these pages. In the midst of the campaign, however, who can say? I'm not a journalism major, nor am I an author by trade. But this I know for sure: no one would have the opportunity to glean anything from this book if it didn't exist.

While David did prove to be a warrior and a mighty man of valor in his great moment in the valley of Elah, he also proved to be a mere man plagued by fear and paranoia, horrendous character flaws, and a life full of fits and starts. The key to living a life pleasing to God is to focus not on perfection, but on devotion.

SIGNIFICANT OBSERVATIONS:

1. David knew without question who he was in Christ.
2. David had a covenant contract with God; anyone uncircumcised didn't.
3. David's reputation preceded him because he chose to let his light shine.
4. David gave God credit for victories in advance of the victory.
5. David spoke to things as they were rather than how they appeared.
6. David spoke boldly and with authority to his enemy.
7. David had an attitude with altitude.
8. David had both great moments and horrendous failures.
9. David always had a heart for God and always came back to Him.

NATHAN:
BOLD AND UNAFRAID SPOKESMAN

*Then the Lord sent Nathan to David. And he came to him,
and said to him: "There were two men in one city, one rich
and the other poor."*

—2 Samuel 12:1

In the last chapter, I said that David's later years were fraught with
fears, failures, and downright bad decisions. These were no doubt his
least noble traits. While we don't hear much about his less than stellar
escapades, they did not go unnoticed by God or man.

> So all the elders of Israel came to the king at Hebron, and
> King David made a covenant with them before the Lord at
> Hebron; then they anointed David king over Israel. David
> was thirty years old when he became king, and he reigned
> forty years. At Hebron he reigned over Judah seven years
> and six months, and in Jerusalem he reigned thirty-three
> years over all Israel and Judah.
>
> —2 Samuel 5:3-5

Meanwhile, David took on more wives from Jerusalem after departing
Hebron, and he had more sons and daughters. Two of his children,

Nathan and Solomon, became quite famous in their own right. Nathan grew up to become a prophet for his own father David, and Solomon became the next king after David passed on.

The warring and the battles between David and the Philistines continued throughout chapter 5 of Samuel. In chapter 6, we begin to see a different side of David, one that features pride more than humility, that led him to rely more on his own understanding, and less on God's instruction.

> Now it came about when the king lived in his house, and the Lord had given him rest on every side from all his enemies, that the king said to Nathan, the prophet, "See now, I dwell in a house of cedar, but the ark of God dwells within tent curtains."
>
> —2 SAMUEL 7:1-2

David was now living comfortably. There were no wars to contend with and David had decided that now was a good time to build a more permanent house for the ark of God. However, God had other plans. God wanted someone who didn't have blood on his hands to be the builder of the house of the ark. This task was given to Solomon, a man of peace. David did not approach God directly about his desire to build a home for the ark; at this point he relied on his own son, the prophet Nathan, to communicate with God.

Here we meet Nathan, who tells his father the king, "Go ahead, pops, do whatever is on your mind, for the Lord is with you." But later on that very same night, the Word of the Lord came to Nathan, saying:

> "Go and say to My servant David, Thus says the Lord, 'are you the one who should build Me a house to dwell in?'"
>
> —2 SAMUEL 7:5

God revealed to Nathan that He never asked for a house to be built. He told Nathan to say to David, "When your days are complete and you lie down with your fathers, I will raise up your descendant after you, and I will establish his kingdom. He shall build a house for My name."

So Nathan, in his first account as a prophet, got the message wrong. Was it because he didn't hear the Lord correctly, or did he speak out before he heard from the Lord in the first place? I think it's the latter. David was telling Nathan, "It's not right that I have a nice home but that the ark of the Covenant rests within tent curtains." Young Nathan, agreeing with his father's reasoning and logic, quickly overlooked his own calling, and without conferring with the Lord agreed with his father's rationale.

How many of us, like Nathan, have taken the path of least resistance, or responded with an answer before checking in with our spirit for peace? Have you, when giving a response, known immediately that something didn't feel right, and that your gut wasn't in agreement?

But Nathan found the courage to share God's message with his father. This wouldn't be the only faith encounter Nathan would have to deal with. In chapter 11, we start to see David make one bad decision after another. These decisions eventually snowball into an act of deceit and murder.

> Then it happened in the spring, at the time when kings go out to battle, that David sent Joab and his servants with him . . . and they destroyed the sons of Ammon and besieged Rabbah, but David stayed at Jerusalem. And when evening came David arose from his bed and walked around on the roof of the king's house, and from the roof he saw a woman bathing; and the woman was very beautiful in appearance.
>
> —2 SAMUEL 11:1-2

That's right. Say hello to Bathsheba, the wife of Uriah the Hittite. As it goes in many other stories, bad decisions bred more trouble, until stupidity ruled the day. David, idle in his duties as king, committed adultery with Bathsheba, and she became pregnant. After learning of this, David sent Joab to fetch Uriah, Bathsheba's husband, supposedly to meet and discuss how the war was going. He encouraged Uriah to go home and enjoy his wife, for his journey had been long. Basically, David hoped that if Uriah slept with his wife, and soon, no one would be the wiser that the child was actually David's. But Uriah, being a devoted soldier, could not justify enjoying the comfort of his wife when all the other soldiers were sleeping apart from their families. So he slept that night with the other servants, not with his wife.

> But Uriah slept at the door of the king's house with all the servants of his Lord, and did not go down to his house.
>
> —2 SAMUEL 11:9

For a second night, David attempted to get Uriah to stay with his wife, and for a second night Uriah decided to stay with the men.

> Now it came about in the morning that David wrote a letter to Joab, and sent it by the hand of Uriah. And he had written in the letter, saying, "Place Uriah in the front line of the fiercest battle and withdraw from him, so that he may be struck down and die."
>
> —2 SAMUEL 11:15

> When the wife of Uriah heard that Uriah her husband was dead, she mourned for her husband. When the time of mourning was over, David sent and brought her to his house and she became his wife; then she bore him a son. But the thing that David had done was evil in the sight of the Lord.
>
> —2 SAMUEL 11:26-27

Enter once again the prophet Nathan, whom God called into service to rebuke David for his actions and behavior.

Nathan undoubtedly struggled with how to confront his father, who was also the king. He decided to craft a story of comparison that his father would be able to relate to. He told a story of two men living in the same city, one rich and the other poor. The rich man had many flocks and herds, but the poor man had only one little ewe lamb. To prepare a meal for a wayward traveler, the rich man decided not to take from his own herd. Instead, he took the one ewe lamb from the poor man. After hearing this account of injustice, David said to Nathan, "As the Lord lives, surely the man who has done this deserves to die." Then Nathan said to David:

> "You are the man! Thus says the Lord God of Israel . . ."
> —2 SAMUEL 12:7

Nathan goes on for several more verses, rebuking his father and reminding him of all the good that God has done on his behalf, and asking why David despised the Word of the Lord by doing evil in His sight? In the story, David is the rich man who takes advantage of poor Uriah, who only had one lamb, his wife. When David recognizes that he is indeed the evil character of this story, he repents of his sin, but not without a price.

Nathan was a brave spokesman for God. He was courageous in sharing the word of God when it wasn't easy or safe thing to do. While we may not be called to be prophets for God, we may find ourselves in a position to speak up for those who have been wronged or who are unable to speak for themselves. Like Nathan, when we hear from God and are asked to defend the weak or even confront the strong, we need to prayerfully consider how best to respond and then be quick to do what God has placed on our hearts.

SIGNIFICANT OBSERVATIONS:

1. David's latter days where not as glorious as his former victories.
2. David's arrogance and pride may have increased after he became king.
3. Pride came before the fall.
4. In idleness and lack of vision, David's eye wandered.
5. Once you start going downhill, it's hard to slow down without falling down.
6. Adultery led to deceit, a plot, and eventually, the death of another.
7. Nathan, despite being in a tough spot, remained a faithful spokesman for God.

HEZEKIAH:
A PRAYER WARRIOR

Hezekiah trusted in the Lord, the God of Israel. There was no one like him among all the kings of Judah, either before him or after him.

—2 KINGS 18:5

Hezekiah came from a very long line of very bad kings. In fact, his lineage hailed from the ten tribes of northern Israel, where twenty bad kings ruled over the people in the territory. A study into Scripture doesn't tell us much about how the son of wicked King Ahab became such a faithful believer. But at age twenty-five, after the death of his father Ahab, Hezekiah crossed the proverbial railroad tracks and left the gang mentality and family baggage behind to reign over Judah for twenty-nine years in Jerusalem, unlike any other king before or after him.

His life and testament are proof that even if you come from a bad line of dudes, even if your heritage isn't anything to write home about, you can, with God's favor, turn your heritage on its ear and start afresh.

> For our fathers have been unfaithful and have done evil in the sight of the Lord our God, and have forsaken Him

and turned their faces away from the dwelling place of
the Lord.

—2 CHRONICLES 29:6

Hezekiah was on a mission to correct and destroy everything his wicked
father had done. Hezekiah made a conscious decision to not walk in the
way of the kings before him. He set out straight away to remove the
pagan idols and places of worship established under his father's rule, and
he destroyed all false objects of worship. In his first year, he reopened
the doors of the house of the Lord and repaired them. Hezekiah was
on a mission. It was a mission to clean house, and to reform and restore
temple worship. He brought all the priests and the Levites into an
assembly in the square and laid out his plan to turn the kingdom around,
to stand for something honorable. He, like Nehemiah, who we will
learn about in the next chapter, had decided to be a difference-maker.

> "Now it is in my heart to make a covenant with the Lord
> God of Israel, that His burning anger may turn away from
> us."
>
> —2 CHRONICLES 29:10

> "Listen to me, O Levites. Consecrate yourselves now, and
> consecrate the house of the Lord, the God of your fathers,
> and carry the uncleanness out from the holy place."
>
> —2 CHRONICLES 29:5

And with that, the house cleaning had begun. The priests went into
the inner part of the house of the Lord and cleansed it. Every unclean
thing that needed to be removed, they brought out to the court, and
the Levites carried it out to the Kidron Valley. The Kidron Valley is
referred to several times in the Old Testament; in each case, someone
is burning something in the brook of Kidron, or dumping trash, so
it's probably safe to say that Kidron was the local dump. It took them
sixteen days to clean house.

> Then they went in to King Hezekiah and said, "We have cleansed the whole house of the Lord, the altar of burnt offering with all its utensils, and the table of showbread with all of its utensils. Moreover, all the utensils which King Ahvaz had discarded during his reign in his unfaithfulness, we have prepared and consecrated; and behold, they are before the altar of the Lord."
>
> —2 CHRONICLES 29:1819

Upon restoring the house of the Lord, Hezekiah set out to restore temple worship. He invited all of Israel to join him in Jerusalem to celebrate Passover. He established a decree and circulated a proclamation that everyone in Israel and Judah should come: "Return to the Lord God of Abraham, Isaac, and Israel, all you who have escaped the hand of the kings of Assyria."

> "For if you return to the Lord, your brothers and your sons will find compassion before those who led them captive, and will return to this land. For the Lord your God is gracious and compassionate, and will not turn His face away from you if you return to Him."
>
> —2 CHRONICLES 30:9

With little insight into how Hezekiah became such a strong believer and advocate for the Lord, we can only speculate and exercise some creative interpretations in hopes of finding connections and deep insights that might help us today. Maybe his personal transformation, his obvious desire to be nothing like his wicked father, was all he needed to boast of in the Lord. Maybe if we were able to read between the lines, or have a conversation with him, he would say, "If God can take me, the son of a very wicked man who went out of his way to displease God and make sport of everything holy, and if God can forgive my upbringing, overlook my dark and nasty lineage, and accept me afresh, even with my father's name, then surely God will hear the prayers of any man."

> And thus Hezekiah did throughout all Judah; and he did
> what was good, right, and true before the Lord his God.
> And every work which he began in the service of the house
> of God in law and in commandment, seeking his God, he
> did with all his heart and prospered.
>
> —2 CHRONICLES 31:20-21

The Scriptures highly praise Hezekiah for his faithfulness and his consistent walk. God blessed him for this, making him successful in his rebellion against the king of Assyria and in his battles against the Philistines. He even heard Hezekiah's prayers when he was on his deathbed, and decided to give him fifteen more years—I am getting ahead of myself. Back to the battlefield and Assyria.

Sennacherib, king of Assyria (which today is modern day Iran), decided to invade Judah and besiege the fortified cities, hoping to take them for himself. But when Hezekiah learned of his intent to make war, he called his officers and all his warriors and together they decided to cut off the supply of water from the springs, which were outside their city walls. They figured that as long as their enemy was parked outside the gate trying to cause trouble, they didn't need to make fresh water available.

> So many people assembled and stopped up all the springs
> and the stream which flowed through the region, saying,
> "Why should the kings of Assyria come and find abundant
> water?"
>
> —2 CHRONICLES 32:4

And so they came. Sennacherib sent many advance servants with warriors in tow to taunt and torment the people of Jerusalem who could hear their enemy's accusations and threats from atop the walls. But King Hezekiah called upon Isaiah the prophet, and together they prayed about this matter and cried out for heavenly intervention. Hezekiah was so serious about his prayers that he actually took a letter he received from Sennacherib, threating God's kingdom, into the prayer room and laid it out for God to see.

> "Incline Thine ear, O Lord, and hear; open Thine eyes, O Lord, and see; and listen to the words of Sennacherib, which he has sent to reproach the loving God. Truly, O Lord, the kings of Assyria have devastated the nations and their lands . . . And now, O Lord our God, I pray, deliver us from his hand that all the kingdoms of the earth may know that Thou alone, O Lord, art God."
>
> —2 Kings 19:16-17, 19

> And the Lord sent an angel who destroyed every mighty warrior, commander and officer in the camp of the king of Assyria. So he returned in shame to his own land. And when he had entered the temple of his god, some of his own children killed him there with the sword.
>
> —2 Chronicles 32:21

> So the Lord saved Hezekiah and the inhabitants of Jerusalem from the hand of Sennacherib the king of Assyria, and from the hand of all others, and guided them on every side.
>
> —2 Chronicles 32:22

In chapter 20 of 2 Kings, we find Hezekiah mortally ill. Isaiah the prophet has already stopped by and told him to get his house in order, for "You shall die and not live." Wow, cold. You would think that Isaiah could at least have shown a little compassion, and said something like, "You did a great job, Hezzie. You were faithful and a mighty prayer partner, and you did a great job restoring worship back into the Temple." With Isaiah's warm and affectionate words, Hezekiah turned to the wall to pray one last prayer:

> "Remember now, O Lord, I beseech Thee, how I have walked before Thee in truth and with a whole heart, and have done what is good in Thy sight." And Hezekiah wept bitterly.
>
> —2 KINGS 20:3

Before Isaiah had a chance to leave the middle court, the Word came unto him from the Lord and said, "Return to Hezekiah, the leader of My people, and say 'Thus says the Lord,'"

> "I have heard your prayer, I have seen your tears; behold, I will heal you. And I will add fifteen years to your life, and I will deliver you and this city from the hand of the king of Assyria, and I will defend this city for My own sake and for My servant David's sake."
>
> —2 KINGS 20:5-6

Talk about God's blessing overflowing. First God heals Hezekiah, and He adds fifteen years to his life. But God's not done. He promises to deliver not only Hezekiah but the city as well. God's still not done. He promises to defend the city for His own sake. All these blessings because Hezekiah decided early on to live his life differently than his father and father's father before him. Hezekiah's life was dedicated to doing good and building up; it was a life of service to God, who could take the stains and sins of Hezekiah's past and wash them pure as snow, making a difference in the lives of many.

SIGNIFICANT OBSERVATIONS:

1. Regardless of your lineage, background, or past, God can start anew with you.
2. How Hezekiah became a believer isn't recorded; what he did as a believer is.
3. Hezekiah was a faithful man of prayer.

4. Hezekiah's entire reign as king was dedicated to reestablishing the house of God.
5. God extended Hezekiah's life by fifteen years.
6. After Hezekiah used what seemed to be his last breath on prayer, God heaped blessings on him.

NEHEMIAH:
DIFFERENCE-MAKER

As for the builders, each wore his sword girded at his side as he built, while the trumpeter stood near me.
— NEHEMIAH 4:18

Much had happened, historically speaking, before Nehemiah came onto the scene. Adam and Eve had already met, ate the fruit, and found themselves running around naked and ashamed in the Garden. Noah had already suffered great ridicule from his fellow villagers and neighbors for building an Ark in advance of the flood. The reigns of Abraham, Moses, and David had come and gone. The kingdom had split off into two sects: Israel to the north, which hosted the ten tribes of Ahab, destroyed in 722 BC; and Judah to the south, which housed the two tribes of Judah and Benjamin until they were destroyed in 585 BC. Jerusalem had also been destroyed and the Jews had been deported to Babylon. In 537 BC, the first group of Jews was allowed to return to their homeland, and in 516 BC, the Temple was rebuilt. In 458 BC, Ezra led the second group of Jews back to Jerusalem, and in 445 BC, Nehemiah asked the king for permission to return to Jerusalem with a third group in tow to rebuild the city walls of Jerusalem and reestablish God's people with their God.

When we pick up the story in Nehemiah 1:1, it's the month of Chislev, or December, in the twentieth year of Assyrian rule in the city of Susa, the capitol city of Persia (modern-day Iran). Nehemiah had just heard from Hanani, his brother, and from other men from Judah that those Jews who had escaped and survived captivity weren't doing so well.

> The remnant there in the province who survived the captivity are in great distress and reproach, and the wall of Jerusalem is broken down and its gates are burned with fire.
>
> —NEHEMIAH 1:3

This news deeply grieved Nehemiah. For four months he wept, mourned, fasted, and prayed on behalf of the sons of Israel, confessing sins on their behalf and reminding God that even though His people were scattered about, if His people returned to Him, He had promised to gather them from their remote dwellings and bring them to the place He had chosen, Jerusalem.

> Let Thine ear now be attentive and Thine eyes open to hear the prayer of Thy servant which I am praying before thee now, day and night, on behalf of the sons of Israel Thy servants, confessing the sins of the sons of Israel which we have sinned against Thee; I and my father's house have sinned.
>
> —NEHEMIAH 1:6

And so in the month of Nisan, the month of March in the twentieth year of King Artaxerxes I, after months of praying and crying out to God for compassion and forgiveness for the sins of his people, Nehemiah found the courage to approach the king. As the king's cupbearer, Nehemiah was often in the presence of the King. But back in those days, being the cupbearer didn't mean you were the headwaiter or maître d'; it meant you were the lucky chap who got to drink from the king's cup before he did, so that the king could be assured his drink wasn't poisoned. How's that for a job? I think I would have rather been the wine-bearer. At least that way you would have greater confidence as to what was going into the king's cup—but that's just me. For those who are sticklers for detail and accuracy, I understand that the cupbearer and the wine-bearer are one and the same, but I invoke the law of creative license, here in the name of humor.

For those familiar with this story, the courage I referred to earlier was not referring to Nehemiah possessing a holy boldness or an authoritative voice in the presence of the king, but rather to the courage one possesses when he is standing in the gap, praying for others and trying to hear from God. The plight of Jerusalem was heavy on Nehemiah's heart, and despite his attempt to carry and conceal the burden; it was obvious to the king that something was weighing heavily on Nehemiah.

> So the king said to me, "Why is your face sad though you are not sick? This is nothing but sadness of heart."
> —NEHEMIAH 2:2

Confronted by the king, Nehemiah told him about the state of Jerusalem, the city of his fathers' tombs, and he gave the king an account of what Nehemiah had heard from his brother and friends. The king responded quite favorably, saying, "What would you request?" I'm thinking this response from the king took Nehemiah a bit by surprise, as the account goes on to say that Nehemiah then prayed to God. No doubt he was asking God, "Okay, now what do I say?"

> "And I said to the king, 'if it please the king, and if your servant has found favor before you, send me to Judah, to the city of my fathers' tombs, that I may rebuild it.'"
> —NEHEMIAH 2:5

One would think that the king would want Nehemiah to stay put. "Keep testing my wine and serving as my cupbearer because thus far, you've done a pretty good job. You are still alive and so am I and I would like to keep it that way." But instead, the king asked him how long the journey would be and when he expected to return. Nehemiah had obviously given this some thought; he quickly gave the king a definite time. The king granted his wish. With this boost of confidence and the obvious favor of the king, Nehemiah managed to summon up some good old-fashioned holy boldness and courage. He proceeded to ask the king for papers to be drawn up granting him not only safe passage with the governors of the providences, but also a special letter written to Asaph, the keeper of the king's forest, stating that Asaph was to supply Nehemiah with timber from the king's forest to rebuild the walls of Jerusalem. Wow, a man with a plan. Through prayer, Nehemiah had thought through many of the challenges he might face later. The king granted him all that he had requested, and then some. In addition to granting Nehemiah permission to go and papers to guarantee safe passage and access to the king's forest for timber, the king also sent with him some officers of the army and some horsemen. Nehemiah certainly did have the king's favor.

I think it's also safe to say that prayer had a lot to do with it. Through prayer, Nehemiah had an idea how long the project might take, and when asked by the king, he had a definite time to give him. Through prayer, God revealed, "You might want to ask for safe passage documents and secure access to timber, because you are going to need some timber." No doubt Nehemiah had prayed in advance for the people of Israel, that their hearts and backs would be in the rebuilding campaign, before he even had permission to go. Suffice it to say that in the business world, in your studies, and in raising a family, great insight, planning, challenges, and solutions can be found through prayer. God obviously believes in planning, so we too should make plans, develop strategy, and form a new game plan to drive us closer to what God has either called us to do, or placed upon our hearts to accomplish.

"For I know the plans I have for you," says the Lord, "plans to prosper you and not harm you, plans to give you a hope and a future."

—JEREMIAH 29:11

"Everything should be done in a fitting and orderly way."
—1 CORINTHIANS 14:40

"Live life then, with a due sense of responsibility, not as those who do not know the meaning of life, but as those who do. Make the best use of your time, despite all the difficulties of these days. Do not be vague but firmly grasp what you know to be the will of God."
—EPHESIANS 5:15-17

Unfortunately, with every good story, there's that other side of the coin called evil. What is true today was true back then. For some reason, when unloving, hostile, and jealous folks see you receiving God's favor and enjoying God's blessings, bitterness and resentment take wing. It seems like the devil always gets stirred up when people of God start to show initiative. The same proved true for Nehemiah. As the story goes, the neighbors weren't too happy about the new development project underway in Jerusalem. Sanballat, Tobiah, the Arabs, the Ammonites, and the Ashodites heard about the Rebuild Jerusalem Campaign, saw that the breaches in the walls were closing, and were not happy about it. In fact, they were downright angry. They decided to conspire together and hinder the progress Nehemiah was making.

And all of them conspired together to come and fight against Jerusalem and to cause a disturbance in it.
—NEHEMIAH 4:8

Yet despite the mocking and harassment of his enemies, the building continued. There were different construction teams assigned to different gates around the city in need of repair. Construction was in full swing. If you want to know in detail who worked on what gate and who was part of which crew, check out chapter three of Nehemiah; all the people are listed right there. As rumors began to surface among the people that the enemy was planning an attack to disturb their progress and tear down the walls, Nehemiah, the simple cupbearer-turned-builder-and-head-foreman transforms into a militaristic tactician and leader.

> "Then I stationed men in the lowest parts of the space behind the wall, the exposed places, and I stationed the people in families with their swords, spears, and bows."
> —NEHEMIAH 4:13

> "And it happened when our enemies heard that it was known to us, and that God had frustrated their plan, then all of us returned to the wall, each one to his work. And it came about from that day on, that half of my servants carried on the work while half of them held the spears, and shields, the bows . . ."
> —NEHEMIAH 4:15-16

And so the construction went until the walls were restored and their enemies were amazed and lost their confidence; they recognized that this work had been accomplished with the help of God.

So who was Nehemiah? He was first a man of prayer. Throughout the book of Nehemiah you'll find that at every turn, Nehemiah prayed. Yes, he was the king's cupbearer; that job alone would cause anyone to highly regard prayer. His deep compassion for God's people and the fallen city of Jerusalem opened the door for him to become the head foreman of a pretty large construction project. With God's vision and favor and with the people of Israel rallying behind Nehemiah, they were able to rebuild in fifty-two days what had taken over 145 years to destroy.

Nehemiah was also a proven militaristic tactician and leader. He acquired his skills via on-the-job training. He also governed over the people; he introduced law and order back to the people, abolished usury, assisted Ezra in restoring worship, conducted a census of the first returned exiles, and instituted many reforms.

Today, we would see Nehemiah as a mover and a shaker, both noble and notable, who decided to make a difference in the lives of God's people. Like Hezekiah, he was a difference maker.

Nothing happens until someone moves. That's what a difference maker is. A difference maker is a person of positive influence. A person possessing a God-given ability and sense of duty to influence people to accomplish God's purpose.

What makes a difference maker unique is not charisma, but character. To quote our current pastor, who is leading us through a study of Nehemiah, a difference maker has "a message worth remembering. He will have a lifestyle worth considering, and faith worth imitating."

> "Remember your leaders who spoke the Word of God to you. Consider the outcome of their way of life, and imitate their faith."
> —HEBREWS 13:7-8

> "Whatever you have learned of me, received or heard from me, or seen in me—put into practice."
> —PHILIPPIANS 4:9

A difference maker is willing to step out of his comfort zone, take a risk, and trust in God. When a difference maker finds that the current circumstances are out of his control, he prays. When he finds the circumstances are under control, he plans.

Through prayer, God not only helps difference makers understand the challenges; He also helps them define solutions and prepare for the questions and challenges that will no doubt naturally arise. A difference maker for God knows he must prepare in advance of opportunities presenting themselves. When these opportunities do present themselves, and we don't feel like we are ready, we need to be willing and ready to move ahead in spite of our fears, trusting that God will make the balance of His plan known, as we advance.

SIGNIFICANT OBSERVATIONS:

1. God chose Nehemiah to be a difference maker because he had compassion.
2. Nehemiah was sensitive and had a broken heart to the needs around him.
3. Nehemiah made himself available to do something for God's people.
4. Nehemiah was dependable and faithful.
5. Nehemiah held many job titles.
6. Nevertheless, Nehemiah was up to every challenge; he prayed all the time.
7. Nehemiah had a lifestyle worthy of consideration and a faith worthy of imitating.

JESUS:
THROUGH THE EYES OF A CHILD

If you abide in My word, then you are truly disciples of Mine; and you shall know the truth, and the truth shall make you free.

—JOHN 8:31-32

Like Nehemiah, Jesus was also a difference maker. In fact, Jesus was and is the ultimate difference maker!

As we conclude our study of biblical legacies of valor, it would be easy to stay on theme and highlight the many acts of courage and valor that Jesus obviously, and most notably, possessed. His entire adult life was a walk of faith, patience, gentleness, and courage. The path to the cross, where He would sacrifice His sinless life for those who persecuted and taunted Him at every turn, must have been most humbling, difficult to bear, and in the end, terrifying and unimaginable for us to fully comprehend. In adulthood, He openly shared the message of hope, love, patience, perseverance, kindness, and compassion to everyone who would listen. He healed those who were sick. He raised the dead. He spoke words of encouragement and faith. He taught the principles of the kingdom, God's kingdom, through ancient Scriptures, stories, and parables.

But Jesus did not come to us as a mighty warrior or a reigning king. Rather, He came as a lamb, the Lamb of God, for all of us, so that through His life and teachings, through his trials and crucifixion, through his death and resurrection, we might come to know our purpose in Him in our lifetime.

Up until now, we have focused primarily on biblical characters of the Old Testament. Ordinary men and women of character, faith, and right standing with God, were called on to be leaders, warriors, prophets, kings, ship captains, messengers of faith, spokesmen, temple builders, and difference makers. To be sure, these were brutal and unsettled times. And then a new covenant with man was born. Enter the New Testament, the one-on-one covenant between God the Father and man, through His Son Jesus.

> This cup which is poured out for you is the new covenant in My blood.
>
> —LUKE 22:20

> Who also made us adequate as servants of a new covenant, not of the letter, but of the Spirit; for the letter kills, but the Spirit gives life.
>
> —2 CORINTHIANS 3:6

> And for this reason He is the mediator of a new covenant, in order that since a death has taken place for the redemption of the transgressions that were committed under the first covenant, those who have been called may receive the promise of the eternal inheritance.
>
> —HEBREWS 9:15

Beyond being our Savior and the hope of the world, there is much to learn of Jesus the man through the eyes of Jesus the young boy growing up in and around Palestine. During His early childhood, Palestine was a place of bloody oppression, an occupied land ravaged by violence and injustice. By the time Jesus was a young boy, the occupiers were the Romans. The area Rome called Palestine was split into three regions. Samaria was centrally located with Judea to the south and Galilee to the north. In the rural area and hills to the south of Galilee lies Nazareth, the town where Jesus grew up.

While we most certainly live in times today that are different from biblical times, it is important to have some understanding of the region, its social and economic influences, and the geopolitical landscape of the day so that we can better comprehend and interpret the parables and teachings of Jesus.

Born in the reign of Jewish king Harold the Great around 4 BC, Jesus lived with his four brothers, James, Joseph, Simon and Judas, along with his sisters. He had spent His entire childhood pulling His weight around the home with family chores and the demands and needs of everyday life. Family life back then was hard. Everyone had chores and families banded together. Nearly half of the children born during biblical times never reached the age of five. Prospects for survival were not very promising. Poverty, hunger, famine, and disease were quite common in the region. Not exactly the kind of lives we enjoy in the west, with our super regional shopping malls, strip-malls, and every convenience one might need within minutes of where we live.

Compounding the daily struggle for survival came the seismic social, economic, and political unrest of the region. The effects of the Roman occupation were felt even in the rural area of Galilee. For years, the Jews had rebelled against their Roman overlords, their quest for land ownership and greater taxes from the Jews. It would have been very difficult not to notice or feel the effects of this oppression, growing up as a young man in this society. But out of hardship grew compassion.

Observing the daily dislocations and injustices would have had a major effect on how Jesus processed everything that happened around Him, as is evident from many of the parables He used to teach justice and fairness when His ministry was in full bloom.

> "I am the true vine, and My Father is the vinedresser. Every branch in Me that does not bear fruit, He takes away; and every branch that bears fruit, He prunes it, that it may bear more fruit."
>
> —JOHN 15:1-2

> Abide in Me, and I in you. As the branch cannot bear fruit of itself, unless it abides in the vine, so neither can you, unless you abide in Me.
>
> —JOHN 15:4

Here is a parable teaching that all of us can understand. It encapsulates all that we are to do; how we are to do it, and the purpose for doing it. Each of us are to walk in such a way as to produce fruit that will feed others and to leave seedlings behind that will further grow and produce abundance for others to enjoy and follow. We have this ability to grow, mature, and produce a harvest because we remain attached and connected to the vine, the life organ and root of the entire vine. Jesus, God the Father, is that vine from which we draw life and the ability to sprout mini-me twigs and branches from our own branch.

And yes, at times we ourselves will be pruned, so that we may bear more fruit. When you find yourself in a position that feels as though you are being trimmed, tested, or shaped by fire, take courage, for the Lord is just beginning a new work in you.

> Rejoicing in hope, persevering in tribulation, devoted to prayer.
>
> —ROMANS 12:12

Hear then the parable of the sower. When anyone hears the word of the kingdom, and does not understand it, the evil one comes and snatches away what has been sown in his heart. This is the one on whom seed was sown beside the road.

—MATTHEW 13:18-19

And the one on whom seed was sown on the rocky places, this is the man who hears the word, and immediately receives it with joy; yet he has no firm root in himself, but is only temporary, and when affliction or persecution arises, because of the word, immediately he falls away.

—MATTHEW 13:20-21

And the one on whom seed was sown among the thorns, this is the man who hears the word, and the worry of the world, and the deceitfulness of riches choke the word, and it becomes unfruitful.

—MATTHEW 13:22

And the one on whom seed was sown on the good soil, this is the man who hears the word and understands it; who indeed bears fruit, and brings forth, some a hundredfold, some sixty, and some thirty.

—MATTHEW 13:23

Ready for some great news? You and I, we are that good soil, for we have heard the word and we now understand it better. Take heart! We will all bear fruit; some a hundredfold, some sixty, and some thirty. Regardless of the amount, increase and blessings are heading our way. Amen and amen.

SIGNIFICANT OBSERVATIONS:

1. Be strengthened by the renewing of your mind.
2. Set a goal to read or re-read the entire New Testament this year.
3. Highlight previous highlights and jot down new observations.
4. Resolve to be a stronger believer in yourself and in Christ.
5. Commit the Word of God to your active thought life.
6. Let the Word flow forth from within to water and encourage others.
7. Know without doubt: if God be for you,; no one can triumph against you.

CLOSING THOUGHTS:
BE MADE COMPLETE

Finally, brethren, rejoice, be made complete, be comforted,
be like-minded, live in peace; and the God of love and peace
shall be with you.

—2 CORINTHIANS 13:11

I hope you have enjoyed reading *Legacies of Valor* as much as I enjoyed writing it. Let me say thank you from the bottom of my heart for reading it. I am most grateful that God led me to a place and granted me the opportunity to write something worthy of publishing, and worthy of note.

Over the span of my career, I have written more marketing messages, business plans, and resumes (lots of resumes) than I care to remember. But after all is said and done, after all I've acquired and passed on to others, I hope that my final resume will simply read:

"Follower of Christ,
Faithful Husband and Devoted Father,
Man of Integrity, Trustworthy and True.
Messenger of Faith and Voice of Hope,
Justified by the Blood,
A Prayer Warrior for the King."

Thirty-one words. One for every chapter in the book of Proverbs. I've never said so much in so few words.

ABOUT THE AUTHOR

David Hammond is the owner and founder of Hammond Ink, a marketing communications consultancy firm. For over thirty years he has helped Fortune 1000 firms design and deploy marketing communications strategies and launch new business ventures. He is highly regarded as a creative communicator, speaker, and motivator. In addition to authoring *Legacies of Valor* and managing Hammondink.com, David is an accomplished psalmist, singer, and recording artist; he released his first full album, *Warrior For The King*, in 2009.

When David isn't consulting to corporate America, or sharing his book and walk of faith at churches seeking a "spark of revival," he is busy promoting his CD to radio stations with the hope of getting God's Word out to those in need of a lift. When he's not working, he can be found hiking the high country trails of Colorado or off-roading in search of the next adventure that's just ahead and around the bend.

Hammond Ink
    www.Hammondink.com
    david@Hammondink.com
    DavidCHammond.com

Warrior For The King
    www.warriorfortheking.com
    david@warriorfortheking.com

ACCEPT THE

LEGACIES OF

VALOR

CHALLENGE TODAY!

Identify one or two folks, besides your kids or family members, folks outside your immediate family, that might be struggling today, that could use an encouraging, uplifting word.

Buy them each a softcover copy of *Legacies of Valor* and sow a seed of hope in their lives.

Start your own Pay-It-Forward Legacy today!

You can find *Legacies of Valor* at your local bookstore or order online at:

WestBow Press
http://bookstore.westbowpress.com/
http://warriorfortheking.com/

If you love Praise Music and can stomach a little country rock vibe, visit my Warrior For The King website.

www.Warriorfortheking.com

For 26 years I carried a hand full of songs I had written in my guitar case before finally deciding to record them professionally with my daughter.

There, you can pick-up a copy of the CD. Don't worry, you can PREVIEW the sound tracks before you buy the entire album or simply download your favorite song.

My personal favorites are *Love Blood* and *Seven Scriptures*. The *Warrior For The King* sound track is the story of my Prayer Room experience set to music.

I hope you enjoy them.

God Bless You!

Victory
Rests
with the
Lord

Victory
Rests
with the
Lord

God in the Vietnam War

JAMES SCHMIDT,
Lieutenant Colonel, U.S. Army Special Forces

WESTBOW
P R E S S®
A DIVISION OF THOMAS NELSON
& ZONDERVAN

WestBow Press books may be ordered through booksellers or by contacting:

WestBow Press
A Division of Thomas Nelson & Zondervan
1663 Liberty Drive
Bloomington, IN 47403
www.westbowpress.com
844-714-3454

ISBN: 978-1-4497-4622-3 (sc)
ISBN: 978-1-4497-4623-0 (hc)
ISBN: 978-1-4497-4621-6 (e)

Library of Congress Control Number: 2012906434

Print information available on the last page.

WestBow Press rev. date: 01/23/2024

This book is dedicated to the men and women around the world who risk their lives for Jesus Christ and the gospel.

Contents

Acknowledgments

I WOULD LIKE TO express my appreciation to my mother for keeping the letters I wrote home before I was married during my first tour in Vietnam, and to my wife, Joyce, for keeping the letters I wrote home to her during my second tour. Without these letters I would not have been able to recall half of the events that took place over forty years ago.

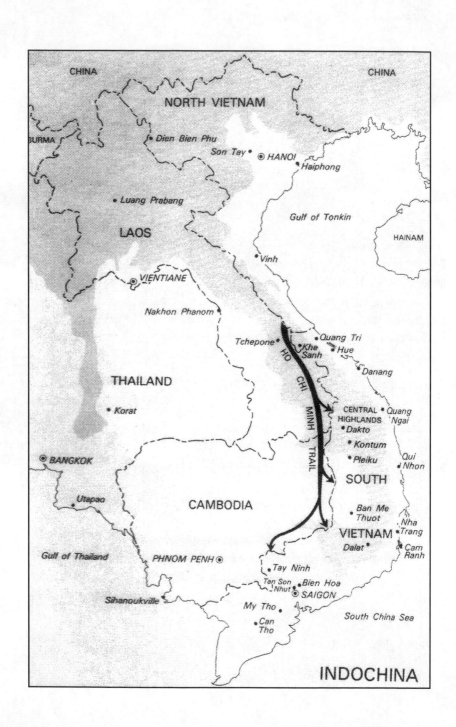

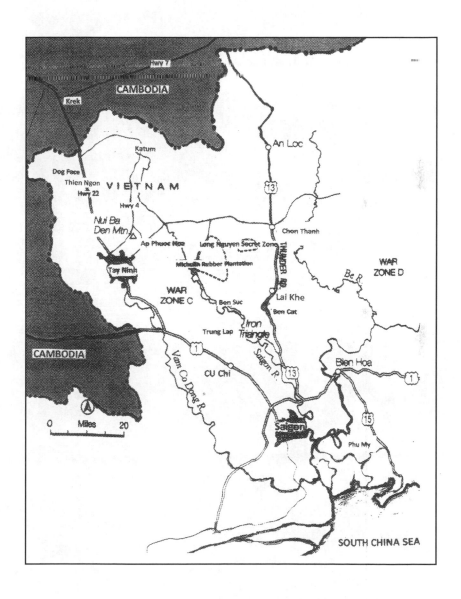

Introduction

The horse is made ready for the day of battle,
but victory rests with the Lord.
Proverbs 21:31[1]

As ONE WHO HAS led and directed men into battle numerous times, I can attest to the validity of Proverbs 21:31. I have found that regardless of how strong one's military is, the outcome of the battle remains in God's hands.

This book provides convincing evidence to the truism that God is in control during war. It shows that God allowed the United States to lose the Vietnam War, yet He also allowed an individual US Army infantry company to achieve victory.

This book is divided into two parts. Part I addresses why and how God denied victory in the Vietnam War to the most powerful country in the world. Part II tells, in chronological sequence, how God blessed the infantry company and task force I commanded in Vietnam with victory and protection.

America's reasons for fighting in Vietnam were honorable and justified. This book proposes that God denied the United States victory not as punishment for fighting, but to discipline America for the disintegration and decay of the nation's moral ethics. As a father disciplines his children because he loves them, God disciplines us out of love so that we will repent and return to Him.

Throughout history God has disciplined nations for their sins, in order to persuade them to repent and return to Him. The following offers an excellent example of how God disciplined America during our Civil War.

One hundred and fifty years ago, the United States was engaged in the Civil War. President Lincoln knew the Bible and understood that victory rested with the Lord. During the first part of the Civil War the Union lost battle after battle to the Confederate Army. Lincoln attributed these defeats on the battlefield to the disobedience and pride of the nation. He declared April 30, 1863, to be a national day of humiliation, fasting, and prayer. The following is part of Lincoln's proclamation:

> It is the duty of nations as well as of men to own (acknowledge) their dependence upon the overruling power of God; to confess their sins and transgressions in humble sorrow, yet with assured hope that genuine repentance will lead to mercy and pardon; and to recognize the sublime truth, announced in the Holy Scriptures and proven by all history, that those nations only are blessed whose God is the Lord.
>
> Intoxicated with unbroken success, we have become too self-sufficient to feel the necessity of redeeming and preserving grace, too proud to pray to the God that made us!
>
> It behooves us to humble ourselves before the offended Power, to confess our national sins and to pray for clemency and forgiveness.[2]

Miraculously, after the nation prayed for forgiveness, the tide of the Civil War turned in favor of the Union Army. Within two days, General Stonewall Jackson, one of the Confederates' best generals, was accidentally and fatally shot by his own men. Within three months, the Commander of the Confederate Army, General Robert E. Lee, who was considered a brilliant military strategist, made the imprudent decision to send his troops across a mile of open terrain to attack Union troops in good defensive positions located on the high ground near the town of Gettysburg. Lee's unwise decision resulted in the Confederates suffering a disastrous defeat. After the Union victory at the Battle of Gettysburg, the war turned around.[3]

Unfortunately, unlike in the Civil War, during the Vietnam Conflict the United States never acknowledged its dependence on the overruling power of God nor did it repent of its immoral behavior at home. As a result it is my belief that out of love God allowed America to be defeated in Vietnam in order to bring us back to Him.

Before I proceed any further in this book, I will address the issue of troops that died or were seriously injured in the Vietnam War. It is imperative that I make my position known upfront so that there is no misunderstanding as to my stance on this very important issue. Even though I believe the nation lost the war because of its disobedience, I want to make it crystal clear that I do not believe troops killed or wounded in the war were the result of their sins. I do believe that God blessed the infantry company I commanded in Vietnam; however, this does not mean that troops killed or injured in other units were less moral or religious than my men or me. I am confident that God's love, blessing, and mercy is disseminated to his children on an individual and personalized bases. Therefore, one's death in combat should not automatically be seen as God's punishment. In Vietnam, as well as in everyday life, individuals who love Jesus and are being obedient to His commandments, sometimes suffer an early death.

Only God knows what each of us was created to accomplish for Him in life. However, the Bible tells us in Romans 8:24: "In all things God works for the good of those who love him, who have been called according to his purpose."[4]

How God blesses an individual varies depending on God's will for the particular individual. Certainly, how long one lives on earth is not an indicator as to how righteous or how blessed he is. Jesus Christ, the only truly righteous person who lived on earth, was only here for a relatively short period.

Because of Jesus' sacrifice, death has lost its sting for those who have accepted Jesus as their savior. They have received victory over death through our Lord Jesus Christ.

Jesus tells us in Mark 8:35, "For whoever wants to save his life will lose it, but whoever loses his life for me and for the gospel will save it."[5] This does not mean that those who risked their lives and were killed earned salvation for trying to protect the freedom of the South Vietnamese to hear the good news of the gospel. We know that Jesus Christ paid for our sins on the cross, so whoever believes in Him as their Lord and Savior already has eternal life. Ephesians 2:8–9 clearly states that salvation is not earned, "For it is by grace you have been saved, through faith—and this not from yourselves, it is the gift of God—not by works, so that no one can boast."[6]

Only our faith in Jesus Christ leads to eternal life, but this does not mean that there is no value in the troops sacrificing their lives for Christ. Jesus told his disciples in Luke 6:22–23: "Blessed are you when men hate you, when they exclude you and insult you and reject your name as evil, because of the Son of Man. Rejoice in that day and leap for joy, because great is your reward in heaven. For that is how their fathers treated the prophets."[7] Even though the troops' sacrifice of their own lives for the gospel is not what gave them eternal life in heaven, it certainly earned them a great reward after their arrival there. I respect and admire these true heroes who died fighting for the Vietnamese's religious freedom. I believe God does as well.

Since a person, who accepts Jesus Christ as their Lord and Savior, goes to paradise in heaven when he dies, a Christian killed while doing God's will is certainly not a punishment. The parents, spouses, and children of Christians who died in Vietnam suffered a tremendous loss. I hope they are comforted by knowing their loved ones are in a much better place.

The success of a strategic plan depends upon how well it is executed. Therefore, the effectiveness of overall United States strategy in Vietnam was significantly influenced by tactics at the military company and battalion level. This book will show that God denied American senior military leaders the wisdom of effectively using tactics to execute their grand strategy.

All good leaders and managers know that one cannot develop the solution to a situation without first understanding the problem. It was vital for the leaders developing military strategy in Vietnam to understand the problems that infantry units were having where the rubber hit the road. This book suggests that Generals Westmoreland and Abrams never fully understood the problems US conventional infantry units had fighting in Vietnam's jungle environment and, as a result, employed incorrect tactics.

To substantiate the claim that there was a better way to fight the war and to show how God blessed the infantry company I commanded during my second Vietnam tour in 1970, I present a chronological account of our extremely successful combat operations in Part II.

The experiences of my first tour in Vietnam (August 1966 to August 1967) had a profound influence on my understanding of both men and of tactics, so I've included many accounts of them throughout this book to complement the descriptions of operations during my second tour. I hope to show how God used earlier events in my life to prepare me for what

He wanted me to accomplish later in life for His honor and glory. These first-tour experiences provide support for my positions on various concepts and help explain why I employed the tactics I did.

Military scholars may find value in the identification of both failed and successful tactics, but the overriding reason for my discussion of them is to provide the reader with evidence regarding which American commanders were denied wisdom and which were given wisdom by God during the Vietnam War. My goal is not to teach military theory, but to provide support for the hypothesis that the Vietnam War could have been won if God had provided the necessary wisdom to senior US commanders.

God denied US senior military leaders the tactical wisdom necessary for the nation to succeed. Likewise, it was God who gave my infantry company the tactical wisdom that resulted in our success and protection. My motivation for writing this book is threefold:

1. To emphasize that it is God who provides or denies wisdom to individuals in war
2. To encourage Christians to actively challenge America's morals and to convince American citizens to re-adopt the Bible as their moral compass
3. To give all the glory for the success of my infantry company to God the Father, Son, and Holy Ghost

PART I

Defeat

CHAPTER I

Why Didn't Victory Go to the Strongest Military?

If my people would but listen to me, if Israel would follow my ways, how quickly would I subdue their enemies and turn my hand against their foes!
Psalm 81:13–14[1]

MANY BOOKS HAVE BEEN written on the Vietnam Conflict by authors such as a former President, Secretaries of Defense, military historians, professors, and key generals. None, however, adequately explain why the United States was unable to prevent South Vietnam from becoming communist. This book provides the answer.

In light of Proverbs 21:31, which states, "The horse is made ready for the day of battle, but victory rests with the Lord,"[2] the short answer to the above question is: because God did not allow the United States to win.

If this is true and God controls the outcome of war, then why did God allow an atheist communist regime that restricts religious freedom to succeed in Vietnam? It would be presumptuous for me to think that I know the mind of God, or to state that I absolutely know why God denied final victory to the United States. Therefore, I'll only suggest what I believe God's reason was, and leave readers to form their own opinions.

However, I will remind readers of God's warning to the Israelites who might disobey Him: "I will set my face against you, and you shall be struck down by your enemies…And if in spite of this you will not obey me, I will continue to punish you sevenfold for your sin."[3] History shows that when the Israelites disobeyed God, He allowed evil and non-believing nations to have victory over them.

In light of this warning from God, and of America's increasing moral decay since the early sixties, it is my opinion that God allowed the United States to be defeated in Vietnam in order to discipline American citizens so that they would turn away from their debauchery and other evil behavior. Tragically, America as a nation has been stubborn and unrepentant, thus putting the nation in jeopardy of God's continuing punishment.

A counterinsurgency war is not won or lost based on the outcome of a single battle, or even on the security of the population and government. To defeat an insurgency, a government must take political, economic, military, paramilitary, psychological, and civic action. The reader will find that God did not intervene in just one battle or event to cause overall defeat or victory in the Vietnam War. This book will reveal that the United States leaders performed many things right in Vietnam; however, two things they failed to do correctly that led to our defeat were ground tactics and physiological operations. Of the two, the one that contributed the most to America's defeat were poor infantry tactics.

This book will show that if God had provided the top brass of the US military with wisdom and insight, they would have adopted tactics that resulted in fewer casualties, and the American public would not have lost their resolve as quickly as they did. With stronger resolve America would have been willing to use its military power to enforce the Paris Peace Accord to lasting victory.

In his 1981 book, *On Strategy: The Vietnam War in Context*, Colonel Harry Summers stated, "On the battlefield itself, the Army was unbeatable. In engagement after engagement the forces of the Viet Cong (VC) and of the North Vietnamese Army (NVA) were thrown back with terrible losses. Yet, in the end, it was North Vietnam, not the United States that emerged victorious. How could we have succeeded so well, yet failed so miserably?"[4]

I believe Colonel Summers provides one of the best analyses written of the Vietnam Conflict; however, his statement that we never lost on the battlefield has led many to assume that our tactics were correct and had little adverse effect on our overall defeat. It is true that we were always able to drive the enemy off the battlefield, but that fact in itself does not necessarily mean we employed the correct tactics. In contrast to the enemy, the United States had overwhelming air and artillery firepower; therefore, even units employing extremely poor tactics succeeded in driving the enemy off the battlefield.

Because of the false assumption that our tactics were good, the tactics used in Vietnam have never been properly analyzed. This question has unfortunately never been asked: *if we had changed our tactics, could we have suffered fewer casualties while still inflicting the same losses on the enemy?* This book provides evidence that the answer is a resounding 'yes.'

The next few chapters outline basic military doctrine. They also present the strategies and tactics employed by the United States and by the North Vietnamese and Viet Cong communists. These chapters will provide the background necessary to understand why some tactics and strategies worked and others did not.

The latter chapters of Part I give convincing evidence that American top brass lacked the insight and wisdom to employ the correct tactics in Vietnam. I also explain how this conclusion is based on analyses of the strategies and tactics discussed in the initial chapters.

Although I contribute the defeat in Vietnam to a lack of wisdom and creativity in America's senior military leaders, I am not suggesting that any of these leaders lacked faith in Jesus Christ, or that they were immoral. Rather, similar to the very Godly and brilliant Robert E. Lee's bad decision at Gettysburg, I believe that God denied them wisdom in order to influence the outcome of the war for His' purpose.

CHAPTER 2

How God Intervenes in War

*By faith the walls of Jericho fell, after the people
had marched around them for seven days.*
Hebrews 11:30[1]

SOME PEOPLE MIGHT BELIEVE that God does not approve of war, and for that reason, that He does not intervene in war. Before we move on, then, I devote the first part of this chapter to the subject of the morality of war from a biblical perspective.

Some say that God only intervened in war prior to Jesus Christ's ministry on earth. They say that Jesus' Sermon on the Mount changed the old law; it now condemns all wars and those who would fight in them. As proof, people quote Jesus: "You have heard that it is said, 'Love your neighbor and hate your enemy.' But I tell you: Love your enemies and pray for those who persecute you, so that you may be sons of your Father in heaven."[2] However, the use of this verse to support the position that all wars are wrong is incorrect.

First of all, Jesus never claimed that it was God who said in the Old Testament that one should hate his enemies. Secondly, as a soldier doing his duty, I had to kill enemy soldiers many times. However, I can truthfully say that even though the enemy's mission was to kill my men and me, I never killed out of hate or revenge. In fact, killing out of revenge and hatred only interferes with clear-headed thinking; therefore, it is counterproductive in war. Finally, there is a vast difference between killing and murdering, just as there is a vast difference between a just war and an unjust war.

To help define a just war, the Chief of Chaplains of the Army published an article in 1982. The views within the article were not necessarily those of the Department of Defense, but they are views on war by very influential individuals. The view of St. Augustine on war (as stated in the article) is provided below:

It was St. Augustine writing in the 5th Century A.D. that provided a moral justification for a Christian fighting in a war. Although St. Augustine would not avail himself of the natural right to repel force by force, he did concede to other men the right of self-defense. However, the moral formula was transformed even for him once a third party was introduced. He reasoned that if he were traveling upon the desert in the company of women and children and they were attacked by brigands, unselfish love for others would this time demand that he sacrifice himself in defense of the innocent victims of unjust attack. He would fight, and if necessary, die to defend them. Resorting to violence under this circumstance was seen as not only serving justice, but as a work of charity. Augustine's logic has dominated Western thought concerning the just and unjust use of force.

The reasoning of St. Augustine enables us to understand the ambivalence experienced in reflecting upon war and upon the profession of arms. For St. Augustine, war was the result of sin; terrible evidence of the disorder of human existence. But war, when viewed as an essential act taken to protect the innocent from an unjust attack, was not the result of the defenders' sin, and, therefore, was not to be considered evil. Hence, under severe necessity, war could be the lesser evil and the morally preferred act.

In a sense, because good and evil were inextricably intermixed in man, St. Augustine regarded war as being at once a result of sin and a cure for sin.[3]

Although the Chaplain's article includes the views of numerous important religious and non-religious individuals throughout history, from 400 BC to AD 1982, I believe the words of Martin Luther in the 16th century are the most succinct summary of the issue: "A defensive war is the only true just war, and any war should be fought in the fear of God."[4]

It is not murder when a soldier takes the lives of enemy soldiers in order to stop armed aggression against one's own or another's country. This is a just war. On the other hand, it is murder when a soldier or non-soldier intentionally takes the life of a civilian or soldier of another country that is not threatening his nation or someone else's nation by armed force, and takes that life due to hatred, revenge, greed, a quest for power, or a desire to impose his own religion on others.

A war fought to defend one's innocent fellow citizens or another nation's innocent citizens from unjustified armed aggression is justifiable. Consequently, it was just to defend the South Vietnamese from armed aggression by a communist government outside South Vietnam's borders.

While for me, South Vietnam's freedom to worship Jesus Christ was cause enough to fight and risk my life, it was also critical to our national security to keep Southeast Asia non-communist. Unfortunately, many Americans did not understand military strategy and what the consequences of a communist Southeast Asia would be during a war with the Soviet Union or China. Therefore, they did not believe the United States had any business fighting for a country halfway around the world.

President Johnson deliberately did not mobilize the American people for fear of adversely impacting his Great Society program. As a result, most Americans were never told how important it was to keep the Strait of Malacca open to US ships and to have access to air and naval bases in Southeast Asia during wartime.

Even though the wars on terrorism and drugs did not have a bearing on the Vietnam War, because they are current threats to the United States, I will briefly address my thoughts on how the issue of a just war applies to them.

As defined above, a just war occurs when a nation's military fights to protect its citizens from being killed. Surely, the United States would be justified in destroying an enemy who was firing missiles into our cities and killing our citizens.

An organization that produces illegal drugs or train terrorists within the borders of a foreign country, but then sends the drugs or terrorists into our cities, is just as deadly. If the government of such a deadly organization is unwilling or incapable of preventing these actions, then the US government has not only the right but a moral responsibility to its own citizens to destroy them.

Individual rights and sovereignty have their limits in our ever-shrinking world. If illegal activities in one country threaten the security of another, then those illegal activities are no longer just the internal concern of that country. Consequently, a policy of noninterference in the internal affairs of drug- and terrorist-producing countries is no longer appropriate.

In the past, a *state of war* was defined as open and declared armed hostile conflict between states or nations. Today, because of the magnitude of organized crime and terrorism, *war* is used to describe the fight against these groups as well. It is important to clarify that even though we use this term to talk about the fight against drug and terrorist organizations, the people in these groups are still common criminals. They should not be considered soldiers or given the rights of soldiers as defined in the Geneva Convention.

So as not to divert focus from the intent of this book, further discussion of the problem of illegal drugs and terrorism will be avoided. Readers interested in my thoughts on dealing with the illegal drugs problem can read my article "Hit Drug Lords' Center of Gravity," published in the July 1992 issue of *Army Magazine*.[5]

We should note that Jesus never criticized those in the military. In fact, Jesus did just the opposite. In Matthew 8:10, a centurion tells Jesus only say the word and the centurion's dying servant will be healed. "When Jesus heard this, he was astonished and said to those following him, 'I tell you the truth, I have not found anyone in Israel with such great faith.'"[6]

Similarly, John the Baptist did not forbid soldiering. John did not condemn men for being soldiers, as we see in Luke 3:14: "Then some soldiers asked him, 'And what should we do?' He replied, 'Don't extort money and don't accuse people falsely—be content with your pay.'"[7]

One last comment before leaving this discussion of the justification of war: I think most people would agree with the well-known statement, *all that is needed for evil to prosper is for good people to do nothing.* If a person sees that something should be done to stop evil and he has the ability to stop it, but does nothing, that is a sin of omission.

God uses natural disasters, weather, plagues, and people themselves (their wisdom, special skills, technology, weapons, etc.) to influence the outcome of war. Certainly, the creator of the world can do all things; God is not limited in the ways He intervenes in war, or in any other events on earth. It is imperative for us to acknowledge God's power to intervene, and for us to call upon the Lord for help in all things.

For example, during the Revolutionary War, George Washington credited God for the safe evacuation of his troops from Brooklyn Heights, Long Island. In 1776, the British had trapped the American army and were about to crush them, which could have resulted in a disastrous end to the war. To save his forces, Washington conducted a risky night withdrawal across the East River the night before the British were to attack. A particularly heavy "black fog" covered their evacuation throughout the night. In the morning, the fog remained; it lasted longer than fog normally does. By the time the fog lifted, the last American boats were out of range of the British guns.

Ironically, when the British were trapped by the Americans at Yorktown, British General Cornwallis attempted a similar nighttime escape by boat; however, instead of fog, he experienced a tremendous storm that eliminated their chance for escape.[8]

In Israel's war against the Philistines, God used David, a small boy with a sling, to defeat the powerful, giant warrior Goliath, causing the Philistine army to retreat in fear. David had a great love for God, and because of his enormous faith, he had the courage to face Goliath. Thus, God blessed David with the skill to use a sling, and He guided the rock to its target.[9]

Although God had numerous methods of influencing the outcome of the Vietnam War, His primary one was to deny the United States military leaders the wisdom to employ the correct tactics.

The senior civilian and military individuals responsible for the strategies used in Vietnam either claim the war was unwinnable or blame others for the defeat. This book will provide evidence that the Vietnam War would have been winnable if God had provided US senior military leaders the insight, creativity, wisdom, and knowledge necessary for them to employ better tactics. The book identifies which strategies, tactics, and actions led to the United States' defeat, and which actions, if taken, could have led to victory.

It is, of course, important to study tactics that have worked in the past and established military doctrine, but it is even more important to ask God to provide us with insight, intuition, and creativity to develop new tactics and technology necessary to defeat our country's enemies in the future. The acclaimed nineteenth-century military theorist Carl von Clausewitz states in his book *On War* that "History provides the strongest proof of

11

the importance of moral factors and their often incredible effect: this is the noblest and most solid nourishment that the mind of a general may draw from a study of the past. Parenthetically, it should be noted that the seeds of wisdom that are to bear fruit in the intellect are sown less by critical studies and learned monographs than by insights, broad impressions, and flashes of intuition." [10]

Where does a military leader obtain these insights and flashes of intuition that Clausewitz writes about? As it is written in James 1:5, they come from God: "If any of you lacks wisdom, he should ask God, who gives generously to all without finding fault, and it will be given to him."[11]

The responsibility of leadership drove young King Solomon to pray to the Lord for a discerning heart to lead the Israelites. Because Solomon asked for this rather than for long life and wealth for himself, in 1 Kings 3:12, the Lord says to Solomon, "I will give you a wise and discerning heart, so that there will never have been anyone like you, nor will there ever be."[12]

In the following chapters of this book, I provide support for the claim that God did not give senior US military leaders the wisdom to employ tactics that could have won the Vietnam War.

Because I experienced the Vietnam Conflict at the point of the spear as an infantry rifle platoon leader and as an infantry company commander, and because later in life I was a key contributor to planning US military strategy and doctrine, I provide the reader insight into the impact that poor company and battalion level tactics had on our overall strategy in Vietnam. Additionally, the infantry company I commanded was considered to be one of the most successful infantry units in the Vietnam Conflict. I not only identify problems in US tactics, but also provide what I believe would have been the solution to the Conflict, if God had provided our senior military leaders with the light to see it.

Contrary to former Secretary of Defense Robert McNamara's opinion that the war in Vietnam was unwinnable, I will make a strong case that the war could have been won if God had provided our leaders with the knowledge and creativity to employ the correct tactics.[13] I identify these flawed tactics as well as which tactics should have been employed instead. I also describe the most effective infantry tactics and techniques that were used in the latter years of the Vietnam Conflict. These tactics and techniques are unknown to most previous authors of books on Vietnam. If these tactics had been used throughout the entire conflict, the United States would have gained enough time to achieve a lasting victory.

CHAPTER 3

Military Strategy and Doctrine

*The fear of the Lord is the beginning of wisdom, and
knowledge of the Holy One is understanding.*
Proverbs 9:10[1]

THIS CHAPTER ON STRATEGY is for those who have not had the opportunity to study military strategy. It provides enough basic knowledge of military strategy and US military doctrine for the reader to be able to question the wisdom of America's civilian and military leadership during the Vietnam Conflict. Basic comprehension of military strategy will also help the reader to understand the reasons why US tactics failed. Finally, and most importantly, this chapter will help the reader see that the war would have been winnable, had God provided US leaders with the wisdom to employ better tactics.

Before one develops a military strategy, one must first understand the process by which a government causes another government to act in a particular way. The diagram below shows the spectrum of actions available to governments, from those with the least amount of pressure to those with the greatest:

SPECTRUM OF FOREIGN DIPLOMACY
Voluntary Compliance - Coerced by Assistance - Coerced by Sanctions - Forced by Military Action

Clearly, military action is the least preferred option, but when less forceful options fail, military action may be the only way to accomplish the desired objective. There is, however, a wide range of military actions from which to choose, such as military presence, show of force, demonstration, special operations, quarantine, blockade, and force entry.

The United States believed it necessary to use the military option *force entry* in order to convince North Vietnam and the Viet Cong to allow South Vietnam to remain an independent democratic nation. Once the decision was made to use military force, the objective should have been to accomplish the mission with a minimum of US casualties.

In discussing military strategy, one needs to be familiar with the US military's Principles of War and Counterinsurgency Principles (COIN).

PRINCIPLES OF WAR[2]

Objective. Direct every military operation towards a clearly defined, decisive, and attainable objective.

Offensive. Seize, retain, and exploit the initiative.

Mass. Concentrate combat power at the decisive place and time.

Economy of force. Allocate minimum essential combat power to secondary efforts.

Maneuver. Place the enemy in a position of disadvantage through the flexible application of combat power.

Unity of command. For every objective, ensure unity of effort under one responsible commander.

Security. Never permit the enemy to acquire an unexpected advantage.

Surprise. Strike the enemy at a time, at a place, or in a manner for which he is unprepared.

Simplicity. Prepare clear, uncomplicated plans and clear, concise orders to ensure thorough understanding.

Department of the Army
Operations Field Manual 100-5, B-1

COUNTERINSURGENCY PRINCIPLES[3]

Legitimacy is the Main Objective
Unity of Effort is Essential
Political Factors are Primary
Understand the Environment
Intelligence Drives Operations
Isolate Insurgents from Their Cause and Support
Establish Security Under the Rule of Law
Prepare for a Long-Term Commitment
Department of the Army
Counterinsurgency Field Manual 3-24, 1-16

The final principle to be considered cannot be found in military manuals; it is one I developed early in my military career, and it has proven extremely useful.

In most military conflicts, the goal is to convince the opponent to surrender. It is my belief that in most cases *an enemy will capitulate when he comes to one of the three following conclusions*:

1. The cost of what he is fighting to gain is more than he is willing to pay (cost-benefit analysis).
2. He has no chance of winning the war.
3. He has no hope of winning a better bargaining position.

To develop a strategy, one must determine which of the above three approaches will convince the enemy to capitulate, as well as which approach the enemy will use against one's own country.

Although the above principle normally works with sane leaders, it will not work with individuals who no longer think in a rational manner, or individuals who know they will be killed even if they surrender because of atrocities they have committed. Hitler, Saddam Hussein, and Osama bin Laden are three examples of individuals who probably fall into both of those categories. Leaders such as these will need to be captured or killed by either their enemies or those of their own fighters who are rational enough to see the futility of continuing to fight.

Because leadership in North Vietnam was sane, the principle for convincing rational leaders to capitulate will be used to analyze strategies in the following chapters.

CHAPTER 4

American and Communist Strategy in the Vietnam War

As I STATED IN the previous chapter, it is my belief that an enemy will normally capitulate when he is convinced either that what he is fighting to gain will cost him more than he is willing to pay, that he has no chance of winning the war, or that he has no hope of winning a better bargaining position.

Because the United States has such powerful military strength, North Vietnam and the Viet Cong knew they could not affect the physical ability of the United States to prosecute the war. Therefore, *North Vietnam's approach was to try to convince the US that it would cost us more than we were willing to pay to keep South Vietnam non-communist.*

The United States, on the other hand, had more than enough military power to defeat North Vietnam. *US leadership, therefore, believed it would be relatively easy to convince North Vietnam that they had no hope of winning.* However, our leaders failed to realize that to successfully persuade an opponent into believing they have no hope of winning, you must convince that opponent not only that you have overwhelming combat power, but *also that you have the will to use it.* For example, during the Gulf War, Operation Desert Shield certainly convinced Saddam Hussein that the United Nations forces had overwhelming combat power; however, it took Desert Storm to convince him that we were willing to use it. In WWII, Japan didn't surrender after we used the first atomic bomb to destroy Hiroshima because they believed that after Americans saw the massive civilian casualties of the bomb, we would not use it again. As a result, we had to convince them that we did have the will to do so by bombing Nagasaki.

Although the US approach in Vietnam was to convince the enemy that they had no hope of winning, our leaders unfortunately adopted the strategy known as *graduated response*; this showed a hesitancy to use our overwhelming combat power. In *Summons of the Trumpet*, Brigadier General Dave Palmer states that the graduated response strategy was initially presented during a debate over bombing: "civilian planners wanted to start out softly and gradually increase the pressure by precise increments which could be unmistakably recognized in Hanoi. Ho Chi Minh would see the tightening pattern, the theory went, and would sensibly stop the war against South Vietnam in time to avoid devastation of his homeland."[1]

Unfortunately, gradually escalating our power led to a protracted war which not only allowed North Vietnam time to replenish their losses, but also to affect America's willingness to continue to fight.

Once government approaches are identified, the next step to developing a military strategy is to identify the enemy's *center of gravity* and develop a means to destroy it. Similarly, one must identify the center of gravity of one's own country that must be protected from the enemy.

In military strategy, the term *center of gravity* is defined by *Department of Defense's Joint Publication 1-02* as "those characteristics, capabilities, or sources of power from which a military force derives its freedom of action, physical strength, or will to fight."[2] In *On War,* Clausewitz describes it thus: "Out of these characteristics a certain center of gravity develops, the hub of all power and movement, on which everything depends. That is the point against which all our energies should be directed ... For Alexander, Gustavus Adolphus, Charles XII, and Frederick the Great, the center of gravity was their army. If the army had been destroyed, they would all have gone down in history as failures. In countries subject to domestic strife, the center of gravity is generally the capital. In small countries that rely on large ones, it is usually the army of their protector. Among alliances, it lies in the community of interest, and in popular uprisings it is the personalities of the leaders and public opinion. It is against these that our energies should be directed."[3]

The US strategy of graduated response played into the hands of the North Vietnamese by allowing them, as stated above, not only time to replenish their losses, but also time to eventually convince the US that what we had to gain was costing us more than we were willing to pay. As Clausewitz stated, in small countries that rely on large ones, it is usually the army of their protector that is their center of gravity. North Vietnam couldn't destroy the army of South Vietnam's protector (the United States), but it could destroy the protector's resolve to provide protection.

Because in a democracy the citizens ultimately make the decisions to capitulate or to keep fighting, *our center of gravity was the US citizens' resolve.* Since US casualties have the greatest influence on the willingness of US citizens to stay in the fight, causing as many American military casualties as possible became a major objective of our enemy and one that we should have done a better job of protecting against.

One way that an enemy can expedite the process of causing an opponent to lose patience is to conduct a large operation that will result in a large number of casualties and prisoners of war (POWs). This was accomplished against the French at Dien Bien Phu in 1954. The NVA attempted to repeat this success in 1968 by overrunning and capturing the US Marine firebase at Khe Sanh, but new technology and greater airpower available to the Americans than the French had available to them at Dien Bien Phu prevented their success. The communists' only option was to fight a protracted war until they could kill enough US soldiers to convince the American citizens that continuing to fight the war was no longer worth the cost.

There was a correlation between the number of US casualties citizens were willing to accept and the importance to national interests of saving South Vietnam from communism. The communists understood this correlation; they initiated an effective propaganda campaign, targeted to US citizens, to discredit the perceived dangers of a communist South Vietnam. Their key theme was to label the war as internal insurgency rather than communist aggression by North Vietnam against South Vietnam. This internal-struggle smokescreen bamboozled many less-informed citizens within the US. It resulted in naïve college professors providing incorrect analyses of the war to their students and in the grandstanding media presenting biased news broadcasts; the resolve of US citizens was thereby weakened. Misinformation spread by professors and the media also led to increased peace demonstrations within the US; this strengthened the enemy's resolve. Napoleon recognized the power of propaganda when he said, "There are only two powers in the world, the sword and the spirit. In the long run the sword will always be conquered by the spirit."[4]

North Vietnam's effective propaganda campaign also caused the US military to focus on a counterinsurgency strategy, thus neglecting a strategy to defeat and destroy the conventional threat that North Vietnam presented.

As previously stated, the North Vietnamese knew that the US had overwhelming combat power, but they also rightly believed we would not use it. The US had the capability to bomb Hanoi into the Stone Age; however, we were not willing to do it. Fear of China entering the war, as they had done in Korea, and humanitarian concerns influenced our decisions about how much of our power we were willing to use against North Vietnam.

The North Vietnamese leaders correctly believed that the US was willing to use its military power only to destroy military targets and military support targets. The US could not win a quick war as long as they protected their war fighting capability; this allowed North Vietnam to fight a protracted war. They knew a protracted war would work to their advantage as long as the US continued to use tactics that allowed North Vietnam to kill large numbers of US soldiers, thereby destroying American citizens' resolve. Unfortunately, the US tactic of using relatively large US ground troops to conduct *search and destroy* operations provided the enemy with enough targets to achieve their objective.

Additionally, North Vietnam's disinformation program gained momentum over time. The propaganda aimed to lower the perceived importance of keeping South Vietnam from becoming communist and to present South Vietnam as a corrupt and illegitimate government in the minds of American citizens. The United States' failure to counter the enemy propaganda or to use effective fighting tactics to reduce US casualties encouraged the communists to fight a protracted war.

With the withdrawal of US ground troops from Vietnam by early 1972, the North Vietnamese believed they had successfully defeated their enemy's center of gravity, the alliance between the United States and South Vietnam. Therefore, they chose a new center of gravity: the destruction of the South Vietnamese Army. In March 1972, North Vietnam invaded South Vietnam in a large scale conventional attack with tanks and heavy artillery. However, they severely miscalculated President Nixon's resolve and the effectiveness of US firepower when American advisors were still in Vietnam to direct it. As a result, North Vietnam suffered a major defeat and withdrew their attack.

North Vietnam had defeated American civilian resolve; however, President Nixon's resolve was not. US advisors and close air support (CAS) aircraft were still in Vietnam. Therefore, these in country US assets as well as the availability of B-52s and naval CAS, allowed President Nixon to provide South Vietnam the military support they needed. North Vietnam realized their mistake. Only after Congress restricted all funding and support to South Vietnam, and Nixon left office, did they attempt another invasion with conventional forces.

When North Vietnam signed the Paris Peace Accord, they may or may not already have been planning to break it and invade South Vietnam with conventional troops. However, I am sure North Vietnam knew that to win an insurgency war, they would have to discredit the legitimacy of the current South Vietnamese government and convince the South Vietnamese that a new communist government was more legitimate. With the US's withdrawal, the South lost its major protector; however, they gained a psychological advantage by increasing their legitimacy in the eyes of their people. The communists could no longer claim the current government was only a "puppet of the Americans." With the legitimacy of South Vietnam's government strengthened, and having developed a relatively good counterinsurgency program, South Vietnam had an excellent chance at winning the war against the communists who were allowed by the Paris Peace Accord to remain in South Vietnam.

I believe North Vietnam knew that to comply with the Paris Peace Accord was to allow South Vietnam to defeat the communist insurgency in South Vietnam. Once North Vietnam knew that they could break their treaty with the US without adverse consequences, they no longer found it necessary to pretend to be fighting an insurgency war, so they planned a large conventional invasion.

North Vietnam tested our new President, Ford, by attacking Phuoc Long in South Vietnam on January 6, 1975. Since the United States didn't retaliate, North Vietnam launched an invasion with twenty divisions into South Vietnam in early March 1975. Without the support of the United States, North Vietnam successfully destroyed the South Vietnamese army, and Saigon fell on April 30, 1975. By seizing and holding Saigon, North Vietnam also effectively ended the internal war. As Clausewitz stated, "In countries subject to domestic strife, the center of gravity is generally the capital."[5]

When it came to resolve, North Vietnam had a significant advantage over the United States. Unlike US leaders who had to answer to US citizens, North Vietnam leaders considered their soldiers' lives of little value, expendable. Because the communist government of North Vietnam controlled their media, they were able to hide their heavy losses in South Vietnam from their citizens. North Vietnam also had a large enough population that they could always replace the soldiers they had lost.

The United States believed the enemy's center of gravity was initially their troops, and later in the war, their supplies. Consequently, General Westmoreland implemented a strategy to attrite the enemy force until they no longer had the capability to continue fighting. Unfortunately, the tactics Westmoreland implemented to destroy the enemies troops also cost an unacceptable number of US casualties.

US military leaders thought that over time, North Vietnam would eventually say they had had enough. However, the longer the war lasted, the more obvious it became that time was not on our side. It was the will of American citizens rather than of North Vietnam citizens that was deteriorating. Time ran out on us.

Many books have been written to argue the wisdom of restricting the US's military power against North Vietnam. For that reason, this book will not discuss the pros and cons of the decision to not attack the North with our full power.

Neither will I discuss the United States' failure to extend the Demarcation Line (DMZ) fortifications along the North-South Vietnam border an additional ninety miles across Laos to the Mekong River and Laos-Thailand border. Limiting the DMZ to Vietnam allowed the NVA to bypass US fortifications much as the Germans bypassed the French Maginot Line by invading via Belgium in World War II.

Even recognizing the disadvantages of the above self-imposed restrictions, not using our full power, the United States could still have won a protracted war against the communists in the Vietnam Conflict.

I will provide evidence with examples that the United States could have won if we had employed tactics that kept US casualties at an extremely low and acceptable level, while still stopping the infiltration of the enemy and destroying their weapons, supplies, and troops in order to provide security to the South Vietnamese. A convincing argument will be made to support the position that with proper tactics, the US military could have protected and kept the resolve of US citizens strong enough to enforce the 1973 US-North Vietnam treaty.

Most military analysts believe South Vietnam was clearly winning the counterinsurgency war against the communist forces allowed by the Paris Peace Accord to remain in South Vietnam. If the United States had been able to convince North Vietnam that the US was committed to stopping any invasion of South Vietnam with conventional forces, there would be a non-communist government in South Vietnam today.

General Westmoreland was replaced by General Creighton Abrams in 1968, and the large scale search and destroy operations that resulted in the majority of US casualties were replaced by *clear and hold* operations. Additionally, maintaining the security of people in hamlets and villages replaced attrition of enemy forces as a primary objective.⁶

Abrams was more focused on the enemy's supply of weapons, ammunition, and food rather than on body count; Abrams *believed the supply was the enemy's center of gravity.* Incursions into Cambodia by US and Army of the Republic of Vietnam (ARVN) forces and into Laos by ARVN forces to destroy enemy supplies proved to significantly damage the NVA/VC's ability to conduct large scale operations within South Vietnam.

By mid-1970, the number of NVA/VC remaining in South Vietnam was at a level low enough that the ARVN could almost handle the threat on their own, with US advisors, equipment, and air support. Consequently, President Nixon's Vietnamization program which required turning the war fighting over to the Vietnamese was in full swing. After the US's Cambodian incursion, US ground maneuver units remaining in Vietnam continued to improve security and pacification within South Vietnam to the point where the ARVN could manage the war on their own.

By 1971, the ARVN conducted most of the search and destroy type of mission, and the number of US combat troops remaining in Vietnam had been reduced significantly. As a result the US experienced a substantial reduction in American casualties. Unfortunately, heavy US casualties in the past had already weakened the US citizens' resolve to the point that America was not willing to take the actions required to enforce the Paris Peace Accord signed on January 27, 1973.

Certainly, North Vietnam would never have invaded South Vietnam with a conventional attack if they thought the US would return to enforce the Paris Peace Accord. For North Vietnam to attack with conventional troops, using tanks out in the open, would have been suicide against the superior airpower of the United States. With US air superiority, the United States would have completely destroyed North Vietnam's army.

I conclude that the United States lost the war because we lost our resolve, and that we lost our resolve because we lost an unacceptable number of US soldiers. In the next chapter, I argue that poor tactics caused higher casualties than necessary.

CHAPTER 5

Flawed Military Tactics

Since they hated knowledge and did not choose to fear the Lord, since they would not accept my advice and spurned my rebuke, they will eat the fruit of their ways and be filled with the fruit of their schemes. For the waywardness of the simple will kill them, and the complacency of fools will destroy them.
Proverbs 1:29–32[1]

THE DECISION MADE BY US civilian leadership to not use our overwhelming combat power within the borders of North Vietnam to destroy their military made the Vietnam Conflict extremely challenging for General Westmoreland, and later, for General Abrams. Even with these self-imposed limitations, I believe both generals had winnable plans at the strategic level; however, at the tactical level, they were executed poorly.

Poor US tactics failed to protect America's center of gravity (our resolve) and also failed to effectively destroy the enemy's center of gravity (military). Thus, the enemy destroyed America's center of gravity before America could destroy theirs.

Both General Westmoreland and General Abrams focused on the security of the people in the hamlets and villages. However, during Westmoreland's command, to keep the enemy from planning and conducting offensive operations that would endanger the villages, the US had to continually search for the enemy and attack him. By the time Abrams took command, there were fewer large NVA/VC camps remaining in South Vietnam. Consequently, Abrams could focus on search and hold and not as much on search and destroy. Although there were fewer large NVA/VC troop bases in South Vietnam, there were still enough to present a threat. Therefore, there remained a need to search them out.

Abrams and Westmoreland understood that it was necessary to go on the offensive and conduct search and destroy operations to win. However, the way they conducted these operations was wrong. The decision to use conventional infantry units to stumble through the jungle searching and closing with the enemy to destroy him proved to be extremely ineffective and costly. Any good infantry officer should have foreseen how difficult it would be to use conventional infantry to surprise, fix and destroy the VC/NVA in their familiar jungle environment.

Unfortunately, Westmoreland was commissioned an artillery officer and Abrams an armor officer; neither had experience as an infantry platoon leader or a company commander in a jungle environment. This is not to say that the overall commander of military forces in Vietnam needed to be an infantry officer with jungle fighting experience. It does, however, insinuate that if one does not have the experience, one must be wise enough to heed the advice of those that do. Proverbs 15:22 states, "Plans fail for lack of counsel, but with many advisers they succeed."[2]

To support the overall hypothesis of this book, that God denied the US top brass the wisdom to employ winning tactics, I present an account of one of the first large US battles conducted in Vietnam. The tragic result of this battle should have sent a clear message to our senior military leaders that the practice of conducting search and destroy operations with conventional infantry units needed to be changed. Instead, Westmoreland and Abrams seemed to have been blinded to this reality, and continued to use the same failed tactics over and over throughout the war.

On November 14, 1965, at 10:48 a.m., the 1st Battalion, 7th US Cavalry conducted a helicopter assault into the LZ X-Ray zone in order to search for an NVA regiment of approximately 1,500 troops believed to be in the area. Rather than one NVA regiment, there were three NVA regiments scattered around the area. Helicopters landing US troops into an obvious Landing Zone (LZ) deep in NVA territory was exactly what the NVA wanted. Almost as soon as the first lift of helicopters arrived, the NVA began moving troops towards LZ X-Ray to kill the Americans. Ironically, 1/7 Cavalry Battalion Commander Lieutenant Colonel (LTC) Moore's order before boarding the helicopters was to "take your battalion in there and find and kill him."[3] LTC Moore did not need to find the enemy; the enemy found him and his battalion. Within minutes, Moore had lost the initiative to the NVA, and within three days and two nights, his 450-man under strength battalion suffered 79 Americans killed and 120 wounded.

Because most of the NVA killed in the battle at LZ X-Ray were by US airstrikes and artillery, there is no way of knowing exactly how many NVA were killed. American units generally claimed that the enemy lost ten times as many as the Americans. Consequently, reported figures were not always close to reality. However, the number of the enemy killed was also not all that important to the American population. They only paid attention to how many Americans were killed. American citizens knew exactly how many Americans had already been killed in the war and how many were killed in the current week, but they had no idea, nor did they even care, how many of the enemy had been killed. Attrition of the enemy was important, but some commanders failed to weigh the cost in American lives of attaining it.

On the afternoon of November 16, the 1/7 Cavalry was extracted from LZ X-Ray along with all their dead and wounded. However, the 2nd Battalion, 7th Cavalry, and 2nd Battalion, 5th Cavalry, who had both marched into LZ X-Ray on foot earlier in the fight to strengthen the 1/7 Cavalry defenses, remained at LZ X-Ray.

Because a B-52 airstrike was scheduled for the area, on November 17, the 2/7 Cavalry moved out of LZ X-Ray and marched to a clearing in the jungle two miles north, called LZ Albany. For the same reason, the 2/5 Cavalry marched two miles northeast to LZ Columbus, where two of the four artillery batteries that supported the operation were located.

Once the NVA saw that the 2/7 Cavalry was moving on foot in the direction of a clearing that could be used as a pickup zone or a night defensive position, they moved their fresh reserve battalion into position to ambush the 600-yard-long US infantry column. They initiated their ambush just short of LZ Albany on the afternoon of November 17, and the attack lasted through the night and into the early morning of November 18. The result was even worse than that at LZ X-Ray: the battalion suffered 155 Americans killed and 130 wounded.[4]

The NVA also attacked LZ Columbus, but the 2/5 Cavalry and artillery units were in prepared defensive positions with good fields of fire. They cranked down the twelve howitzer barrels and fired beehive rounds (thousands of small nail-shaped darts) directly into the enemy. The NVA attackers were driven off with heavy losses. This is a clear example of the benefit of fighting the enemy from an advantageous position.

Sadly, even though most heavy American casualties were the result of search and destroy operations similar to the one described above, this method of operation was never changed. How could intelligent generals like Westmoreland and Abrams not have seen the obvious reasons for the tragic results of the battles at LZ X-Ray and Albany? How could they not have changed their method of finding and destroying the NVA/VC in the jungles of Vietnam? My intent is not to convince the reader that searching for the enemy and killing him was unnecessary, but that there could have been a better way to do so that would have caused fewer US casualties.

I identify a concept that could have accomplished the search and destroy missions with fewer casualties. Throughout the Vietnam War, though, God did not provide our senior military leaders with the insight to see it.

During his time as the overall commander in Vietnam, General Westmoreland never did change how search and destroy operations were conducted. General Abrams finally realized that battalion-size units searching for the enemy in jungles that were familiar to the NVA/VC could not employ the element of surprise. However, he never fully understood just how difficult it was for US conventional troops to search and fight in this environment against the NVA/VC, regardless of unit size. Ultimately, neither Westmoreland nor Abrams ever discovered a better way of conducting search and destroy operations.

When General Abrams took overall command in Vietnam, he claimed to have devised new tactics. Abrams's new tactics called for getting out in smaller ground units to make contact with the enemy, and then moving unengaged units in to pile on the area. In the book *A Better War*, Abrams is quoted describing his concern over getting the ARVN to adjust to his new tactic: "The idea of going out in company strength, or platoon strength—whoo!—only battalions! That was the only way they wanted to go. Well a battalion—it's like trying to sneak up on the enemy with a tank, it's just too damn noisy. If you want to get him, if you want to find him, you've got to do it with these small outfits. And then, once you get him, then everybody jump in! Well, they've been working on it."[5]

Abrams knew correctly that US and ARVN battalion-size search and destroy operations always failed to surprise the enemy. Unfortunately, he incorrectly believed an infantry platoon or company was small enough to sneak up on the enemy. My experience from my first tour as a leg infantry platoon leader taught me that even a platoon usually made too much noise when moving through the jungle to actually surprise the NVA/VC in their base camp. The enemy commander usually had a choice—either to immediately leave the area, or to set up an ambush. The US unit would either find an empty base camp full of booby traps or run into an enemy ambush.

During my first tour, I conducted numerous search and destroy operations and located many enemy base camps; all of them were empty of the enemy and full of booby traps. There was one exception, and that one had a few VC stay behind to set off Chinese Communist (CHICOM) claymore mines to kill any US troops searching their evacuated camp. To the infantryman, the CHICOM claymore mine was possibly the enemy's most devastating and feared weapon. Unlike a conventional land mine, the claymore is usually command-detonated and directional, meaning it is fired by remote-control and shoots a pattern of metal balls into the kill zone like grape shot fired out of a cannon (See figure 1).

I located the VC base camp mentioned above during my first tour, when I was searching a jungle with my infantry platoon. The VC base camp had a number of huts that appeared to have just been evacuated. I put out security and began searching the huts for documents, weapons, and equipment when I heard one of the men that I had on security yell: "Claymore!" I hit the ground. My security man, who had yelled the warning, tried to run, and when the claymore detonated, he was hit and fell to the ground. The claymore was command-detonated by a VC hiding in a spider hole (a small tunnel with a camouflaged trap door). I immediately went to where my man went down. As I looked up, I saw another claymore facing in our direction. Because a CHICOM claymore is attached to the top of a tripod, I was able to shoot it over with my M-16. I then attempted to provide aid to my man—unfortunately, he was already dead. I retrieved him and pulled my platoon out of the camp. I called in airstrikes and artillery on the camp, moved back in and continued the search without further incident. I didn't realize how close I came to dying that day until my Vietnamese scout dog-handler went into his rucksack for a dog food can. When the claymore detonated, the dog handler was behind me. We both hit the ground and I saw leaves falling down on me. I hadn't known just how close the projectiles were until I saw the holes in the dog food cans that were in the dog-handler's rucksack.

Another time, in 1966, while searching an enemy base camp along with the entire company, I saw a sergeant from another platoon about to pull a wire that ran across a tunnel entrance. He was about to do so with his bare hands, rather than using a grappling hook and rope. I yelled, "Don't pull that wire!" To this day, I don't know why, but he pulled it—there was an enormous explosion. The sergeant literally disintegrated.

During my first tour, I also experienced the consequences of an enemy commander opting to conduct an ambush against a US unit searching through the jungle for his camp. In 1966, our entire infantry battalion conducted an air assault into a dried-up lake deep in the jungle, and set up a Night Defensive Position (NDP). Each day over the next week, the three line companies would conduct company-size search and destroy operations using the cloverleaf technique from the battalion NDP. My company commander rotated the lead platoon each day when conducting these movements. On this particular day, my platoon was the rear platoon in the file. We had traveled approximately two kilometers into the jungle when I noticed that the underbrush was turned down and tied to create an area of *tangle foot*. Except for my platoon, the entire company had already moved into the area. I knew the underbrush didn't grow this way. I had just asked my radio operator for the handset in order to tell the company commander that they had walked into the kill zone of an ambush, when the enemy initiated their attack.

The enemy conducting the ambush stayed hidden in camouflaged spider holes, and set off command-detonated claymores and other types of explosives. Because we couldn't see the enemy, we fired out to our flanks and walked artillery in on both sides of our file as close as we could. The company ended up with eighteen casualties before the NVA pulled back. Because my platoon was not in the kill zone, we hadn't suffered any casualties, and we provided front, flank, and rear security for the company while also cutting an ankle-high trail out of the jungle so that the wounded and dead could be carried out on field expedient poncho stretchers. As we moved back, enemy snipers fired into the battalion perimeter, hoping that our battalion would fire in our direction as we returned. I had good radio communication with the battalion, though, so their trick didn't work.

I conducted a head-count as the company came out of the jungle back into our night defensive position. A man from one of the other platoons passed by, smiling but smelling terrible. I asked what he was smiling for and he said that when he hit the ground during the ambush, he looked up and saw a CHICOM claymore staring him in the face. All of a sudden he heard a pop—the claymore's electric blasting cap went off, but it didn't detonate the claymore. The man literally shit in his pants, but he was a happy and very lucky soldier.

General Abrams's quote above recommends that once you find the enemy, everybody should jump in. Piling on in a jungle battle, in the enemy's territory, can have disastrous results. It usually only provides the enemy more targets to shoot at. Although "massing your force at a specific location to overwhelm the opponent" is one of the Principles of War, with the devastating lethality of today's weapon systems, massing dismounted troops is a bad idea when attacking a guerrilla force in the jungle. The principle of massing is still valid, but, massing firepower rather than troops usually makes for a better outcome.

Even for General Abrams's clear and hold strategy, some commanders failed to understand the danger of the jungle. The battle of the 101st Airborne Division's 3rd Brigades on May 10, 1969, up Hill 937 (known as "Hamburger Hill" because troops felt they were attacking into a meat grinder), resulted in 47 US killed in action (KIA) and 308 wounded in action (WIA). Most of the 691 enemy dead found on the battlefield were killed by artillery, tactical air, helicopter gunships, and B-52 bombers.[6] I do not know of any battle against the NVA/VC in an enemy jungle base area in which the US infantry was able to surround the enemy and fix them in place so they could be destroyed with direct or indirect fire. The NVA/VC was not stupid. They always had the flexibility to slip away from American troops unfamiliar with their defenses and tunnel systems located deep within the heavy jungle.

It was no secret that some generals and colonels were willing to send infantry companies or platoons into the jungle as bait. They hoped the unit would be ambushed so they could pile on additional troops in order to obtain a large enemy body count. In his 1989 book *Mud Soldiers: Life inside the new American Army*, George C. Wilson quotes a conversation between First Infantry Division Commander General DePuy and Lieutenant Libs immediately after the two-day battle of Xa Cam My April 11 to April 12, 1966). The 134 men of Charlie Company, 2nd Battalion, 16th Infantry, First Infantry Division were ambushed by the Viet Cong while conducting a search and destroy operation approximately 42 miles northwest of Saigon. They suffered 35 killed and 72 wounded. Libs is quoted as saying to General DePuy, "You put us out there as bait." General DePuy said he wanted to know exactly what happened, so Libs went through every phase of the battle. The lieutenant ended his briefing by saying, "You walked us into a goddamn holocaust, General." The General replied, "Yeah, but there's no other way to get a goddamn fight going." The after-action report of the battle estimated 150 Vietcong were killed and driven off the battlefield.[7]

The question, therefore, is not whether the objective was important or whether the mission accomplished, but whether it could have been achieved with fewer US casualties.

There are many ways to accomplish a mission, but there is only one best way. At the operational level of planning, a commander should develop a *commander's estimate*. This requires considering all courses of action (C/A) that are possible to accomplish the mission, listing all the advantages and disadvantages of each C/A, and then determining which C/A provides the *best* results. In the Vietnam Conflict, the best C/A was usually the one that eliminated the threat/enemy and resulted in the fewest US casualties. C/As that worked in the past should always be considered and evaluated; however, the more diverse and out-of-the-box C/As considered, the better the results of the final decision.

Throughout the war, US commanders in Vietnam continually selected the same costly C/A to find and kill the enemy. The C/A used over and over was to insert an infantry platoon, company, or battalion by helicopter into a dried-up lake or other obvious Landing Zone, and then search the jungle for enemy base camps. This repetition established a pattern and lost us the element of surprise. Consequently, the NVA/VC were able to anticipate US actions, and gain the initiative.

Sun Tzu's *The Art of War*, written twenty-five hundred years ago, is the earliest existing book of strategy. It warns commanders not to use the same tactic over and over again. Sun Tzu says, "Everyone may know the control through which we are able to achieve victory, but cannot know the control through which we are able to determine victory. So, our victories in battles will not be repeated and our responsive control will be unlimited."[8]

I personally met General DePuy once while I was in Vietnam. That was approximately seven months after the battle of Xa Cam My. In October 1966, I had a tank platoon attached to my leg infantry platoon. We were given the mission of conducting a search and destroy operation in a jungle area close to the 3rd Brigade, First Infantry Division's headquarters in Lai Khe, not far from where the battle of Xa Cam My took place. I was about to bust into the jungle with my five attached tanks positioned in a V-formation and my infantry platoon deployed behind the tanks, when General DePuy's helicopter landed behind us. He asked what we were doing and I told him that a recon aircraft had detected an ox-cart going into the jungle area the night before, and we were tasked to see what we could find. DePuy said that a US unit had run into a large VC unit a number of months ago and took heavy casualties, so if we ran into any enemy we should back off and call in air and artillery. I said we would and he took off again in his helicopter.

It turned out that we found a large VC base camp, but it was empty. If there had been any enemies in the base, they had probably heard the roar of the tanks and the sound of trees falling and decided to run. I had the tanks run through the camp a few times to destroy it and then we pulled back out of the jungle. As long as the terrain was not too marshy or mountainous, the combined armor and infantry team proved to be extremely effective. Tanks could knock down trees and brush and set off booby traps and mines. The infantry provided the tanks flank and rear security as we moved through the jungle. Although a combined infantry and armor force will never surprise the enemy in his base camp, it is a very difficult unit to successfully ambush in the jungle. Unfortunately, following tanks as they moved through the jungle was like climbing over a brush pile all day long. I went through three radio operators (RTO) while on this particular operation.

General Depuy's directive for me to pull my force back and call in air and artillery leads me to believe the General had changed his view on how to deal with the enemy after the battle of Xa Cam My. I believe that, overall, General Depuy was a good division commander, and the First Infantry Division was one of the finest divisions in Vietnam. In all fairness, some of Lieutenant Libs' men were killed by friendly artillery fire during the battle of Xa Cam My. General DePuy could not be blamed for the US casualties that were caused by the artillery unit's mistake.

General Depuy was right about needing to get the enemy to fight. Almost all contact with the NVA/VC during the Vietnam Conflict was enemy initiated; using bait was a way to engage them. However, putting the bait in the jungle where the enemy had the advantage was a bad idea. On the other hand, using some form of bait to draw the enemy into a vulnerable situation is wise as long as it doesn't actually put friendly troops into a vulnerable position. The enemy can be tricked into thinking the friendly troops are vulnerable; in reality, they should actually be in an advantageous position. I describe such an operation later in the book, at the beginning of the Katum chapter, when the construction of a US Special Forces camp was used as bait.

Sun Tzu writes, "To weaken the enemy exercise unconventional means. Through enticement with advantages, show gains to lure them."[9] Tricking the enemy into doing something that will put him at a disadvantage is a major part of warfare. Even at platoon level during my first tour, we were always looking for ways to trick the enemy into making deadly mistakes. For example, in 1966, I placed-three man listening posts (LP) out around our night defensive position each night. Because our mission at the time was the pacification of a particular Vietnamese village, our NDP was semi-permanent. Consequently, the VC would target our LPs at night. One of the three men I lost during my first tour was killed after a VC located one of our LPs and threw a grenade at it. To counter the enemy's assault on our LPs, I had my men set out two LP decoys. They dug two foxholes and placed three manikin dummies in the bottom of each. The plan was to go out to the decoy positions as soon as it became dark, set up the dummies, then low crawl to an ambush position and wait for the VC.

As soon as it was dark, the two LPs left the NDP perimeter. As one of the LPs approached its decoy site one of the men using his starlight scope saw a VC crouched down behind some bushes, and rather than immediately shooting the VC he yelled, "I see VC!" Unfortunately, the VC immediately threw a hand grenade and it severely injured my man's leg. It was common for a VC traveling in areas where he might have contact to hold a US grenade in his hand with the pin already pulled so that he could immediately throw it and break contact. If he didn't have contact and was no longer in a dangerous area, he would bend the end of the grenade handle-up and put a rubber band around the grenade to hold the handle down.

The other LP that went out successfully set up their decoy LP as planned and moved to their ambush site, which happened to be in a Vietnamese cemetery. At approximately 0200 hours, a VC threw a grenade into the decoy LP, and as he attempted to run away, one of my men popped up from behind a grave and killed the VC with his shotgun.

The next morning, we searched the area where the first VC was sighted, and found a CHICOM claymore mine (See figure 1). The wire had not yet been rolled out. If the LP had not seen the VC while going to their decoy, they may have been able to successfully move to their ambush site and ambush the VC. On the other hand, if the LP hadn't seen the VC and hadn't been required to set up a decoy LP, but rather move into a real LP, the claymore surely would have killed all three men.

The point to be made in studying these examples is that tricking the enemy by using bait is good; however, using a vulnerable leg infantry unit in the jungle as bait usually proved disastrous. Conventional mechanized or leg infantry units seldom surprised the VC/NVA in the jungle, and when contact was made, most of the enemy casualties were not the result of small arms fire from the infantry force, but rather from airstrikes and artillery.

Neither Westmoreland nor Abrams understood this. According to David Maraniss in his book *They Marched into the Sunlight*, Westmoreland would ask the First Infantry Division commander General Hays why his troops did not pursue the enemy at the end of the battle and instead allowed them to slip away. Hays is quoted as telling Westmoreland, "we pursued by fire [artillery and air] and that risk to troops pursuing overland into the territory more familiar to the Viet Cong was not worth it unless we knew where they were."[10]

Both Westmoreland and Abrams underestimated the capability of the enemy and the advantage they had when fighting in familiar jungle. They put pressure on their subordinates to be more aggressive against the enemy in the jungle. What these two generals did not understand was that when fighting in the jungle, no matter how aggressive US ground forces were, they could never outmaneuver the NVA/VC in their own familiar terrain.

Although official military reports on battles resulting from search and destroy operations claim victory over the VC/NVA, most lacked the element of surprise and were enemy-initiated. US troops suffered large numbers of casualties in the initial phases of the battles. *They Marched into the Sunlight* provides an understanding of how most search and destroy operation's battles were initiated in Vietnam. Maraniss includes an interview taken after the war with General Vo Minh Triet. Triet was a Lieutenant Colonel and the commander of the Viet Cong's First Regiment, which battled the 2nd Battalion, 28th Infantry of the First Infantry Division at Long Nguyen Secret Zone, 12.3 miles north of Lai Khe during Operation Shenandoah II.

On October 17, 1967, the 2/28 Infantry conducted a battalion-size search and destroy operation in the Long Nguyen Secret Zone. Shortly after entering the jungle from their NDP, they saw fresh tracks and enemy troops further in the jungle, and immediately pursued them. Within minutes they started to receive a heavy volume of fire from both the trees and bunkers in the ground. After a two hour battle 58 US soldiers were dead and 31 wounded. Surprisingly, Westmoreland called the battle a meeting engagement and a success, rather than an enemy ambush and US defeat. Although only a few enemy bodies were found, the official report claimed 103 VC were killed.[11]

In Triet's interview, he said the Americans were kept under observation as soon as they moved into the area. He said, "The fresh tracks along the trail, the sighting of enemy soldiers in the distance—these were lures designed to draw the Americans deeper into a trap." Triet already had two of his battalions in position in the west and a third moving into position from the east. When the American soldiers were just where Triet wanted them, which was in front of his camouflaged bunkers, machine guns, and preset claymore mines—he gave the signal to fire.[12]

This chapter claims that because of flawed tactics used to conduct search and destroy operations, the US suffered a larger number of casualties than necessary. The following chapter provides evidence to support this claim and verify that the tragic scenario described in the preceding paragraph was played out over and over throughout the war.

CHAPTER 6

Search and Destroy Operations

To PROVIDE THE READER with a clearer understanding of how ineffective search and destroy operations were, and of the failure of senior leaders to change their flawed tactics, I have included examples of numerous US search and destroy operations conducted, ranging from one of the first operations in Vietnam to one of the last. My intent is not to convince the reader that searching for the enemy and killing him was unnecessary, but rather that there could have been a better way to do so that might have resulted in fewer US casualties.

Not all failed search and destroy operations that took place in Vietnam are presented below, but I have included enough of them to show that failed operations were not restricted to the Army, the Marines, a specific division, or a specific regiment.

Because US commanders did not change their search and destroy tactics, the tragic scenarios of most failed search and destroy operations are very similar. To avoid redundancy, I refer the reader to the detailed information provided in the previous chapter on the November, 1965, LZ X-Ray/LZ Albany operation[1] and the October, 1967, Long Nguyen Secret Zone operation.[2]

On November 14–16, 1965, the 450-man 1st Battalion, 7th U.S. Cavalry suffered 79 Americans killed and 120 wounded during a search and destroy operation in the Ia Drang.[3]

On November 17–18, 1965, the 2nd Battalion, 7th U.S. Cavalry was ambushed moving to their pickup zone (PZ), LZ Albany, and suffered 155 Americans killed and 130 wounded.[4]

On April 11, 1966, the 134-man Charlie Company, 2nd Battalion, 16th Infantry, First Infantry Division conducted a search and destroy operation near Xa Cam My, 42 miles northwest of Saigon. The company ran into a VC ambush and suffered 35 killed and 72 wounded. The after-action report of the battle estimated 150 VC were killed.[5]

On April 24-May 5, 1967, two battalions of the 3rd Marine Regiment lost 160 men and 746 were wounded in a twelve-day battle to drive NVA troops off three hills near Khe Sanh in Quangtin Province.[6]

On May 9, 1967, a 3rd Marine Regiment unit was attacked by the NVA nine miles northwest of Khe Sanh. In the five-hour battle, the US Marines suffered 24 casualties.[7]

On May 18–31, 1967, the 26th Marines conducted Operation Prairie IV east of Khe Sanh to clear the DMZ. Two fortified hills occupied by the NVA were stormed by the Marines and captured. The operation resulted in 164 Marines killed and 999 wounded.[8]

On June 2, 1967, a US 5th Marine battalion was ambushed in the Hiepdus Valley by a 2900-man NVA regiment. The Marines report killing 540; however, they suffered 73 dead and 139 wounded.[9]

On June 12–17 1967, the US First Infantry Division conducted a drive into the jungles of War Zone D, 50 miles north of Saigon, in an attempt to trap three VC battalions. The First Infantry Division claimed to have killed at least 150 VC during the five-day operation. Unfortunately, the VC ambushed one of the US units while they were moving to their PZ. The ambush cost the Americans 31 dead and 113 wounded.[10]

On June 22, 1967, a 130-man infantry company of the 173rd US Airborne Brigade was ambushed by the NVA near Dakto 28 miles northeast of Saigon. 88 Americans were killed and 34 wounded. Only 106 NVA were reported killed.[11]

On July 2, 1967, a platoon of the 9th Marine Regiment was ambushed by 500 NVA just south of the DMZ, and 35 Marines were killed. Marine reinforcements were rushed in. After intense fighting, Marine casualties totaled 96 killed and 211 wounded.[12]

On July 2, 1967, two companies of the 9th Marine Regiment were attacked by the NVA and suffered heavy losses. Four battalions were helicoptered into the area to reinforce the two companies and maneuver against the flank of the enemy. On July 14, the NVA slipped away after losing an estimated 1301. The US losses were 159 dead and 45 wounded.[13]

On July 10, 1967, while conducting a sweep of the Dakto area near Kontum, a 173rd Airborne Brigade battalion was ambushed by the NVA. The American losses were 26 killed and 49 wounded.[14]

On July 11, 1967, while conducting a search and destroy operation, a US 4th Infantry Division unit was ambushed five miles south of Ducco in the Central Highlands. American losses were 35 killed and 31 wounded.[15]

On September 4–7, 1967, units of the US 5th Marine Regiment fought the NVA in the Queson Valley, 25 miles south of Danang. During the battle, 114 Americans were killed and 376 NVA died. [16]

On November 19–22, 1967, the 173rd Airborne Brigade attacked Hill 875, while defended by NVA occupying dug-in positions. The NVA eventually abandoned their positions, but not until the Brigade suffered 158 men killed. The attack on Hill 875 was part of a larger battle that started on November 3 when approximately 4000 US troops from the 4th Division and the 173rd Airborne Brigade fought about 6000 NVA troops in the Central Highlands around Dakto. During the nineteen-day battle, an estimated 1455 NVA were killed while 285 US troops were killed, 985 were wounded, and 18 went missing. Westmoreland briefed officials at the Pentagon on November 22, 1967 and said that the battle was "the beginning of a great defeat for the enemy." [17]

On March 2, 1968, US troops were ambushed four miles north of Tansonnhut Air Base while conducting a search and destroy operation. The US suffered 48 men killed and 28 wounded. [18]

On May 10, 1969, the 101st Airborne Division's 3rd Brigade, while searching the jungles of the Ashua valley, found the NVA entrenched on Apbia Mountain (Hill 937). After 11 infantry assaults, air strikes, and artillery fire the stronghold was captured. The 11 infantry assaults up the hill resulted in the US suffering 47 killed and 308 wounded. Most of the 691 enemy dead found on the battlefield were killed by artillery, tactical air, helicopter gunships, and B-52 bombers.[19]

On August 17–26, 1969, 1200 US Americal Division and ARVN troops ran into a well-defended NVA complex of tunnels and bunkers. The result was 60 Americans killed and an estimated 650 NVA killed. During the battle on August 24, the men of Alpha Company of the 196th Light Infantry Brigade refused an order from their commander to continue combat operations to reach a downed helicopter. The company had attempted to reach the helicopter during the previous five days and received heavy losses. The battalion commander sent his executive officer to the field to give the men a pep talk. The men fought their way to the helicopter the following day; however, all eight men were dead. [20]

On October 24, 1969, a US 25th Infantry Division unit of 200 troops ran into a NVA/VC unit 28 miles north of Saigon. American losses were 10 killed and 12 wounded while enemy losses were estimated at 47. [21]

On February 13, 1970, US Marines were ambushed in the Queson valley. Marine losses were 13 killed and 12 wounded while 6 enemy were killed. [22]

On February 14, 1970, eight US soldiers were killed and 30 wounded in a NVA ambush near the Cambodian border. NVA losses were estimated to be 31 killed. [23]

As evidenced from the tragic results of the above examples, using conventional leg infantry units to conduct search and destroy operations resulted in large numbers of US casualties. The fact that almost all of the enemy casualties suffered in the above battles were the result of US artillery and air strikes, rather than infantry light weapons, makes the heavy loss of US infantry troops even more tragic.

I believe all would agree, after an honest review of the battles that took place in Vietnam, that the tactic of using conventional infantry units to find the enemy in the jungle and destroy him was seriously flawed. It should be noted that because most of the above battles were enemy initiated, most of the American casualties happened within a few hours, and in some cases minutes. Clearly this tactic caused extremely high numbers of American casualties; obviously, it was wrong. The fact that America's senior leaders did not see this obvious mistake and change their tactics supports my position that God denied them wisdom.

The next chapter does not suggest that search and destroy operations should not have been conducted; rather it identifies better tactics that should have been used to conduct them.

CHAPTER 7

Better Search and Destroy Tactics

*The general who can assess the value of ground maneuvers his enemy into
dangerous terrain and keeps clear of it himself. He chooses the ground on
which he wishes to engage, draws his enemy to it, and there gives battle.*
Sun Tzu[1]

IN LIGHT OF THE ineffective and disastrous results of conducting the search
and destroy operations with conventional infantry units, it would have
been better to have infiltrated quiet five-man Long Range Reconnaissance
Patrols (LRRP) to search for enemy base camps. If an LRRP found an
enemy base camp, they could call in a B-52 strike.

If B-52 strikes were no-notice surprise attacks as in Cambodia, they
were extremely effective. When we searched base areas in Cambodia after
B-52 strikes, most of the NVA were dead and those not dead were in no
condition to fight.

Attached to my infantry company I had ten former NVA and VC who
had changed sides to work for the United States military called Kit Carson
Scouts. Some of them were excellent and others were similar to Gomer
Pyle. When I asked them if they were afraid of B-52 strikes they told me
because of a requirement to notify the Vietnamese province chief three
days prior to a strike, the NVA/VC never feared a B-52 strike in South
Vietnam. They always received a three-day warning from their spies and
were able to move out of the area.

In addition to poor operational security (OPSEC), B-52s remained under the control of the Strategic Air Command (SAC) and were not responsive to the ground commanders in Vietnam.

Current examples of the effectiveness of B-52 strikes when responsive to the ground commander are the B-52 strikes in the early stages of the 2001 Afghanistan War. With only 300 US Army Special Forces and CIA men on the ground traveling in small teams with the Northern Alliance units, the Taliban was driven out of power in Afghanistan. The United States was able to accomplish this because they had B-52s continually circling above Afghanistan and ready to immediately respond to the Special Forces team on the ground. The B-52s could either drop a 2000-pound GPS-guided bomb onto a specific point target or carpet-bomb an entire ridge line with 500- and 750-pound dumb bombs when the Northern Alliance needed them. When the enemy was not given a three-day warning, B-52 strikes proved highly effective.

Since OPSEC was a major problem in Vietnam, *restricted areas* needed to be assigned to LRRPs for extended periods of time, and B-52s had to be kept on standby to immediately respond to any LRRP's find. Using B-52 strikes in restricted areas would have eliminated the requirement of notifying the Vietnamese ahead of time.

In Vietnam, LRRPs emplaced beacons to direct the aircraft to the targets. The beacons provided the pilots with a relatively accurate method of finding the enemy in jungle-covered terrain. Today, however, with new GPS technology and improved smart bombs, using LRRPs to locate the enemy and keeping B-52 bombers on standby would prove to be even more effective.

Because of the importance of establishing restricted areas in a counterinsurgency, a further definition is provided. A restricted area is not to be confused with a *free-fire zone*. A restricted area is one where all personnel are restricted from entering unless they receive approval from the headquarters that designated the area. No one can enter or fire into the designated restricted area unless the commander assigned the restricted Area of Operation (AO) is notified.[2]

The restricted area control measure, therefore, allows the assigned commander to employ tactics and weapon systems without the fear of killing or injuring civilians or friendly troops. For civilians' own protection, establishing control measures such as restricted areas and curfews is critical in counterinsurgencies. Civilians must be informed that in this type of warfare, some of their freedom of movement will be restricted until the war is over.

Unlike a restricted area, a free-fire zone does not restrict the movement of civilians and other friendly forces within its area. Therefore, one cannot assume that anyone found in a free-fire zone is an enemy. In Vietnam, this meant that a soldier was authorized to fire at any person who could be identified as an enemy soldier without receiving permission from a higher headquarters.[3] Therefore, the distinction between a restricted area and a free-fire zone is huge. While commanding a Navy fast boat, Senator John Kerry ordered his crew to fire at a *sampan* on a river in Vietnam; an unarmed man and child were killed. Contrary to Kerry's justification that they were in a free-fire zone, the shooting of any individual who *is not* carrying an enemy weapon, wearing an enemy uniform or clearly identified in another way as an enemy soldier within a free-fire zone is a crime.[4]

This commentary on the usefulness of LRRPs in searching for the enemy is not meant to suggest there is no use for conventional leg infantry units. Because conventional leg infantry units can either quickly airmobile into position or quietly walk into position without being detected at night, the following missions were very effective and resulted in light casualties:

1. Hammer and Anvil: use leg infantry as a blocking force and mechanized and armor teams as the pushing force.
2. Providing the cordon around villages while ARVN troops search the village for enemy troops and supplies.
3. Conducting day and night ambushes.
4. Providing a quick reaction force when the enemy is in a vulnerable position or friendly forces need reinforcement.

Additionally, leg infantry units are necessary in operations such as airbase, firebase, and supply depot security, as well as urban warfare. However, searching the jungle for the enemy in hopes of finding him and destroying him can be better accomplished with LRRPs and on-call B-52s.

If it was required for conventional troops to enter the jungle, and the terrain was not mountainous or marshy, a combined mechanized infantry and armored team or task force tended to be more effective than a leg infantry unit. A mechanized infantry unit with tanks attached could bust through the jungle to locate the enemy base camps. Although the enemy troops would be gone, the US unit could destroy the enemy's supplies and camp. Enemy booby traps were not effective against armor and the enemy was normally smart enough not to engage a mechanized infantry unit, knowing about the heavy firepower that they could deliver. The enemy usually returned once the US units pulled out of their base camp. *Mechanical ambushes* (MA) could be left behind to kill some of the enemy and demoralize many more. (Mechanical ambushes will be explained in chapter 11.)

These tactics address the use of US conventional maneuver units. However, if the host nation had maneuver units such as armor and infantry units, then it would be wise to provide each of their battalion-size maneuver units with a US liaison/coordination team of approximately six men, and use them in place of a US maneuver unit. The US liaison team would be able to call in US artillery, close air, lift helicopter, and resupply support. In other words, US ground combat maneuver units are a last resort. This policy would provide US airpower and supplies to an ally force that lacked it, while keeping US ground forces out of harm's way. It would produce fewer US casualties, thereby protecting the United States' center of gravity.

How could two intelligent commanders like Westmoreland and Abrams not have seen that their tactics were allowing the enemy to successfully attack the United States' center of gravity? The manner in which search and destroy operations were conducted was not only flawed, it was too predictable; the enemy took advantage of this. Leaders in combat should be, as Sun Tzu says, "as unpredictable as rain clouds, striking like thunder and lightning."[5]

Chapter 8

Consequences of America's
Lost Resolve

We tested Ford's resolve by attacking Phuoc Long. When Ford kept American B-52s in their hangers, our leadership decided on a big offensive against South Vietnam.
North Vietnam's Bui Tin[1]

WHEN US GROUND COMBAT troops departed Vietnam, the ARVN did relatively well at fighting the counter guerrilla war. As long as the US was still providing advisors and air support, the ARVN even countered the larger conventional attacks by the NVA.

After the US completely withdrew, for as long as North Vietnam complied with the January 1973 Paris Peace Accord, the ARVN seemed able to hold their own against communist forces. By many accounts the South Vietnamese were winning the counterinsurgency war in South Vietnam against the communist forces that were authorized to remain in South Vietnam by the Paris Peace Accord. However, when Nixon resigned, the North Vietnamese believed they could break the treaty with the US without any adverse consequences, and gain a chance of winning the war in South Vietnam.

In early December, 1974, North Vietnam tested the United States' commitment to South Vietnam by breaking the Paris Peace Accord. They sent conventional forces from North Vietnam into South Vietnam and attacked Phuoc Long. Because the United States refused to come to South Vietnam's assistance, on January 6, 1975, Phuoc Long Province fell to the enemy.

Unfortunately, the United States' failure to respond to North Vietnam's blatant disregard for the Paris Peace Accord and their attack on Phuoc Long, North Vietnam rightly believed that the US would not retaliate against them, even with B-52s, if North Vietnam conducted an all-out invasion. Consequently, in early March, 1975, North Vietnam conducted a massive conventional attack into South Vietnam, and Saigon fell.

The United States lost an enormous amount of credibility and status in the world when we failed to enforce the Paris Peace Accord. This emboldened tyrants such as Saddam Hussein and convinced them that the United States lacked the willingness to stop their aggression.

I believe the US's goals in Vietnam were honorable; however, our failure to take any action against North Vietnam when they broke the treaty was shameful. Those who actively spread the communists' false propaganda and bamboozled Congress and the American people about US efforts in Indochina share much of the responsibility for the blood and the enormous scale of suffering inflicted by the communists not only in Vietnam, but in Cambodia and Laos as well.

False information about Vietnam, however, was not the only or primary contributing factor to America's defeat. Much of this book is based on the hypothesis that flawed tactics were used during most of the Vietnam Conflict, and that better tactics would have prevented the United States' defeat. I define better tactics as tactics that accomplish a mission more effectively and with fewer US casualties. Since the number of US casualties had a major impact on America's lack of resolve or willingness to enforce the Paris Peace Accord, US senior leaders' failure to employ tactics that would have significantly reduced US casualties, was the overriding cause of America's final defeat in Vietnam.

As an infantry officer who served in Vietnam in 1966–67 and then again in 1970–71, It was obviously to me that the communists were being defeated in South Vietnam. Unfortunately, as I've mentioned, the misinformation spread by the media and naive peace demonstrators, the failure of the government to mobilize the public, and an unacceptable number of American casualties significantly affected US citizens' willingness to stay in the fight.

Interestingly, we won a victory in January, 1973, but because US citizens' resolve was at such a low level after ten years of fighting, Congress was not willing to resume combat operations in order to enforce the hard-won Paris Peace Accord. North Vietnam was allowed to break a treaty with the most powerful nation in the world, and lasting victory was not achieved. In his book *The Real War,* President Nixon correctly stated, "We won a victory after a long hard struggle, but then threw it away."[2]

Certainly, the North Vietnamese knew that the United States had overwhelming combat power to enforce the Paris Peace Accord. However, the American citizens' resolve was the United States' Achilles heel and North Vietnam rightly assumed that we no longer had the will to use our military power.

CHAPTER 9

Part I Reflections

If my people, who are called by my name, will humble themselves and pray and seek my face and turn from their wicked ways, then will I hear from heaven and will forgive their sin and will heal their land.
2 Chronicles 7:14[1]

THE CHAPTERS OF THIS book are not meant to teach military tactics, but rather to be a confirmation of biblical truths. Victory rests with the Lord; therefore, if we as a nation expect success, we must pay attention to 2 Chronicles 7:14, quoted above.

This book provides support for the position that the Vietnam War would have been won if the correct tactics had been employed by the United States. The Bible tells us that it is God who provides men with the wisdom to win in battle, and this book provides clear evidence that God denied America's senior commanders the wisdom to employ sound tactics in Vietnam. It not only explains how these failed tactics contributed to the United States' tragic defeat, but it identifies better tactics which, if used, could have led to victory.

The verse in the Bible from which the title of this book is derived states, "The horse is made ready for the day of battle, but victory rests with the Lord." [2] Because the verse insinuates that God allowed America to lose in Vietnam, this book evaluates the reasons why God denied the United States victory.

Part I identified that the failed tactic that had the greatest negative impact on the final outcome of the Vietnam War was the tactic used to conduct search and destroy operations. The astonishing failure of the senior military leaders to see the futility of the tactic was the result of God denying them the wisdom to understand the problems of fighting in the jungles of Vietnam. A short review of the analysis to support this position is provided below:

Search and Destroy operations in the Vietnam War should not have been conducted using conventional leg infantry units. Rather, they should have been conducted by small five-men Long Range Surveillance Detachments to locate the enemy and mark targets for immediate B-52 airstrikes.

Chapter seven provides examples of heavy US casualties resulting from using conventional leg infantry units to conduct search and destroy operations in the jungles of Vietnam. These examples are evidence that these operations were flawed.

The high number of casualties sustained by conventional infantry units while in contact with the enemy in their own jungle environment, and the fact that these relatively large US units had to be extracted out of the contested area prior to being able to employ the most effective weapon system against the NVA/VC in the jungle, which was a B-52 strike, should have been reason enough not to use conventional infantry units to search for the enemy in this type of environment in the first place.

Part I suggests that Long Range Surveillance Detachments would have been a better element to conduct the search and destroy operations. However, for those operations to have been effective, a number of high level command and control changes would have been needed. The primary change required would be for the SAC commander to chop operational control (OPCON) of a portion of the B-52 force to the commander in Vietnam. Secondly, to ensure OPSEC and immediate responsiveness of B-52 firepower to the patrol on the ground, Long Range Surveillance Detachments would need to be assigned designated restricted areas in which to operate, and B-52 bombers would need to be on standby in order to respond to the discovery of a large concentration of enemy troops.

When I was Chief of Operations for Special Operations Command, Pacific, I was tasked with helping the United States Special Operations Command prepare the *Joint Special Operations Force Readiness Study* that was presented to the Joint Chiefs of Staff on April 6, 1988. One of my major contributions to the study was the concept of using Special Forces

Operational Detachments to coordinate US airpower for foreign maneuver units that lacked their own. In 2001, during the invasion of Afghanistan, Special Forces teams linked up with the Northern Alliance and coordinated US airpower. The success of their mission demonstrated the effectiveness of B-52s when they are available to provide direct support to the ground commander.

Many commanders set a pattern when they conducted search and destroy operations in Vietnam. They inserted troops into obvious LZs and commenced to search the surrounding jungle for the enemy base camp. The enemy capitalized on their mistake by either setting up an ambush or an empty camp full of booby-traps for the Americans.

Clearly, using the same concept over and over failed to follow the *surprise* Principle of War, or, as Sun Tzu states, "All warfare is based on deception. A skilled general must be master of the complementary art of simulation; while creating shapes to confuse and delude the enemy he conceals his true dispositions and ultimate intent."[3]

Although the helicopter was used in the Korean War, it was not used to move large combat troops around the battlefield until Vietnam. The helicopter was a wonderful way to maneuver troops around Vietnam. Unfortunately, because commanders underestimated the enemy's ability to adjust to our use of the helicopter, the US failed to change the way it inserted troops into battle. The helicopter became, in many cases, a means by which targets were brought deep into the jungle for the VC/NVA to easily engage and thereby destroy the United States' center of gravity.

I believe many commanders were overly anxious to engage the enemy in a large ground battle with infantry companies and battalions that could be maneuvered around the battlefield to destroy the enemy. Sadly, because the enemy normally only moved in the open at night and stayed in the jungle during the day, these battles needed to be fought in the jungle where the VC/NVA had the advantage. In Vietnam, most officers at the rank of colonel and above never fought in the jungle. They did not understand the difficulty of fighting in it. Many of their orders were unrealistic, and led to unnecessary US casualties.

PART II

Victory

CHAPTER 10

Duty

*And like the old soldier of the ballad, I now close my military
career and just fade away, an old soldier who tried to do his duty
as **God gave him the light to see that duty**. Good bye.*
General MacArthur[1]

LIKE GENERAL MACARTHUR IN his eloquent farewell speech to Congress,
I believe we each have a God-given duty in life, and those who surrender
their lives to God will be *given the light to see their duty*. This chapter will
tell when and how God turned on the light for me to see my personal
duty.

I received enlightenment at the age of twenty-six. Because it had a
profound influence on my motivation and willingness to fight in Vietnam,
I will present the personal background that led me to this insight and
enlightenment. This background will also provide the reader with a better
understanding of why I made the various decisions I did in combat.

In addition to testifying to the validity of Proverbs 21:31, this book
serves as a testament to the validity of two excellent books which I
recommend to the interested reader: Charles Stanley's 2000 book *Success
God's Way*[2] and Rick Warren's 2002 book *The Purpose Driven Life*.[3] Both
Stanley and Warren explain in great detail why it's important to find out
God's purpose for your life and then follow it. They conclude that you
receive power from the Holy Spirit to accomplish God's purpose for your

life and for true joy. This chapter provides information about how, forty-four years ago, I came to the same valuable conclusion.

In June of 1964, I graduated from Southeast Missouri State College with a Bachelor of Science in Business Administration. Within five months after graduation I was drafted into the Army and given the opportunity to become an officer by attending Officer Candidate School (OCS) at Fort Benning, Georgia. Although OCS added ten months to my military draft obligation, I accepted the OCS challenge and was commissioned an infantry second lieutenant in August 1965. I spent one year at Fort Hood, Texas and was sent to Vietnam in August 1966.

In Vietnam I led an infantry rifle platoon and an 81mm mortar platoon in the First Infantry Division. The nine months that I was on the front lines, the platoon I led lost only three men. Although I was wounded during this first tour, I completed my full-year tour in Vietnam, and in August of 1967, I returned home.

When I returned from Vietnam my draft obligation was over and I enrolled in the University of Missouri's Graduate School of Business. After one year in graduate school I became anxious to start working and make my fortune. I decided southern California was where I wanted to live and work. My goal was to eventually have my own land development company in the San Diego area and become a millionaire by age thirty. Because I wanted to live in the San Diego area, I took a job as a marketing coordinator with the San Diego Gas and Electric Company (SDG&E) in July 1968. SDG&E not only was a great place to work, it allowed me the opportunity to become familiar with the area. While I worked weekdays at SDG&E, I earned a California real estate license in the evenings and sold real estate for La Jolla Sales and Exchange on the weekends. Within a year I met my wonderful wife Joyce while working at SDG&E and married her June 7, 1969.

In a very short period of time after moving to the San Diego area, I had the perfect wife and obtained the jobs that I thought would eventually lead to a successful life and to happiness (i.e. an expensive house on the ocean, cars, boats, plenty of money to travel, and a great wife and children to enjoy it all).

Although I had accepted Jesus Christ as my Lord and Savior as a child, it was at this point that God provided an occasion that helped change my perspective on life, as a result, giving me a life of joy beyond my wildest dreams. While attending a real estate cocktail party, I listened to an extremely wealthy and successful real estate developer complain about his son wanting to become a social worker in Los Angeles. This man was bitter because his son would rather spend his life helping poor people than taking over the real estate business he had worked all his life building. As I listened to him complain, I realized that this could be me in twenty years.

Obviously, the disgruntled father missed what was really important in life. I am sure the father loved his son and in the world's view he felt that he was providing the best thing for him; however, the father failed to understand that each of us is created by God for a specific purpose. The father's focus was on what the world considered success, rather than what God views as success. The Bible tells us that God's purpose for each of us is unique and different based on the talents God has given us. That means that all types of jobs and professions are necessary in order to satisfy society's needs, except for those that are harmful or illegal. Certainly, providing homes for people is a valuable service. The father's profession was not the issue, but rather his attitude and motivation.

To find God's purpose for your life, one must first acknowledge that we were created for God and to do His will—not the other way around. Then, surrender your life to Jesus Christ by focusing on how you can use the talents God gave you to best please Him, rather than for your own personal pleasures. Ephesians 2:8–10 states, "For by grace you have been saved, through faith; and that not of yourselves, it is the gift of God; not as a result of works, so that no one can boast. For we are His workmanship, *created in Christ Jesus for good works*, which God prepared beforehand so that we would walk in them."[4]

When I came home that evening, the Holy Spirit led me to re-evaluate what really was important to me in life and instilled in me a tremendous desire to please God. I had a new desire to read the Holy Bible and find out what pleases God, as well as a desire to bring Him glory and honor.

The United Nations' *Universal Declaration of Human Rights* lists a number of human rights that all nations should guarantee their citizens. Because an individual's knowledge and faith in the one true God has eternal consequences, the United Nations' *Article 18* is the most important. *Article 18* states, "Everyone has the right to freedom of thought, conscience and religion; this right includes freedom to change his religion or belief, and freedom, either alone or in community with others and in public or private, to manifest his religion or belief in teaching, practice, worship and observance."[5] Jesus tells us this right is the most important human right when He says, in Mark 8:38, "What good is it for a man to gain the whole world, yet forfeit his soul?"[6] Other rights such as the right to choose one's spouse, government leader, or even profession, cannot compare to the right to find the one true God and eternal life. It is blasphemy and a lack of faith to think that God does not have the power to provide those He chooses with the wisdom to discern what is true and what is false. Therefore, no man—whether Christian Catholic, Christian Protestant, Muslim, Buddhist, Mormon, Hindu, or atheist—has the right to restrict another human's freedom to hear all theologies in order to find the one true God. Similar to most Islamic nations, communist nations do not comply with the United Nations' *Universal Declaration of Human Rights, Article 18.* Therefore, when communist insurgents or governments take over a country by force, they restrict freedom of religion and deny the population the opportunity to hear about Jesus Christ.

In light of the above, I concluded that communist military aggression was a major threat to religious freedom. Knowing that citizens within a communist nation are prevented from knowing Jesus Christ as their Lord and Savior, and as a result denied an opportunity to receive eternal life, I decided I would be doing God's will in helping to stop the spread of communism being forced upon people around the world *through the barrel of a gun.*

Even though three of my men from the infantry rifle platoon that I led during my first tour in Vietnam were killed and I myself was wounded, my platoon performed extremely well. I believed I was an effective leader and that I had gained valuable counterinsurgency experience and knowledge that would be useful.

God created each of us with specific abilities to do good works. Having served a tour in Vietnam leading an infantry platoon in combat, I was convinced that God had given me the physical and mental ability for military service. Jesus makes it clear in the following parable that we should not be lazy, and that He expects us to fully use our talents to accomplish the works for which He created us:

> "For it is as if a man, going on a journey, summoned his slaves and entrusted his property to them; to one he gave five talents, to another two, to another one, to each according to his ability. Then he went away. The one who had received the five talents went off at once and traded with them, and made five more talents. In the same way, the one who had the two talents made two more talents. But the one who had received the one talent went off and dug a hole in the ground and hid his master's

money. After a long time the master of those slaves came and settled accounts with them. Then the one who had received the five talents came forward, bringing five more talents, saying 'Master, you handed over to me five talents; see, I have made five more talents. His master said to him 'Well done, good and trustworthy slave; you have been trustworthy in a few things, I will put you in charge of many things; enter into the joy of your master.' And the one with the two talents also came forward, saying, 'Master, you handed over to me two talents; see, I have made two more talents. His master said to him, 'Well done, good and trustworthy slave; you have been trustworthy in a few things, I will put you in charge of many things; enter into the joy of your master.' Then the one who had received the one talent also came forward, saying, 'Master, I knew that you were a harsh man, reaping where you did not sow, and gathering where you did not scatter seed; so I was afraid, and I went and hid your talent in the ground. Here you have what is yours.' But the master replied, 'You wicked and lazy slave! You knew, did you, that I reap where I did not sow, and gather where I did not scatter? Then you ought to have invested my money with the bankers, and on my return I would have received what was my own with interest. So take the talent from him, and give it to the one with the ten talents. For to all those who have, more will be given, and they will have an abundance; but from those who have nothing, even what they have will be taken away. As for this worthless slave, throw him into the outer darkness, where there will be weeping and gnashing of teeth.'"

Matthew 25:14–30[7]

I also believed that if God gives a person a particular duty to accomplish, then He will provide that person the wisdom and ability to achieve it. In Philippians 4:13 Paul says, "I can do everything through Him [Jesus Christ] who strengthens me."[8]

After discussing it with Joyce, I decided to go back on active duty and devote my life to fighting communism so that not only my future children and grandchildren, but all people in the world, would have an opportunity to learn about Jesus and receive eternal life.

Within a few months of making the decision to return to the military, I was back in the Army, promoted to captain, and sent to Airborne School at Fort Benning, Georgia to become parachute-jump qualified. After graduating from Airborne School I was assigned to Fort Bragg, North Carolina, for a few months before being sent back to Vietnam.

Part I of this book provided information to support my belief that if God had provided US senior commanders with the wisdom to use the correct tactics in the Vietnam War, America would have been blessed with a lasting victory. The reason God denied wisdom to the military senior commanders was because of the nation's disobedience to God.

Part II will provide the reader with a view of combat in Vietnam different than the one presented by the media. It will show how God blessed my decision to change my worldly focus and follow His purpose for my life by providing the infantry company I commanded in Vietnam with unparalleled success and protection.

Figure 1: Company Vietnamese interpreter next to the CHICOM claymore mine left behind by the VC when Schmidt's LP spotted him attempting to set it up

Figure 2: US claymore mine used in Mechanical Ambushes

Figure 3: Alpha Company's APCs herringboned after one of the tracks hit a mine in the road near Katum. Men of Alpha Company cooling off the barrel of their .50 cal MGs

Figure 4: After treating an NVA soldier's wounds, the Alpha Company medic compassionately gives the NVA a cigarette

Figure 5: LTC Schmidt with a Vietnamese interpreter interrogating a captured NVA female soldier who was found hiding in a tunnel

Figure 6: Men of Alpha Company taking a much appreciated swim in a B-52 bomb crater after a successful operation

Figure 7: Schmidt with some of his men hauling out 170 rounds of 57 mm recoilless and 17 rounds of 75 mm anti-tank ammunition discovered in an NVA/VC tunnel

Figure 8: Schmidt holding 3 AK-47s and a RPG after a successful ambush which resulted in one NVA KIA and two wounded NVA prisoners

Figure 9: Test firing a 7.62 Gatling mini-gun taken off a helicopter and mounted on an Alpha Company APC

Figure 10: Schmidt teaching the Mechanical Ambush to the 7th Special Forces Group at Fort Bragg, NC.

Figure 11: Captured NVA weapons and equipment from a successful ambush

*Figure 12: Alpha Company returning from a dismounted search of
a marshy jungle area near Katum and the Cambodian border*

Figure 13: Helicopter extraction after a dismounted search operation between Katum and the Cambodian border

Figure 14: Just another day at the office

Figure 15: Something worth fighting to protect

*Figure 16: Schmidt is searching the area
along the Saigon River that ran adjacent to
the area known as the Iron Triangle*

Figure 17: Vietnamese patrol boats picking up elements of Alpha Company. Alpha Company was used to search out areas along the shores of the Saigon River. The operation lasted only one day and had negative results

Figure 18: Alpha Company busting through bamboo during a search for NVA/VC base camps

*Figure 19: Alpha Company Armored Personnel
Carriers staying off the roads near Katum*

*Figure 20: Shortly before retiring Schmidt served three years
as Special Operations Command, Pacific's (SOCPAC's) Chief
of Operations, where his vast experience in counter-guerrilla
operations was of immense value in the Philippines*

CHAPTER 11

The Mechanical Ambush and the Automated Battlefield

*But whoever listens to me will live in safety and
be at ease, without fear of harm.*
Proverbs 1:33[1]

THE MOST SUCCESSFUL TACTIC that the Lord provided my infantry company the wisdom to use was the mechanical ambush (MA). Information about this effective weapon system is provided prior to the chapters which will present the day-by-day operations of my company in combat.

A mechanical ambush is a sophisticated unmanned ambush constructed of claymore mines daisy-chained or wired in parallel and placed along a trail or location used by or visited by the enemy. Troops in the field refer to these modified mines as mechanical ambushes or automatic ambushes. For the purpose of this book, I will use the term mechanical ambush. In this unclassified book, it would be irresponsible for me to elaborate any further on the specific details of the MA's design and the various techniques used with it; however, suffice it to say the MAs used during the latter days of Vietnam were significantly more advanced than those found in current unclassified US military field manuals.

What most people, including the majority of our military leaders, are not aware of is how effective the MA was, and how much the US infantry depended upon it in the latter years of the Vietnam Conflict. The mines normally used were claymore (M-18A1) anti-personnel mines. The US claymore antipersonnel mine contains C-4 explosive behind a matrix of about 700 1/8-inch-diameter steel balls. When detonated, it propels these 700 steel balls in a 60-degree fan-shaped pattern to an optimum range of 50 meters and a maximum distance of 100 meters (See figure # 2).

Even though this mine is designed to be detonated by an electrical firing device (M57) actuated by the soldier employing the mine, soldiers in the field modified the mine so that it would detonate when an enemy soldier tripped a tripwire. Unlike most anti-personnel land mines that kill or wound one or two enemy soldiers, the MA could be constructed to destroy an entire enemy patrol.

During my first tour in 1966, when I was an infantry rifle platoon leader in the 1st Infantry Division, I employed a rather unsophisticated MA that used a mouse trap or clothespin as the firing device. However, MAs didn't evolve into an accepted method of conducting ambushes until 1970. During my second Vietnam tour in 1970, I commanded Alpha Company, 2nd Battalion (Mechanized), 22nd Infantry in the 25th Infantry Division. Not all units were using MAs, and the effectiveness of the MAs that were used depended on the skill of the unit members emplacing them. Fortunately, God blessed my company with two brilliant sergeants: Sergeant Henry Smith and Sergeant James McDonnell. Although most of the men in Alpha Company were proficient in setting out mechanical ambushes, these two sergeants were extremely innovative and in a league of their own.

My company's mission was to stop the infiltration of communist soldiers into the hamlets and villages, and to protect Vietnamese civilians so they could freely exercise their democracy and liberty. The MA provided Alpha Company the capability of establishing an automated battlefield, and of successfully protecting an area three times the size that most companies protected. The automated battlefield allowed Alpha Company the ability to maximize its combat power, while minimizing the risk to its own troops.

Because MAs allowed us to ambush deep into enemy controlled territory for long periods of time while protecting the United States' center of gravity by keeping US troops out of harm's way, the MA became our primary weapon system. As a mechanized infantry unit, we were able to systematically search large restricted AOs assigned to us, and at every enemy base camp we found, on every trail we crossed, a manned ambush or unmanned MA could be emplaced.

There were significant advantages in using MAs in this kind of warfare. Initially, senior officers assumed that enemy movement over trails could be stopped by manned ambushes. Unfortunately, most US units that were tasked to conduct these night ambushes were either detected or were not dedicated enough to the mission to go where they were directed. Consequently, this failure permitted the VC/NVA to move about at night with relative freedom, giving them an advantage over US and ARVN forces.

This freedom to move at night allowed them the ability to achieve three important Principles of War: maneuvering, massing of troops at key locations, and the element of surprise. The MAs, where they were employed, clearly denied them this very important advantage.

The MAs were extremely effective for enemy interdiction and attrition. Both the physical and psychological losses to enemy forces caused by MAs were significant. The MAs didn't make noise, fall asleep, eat, or initiate an ambush too early.

To avoid killing any civilians or friendly troops, it was imperative that MAs be employed responsibly. They were only emplaced in designated restricted areas and removed before the troops that employed them departed the AO. In my two tours in Vietnam, I emplaced hundreds of MAs. Not one civilian or friendly soldier was killed by an MA emplaced by my unit.

There is a notion that anti-personnel mines are evil and should be banned. In fact, anti-personnel mines, if used responsibly, save civilian lives and can lead them to freedom. All weapons used in war can be deadly and evil if used irresponsibly or by ruthless people. It is the irresponsible and callous use of anti-personnel mines that should be banned, not the mines themselves.

As I mentioned, when assigned a restricted AO, I would usually conduct patrols within so as to encircle the entire AO. On every trail that a patrol crossed, I would have them emplace an MA, thereby effectively killing or wounding any enemy entering, leaving, or passing through the AO. Then we would systematically search the area for enemy supplies and base camps. If an enemy base was found, I would have an MA emplaced to kill and wound any enemy soldiers returning to the base. The initiative in my AO no longer belonged to the enemy; the entire AO became a huge trap.

While Alpha Company operated in a restricted area, we usually had ten to fifteen MAs employed at all times. I required at least two soldiers to emplace an MA. They were also required to draw a detailed map of the location of the tripwire, claymores and battery in case those emplacing the MA were medevaced out of the area. Each MA was assigned an alphanumeric identification and the eight-digit coordinate of its location.

This detailed information on each MA was given to my 81 mm mortar platoon to plot and work up the firing data to each active MA. I plotted the azimuth and distance to each MA so that when we heard an explosion or saw the black smoke rising from the jungle, I would know which ambush had been detonated. Consequently, we were able to immediately respond to the site with accurate 81 mm mortar fire and troops on the ground.

The mortars not only provided immediate indirect fire support for the troops on the ground, but they also increased the effectiveness of the MA by killing more of the enemy, and by keeping the enemy from removing weapons and documents. Because the impacting mortar rounds disguised what caused the claymore explosions, firing them into the area also allowed us to emplace additional mechanical ambush on the same trail.

The reason no civilian or friendly soldier was ever killed or injured by any MA employed by my company was because we established procedures and strictly followed them. For example, MAs were only employed after the civilian curfew or in restricted areas; two individuals were required to be familiar with each MA; detailed diagrams and grid coordinates of each MA were provided to the company and battalion headquarters; all MAs not detonated had to be retrieved when the ambush was no longer needed or if our unit was to move out of the area.

The use of MAs was not an established US military doctrine; however, its use demonstrated the effectiveness of flexibility and irregular actions in combat. Sun Tzu said, "Prerequisite for the exercise of combat power: The ability to exercise flexible actions in combat … the armies' legions can be sent to fully engage the enemy and will never be defeated—through irregular and regular actions."[2]

To give the reader a better understanding of the effectiveness of the MA and the tactics used during the latter years of Vietnam, the following chapters chronologically present the events of my second tour in Vietnam from May 1970–May 1971.

CHAPTER 12

Cambodia

The Lord is my shepherd, I shall not be in want. He makes me lie down in green pastures, he leads me beside quiet waters, he restores my soul. He guides me in paths of righteousness for his name's sake. Even though I walk through the valley of the shadow of death, I will fear no evil, for you are with me; your rod and your staff, they comfort me.
Psalm 23:1–4[1]

ON MAY 16, 1970, I was back in Vietnam for my second tour. When I arrived at the in-processing station, I was asked to which infantry division I wanted to be assigned. During my first Vietnam tour I had been assigned to the First Infantry Division and would have selected it again, but under the Vietnamization program, the First Infantry Division had already been pulled out of Vietnam.

The 25th Infantry Division took over the same area the First Infantry Division was responsible for during my first tour. Since I was already familiar with this area, I chose the 25th Infantry Division. Because I already had experience with mechanized infantry operations, I was further assigned to the 2nd Battalion, (Mechanized), 22nd Infantry (2-22 Mech) of the 25th Infantry Division.

The 2-22 Mech, also referred to as the Triple Deuce Battalion, played a key role in the May 6, 1970, Cambodian incursion to clean out NVA/VC sanctuaries. Because I had to first in-process and attend a required orientation school for all new arrivals, it wasn't until May 26 that I was able to join the Triple Deuce in Cambodia.

On May 6, 1970, the Triple Deuce crossed into Cambodia from positions west of Thien Ngon village in South Vietnam to destroy the NVA Base Area of the 95C NVA Regiment and the headquarters (HQ) of the 9th NVA Division. Other than losing two armored personnel carriers (APC) to mines, the 2-22 Mech didn't suffer any losses. The Triple Deuce claimed 4 enemy dead, 1,500 NVA uniforms, 1,200 pounds of rice, and 200 gallons of gasoline and kerosene.

On May 10, the 2-22 (Mech) moved back south across the border to prepare for another operation in Cambodia, and on May 11, they joined an operation in Cambodia to destroy the communist headquarters for ground operations within South Vietnam, known as the Central Office of South Vietnam (COSVN).

As previously mentioned, B-52 strikes in Cambodia were extremely effective because they were no-notice and the NVA didn't have time to move out before the bombs arrived. The excellent results of the attack on a part of the COSVN headquarters are a prime example of the effectiveness of a no-notice B-52 strike. Prior to initiating the ground attack on COSVN, at least four waves of US B-52s, with six bombers per wave and each carrying a mix of over a hundred 500- and 750-pound bombs, hit the jungle where COSVN was believed to be located.

When the infantry battalions of the 25th Division moved in and searched the area, they found numerous dead NVA, an underground hospital, a motor pool of trucks, a communication repair shop stacked with radios, caches of weapons, ammunition and rice, and a field desk containing a COSVN stamp. The official count was 146 NVA killed by the B-52 strike. After the heavy bombardment, the NVA headquarters, hospital, and security personnel who survived the bombing were either suffering concussions, with blood coming out of their noses, unable to fight, hiding, or running. Consequently, when the 2-22 (Mech) searched the area they did not receive any resistance and did not suffer any casualties.

Ten days from the initial incursion, it was evident that the advantage the US had gained from the element of surprise was over. Although the NVA could not protect their supply bases, they were able to reorganize their forces and go back on the offense. No longer surprised and having the advantage of knowing the terrain, they were able to take the initiative of the fight back away from the US. Subsequently, most contact was NVA-initiated during the remaining time in Cambodia.

On May 16, 1970, 2-22 Mech had road-marched into an area which became known as Ambush Alley to search for the elusive HQ of the 9th NVA Division. It was approximately eight kilometers northwest of Krek and the area was a thick marshy jungle area with a stream running across an elevated dirt road. The monsoon season had just begun and heavy rain turned the road into mud.

The Triple Deuce laagered in a large clearing near the end of the small muddy road on the evening of May 16. Unfortunately, the commander made the mistake of staying there until May 21, thereby setting a pattern for the NVA to take advantage of. Mechanized infantry night defensive positions, or what mechanized infantry and armor units call laager positions, should be moved every one or two days to prevent the enemy from having time to plan an attack on the NDP or an ambush against units required to use the same route over and over to come in and out of the NDP.

On May 18, returning from another day of reconnaissance-in-force (RIF), Charlie Company was traveling on the only road that entered the Battalion Command Post (CP) and was ambushed. Close air support, artillery, and Alpha Company came to Charlie Company's rescue and after two hours of fighting, the NVA disappeared into the jungle. Charlie Company had 13 WIAs and 3 KIAs, but only found 1 dead NVA.

The NVA were now actively targeting US units in Cambodia, not only by ambushes, but also by deception. The night of May 19, the Triple Deuce's Operations Officer received a request over the radio for artillery fire. The coordinates were on a battalion position; therefore, the Operations Officer asked the individual, who spoke English, to authenticate. The individual responded with, "GI die."

On May 20, Alpha Company was ambushed while traveling down Ambush Alley, but only received a few men wounded. Most NVA ambushes were conducted by squads; they were able to slip up to the road, dig in, fire their RPGs at US vehicles coming down the road, and disappear back into the marshy jungle.

On May 21, the Triple Deuce began withdrawing down the muddy road back to Krek with its Scout Platoon on point. They hadn't gone far when another ambush was initiated by the NVA. The Scout Platoon suffered 4 WIA's and 1 KIA from RPG shrapnel. The NVA ambush quickly disappeared back into the jungle when the platoon leader brought in artillery and close air support. The battalion continued on after the ambush, and laagered in a small clearing down the road.

On May 22, Charlie Company took point and no further than two hundred meters down the road, they ran into another NVA ambush. They lost 2 APCs and suffered 9 WIAs and 6 KIAs.

Again the NVA disappeared when the close air support arrived. The burned-out tracks were pushed out of the road and the battalion continued down the road.

Alpha Company, near the rear of the column, had stuck several tracks crossing a small stream and stopped to wait for an Armored Vehicle Launched Bridge (AVLB). The AVLB was put over the stream and the column continued on. Within minutes, the Scout Platoon at the end of the column was ambushed. The Scout Platoon had 8 WIAs and 2 KIAs. As before, the NVA slipped back into the jungle when the close air support arrived. After the ambush the battalion continued to move. However, rather than stopping at Krek, the battalion continued back into Vietnam for a few days of recovery.

The initial phases of the Cambodia incursion went well for the Triple Deuce. Because of the element of surprise and the use of preplanned B-52 strikes on NVA/VC targets prior to conducting the ground attack, friendly casualties were extremely light. However, once the NVA recovered from the initial surprise incursion, they began to inflict relatively heavy casualties on the 2-22 (Mech). The men of the battalion needed a couple days of rest.

While taking the two-day breather on the Vietnam side of the border, Triple Deuce Battalion Commander Lieutenant Colonel Parker was replaced by Lieutenant Colonel Vail. After the two-day recuperation, the 2-22 (Mech) headed back to Cambodia on May 25. The battalion moved back to the same laager astride Ambush Alley that they occupied three days earlier. Within minutes after the battalion arrived, the NVA opened fire on the rear of the column. Luckily;, there weren't any casualties.

The reason the battalion returned to the same area was because the AVLB that they had put in prior to leaving the area three days earlier had become stuck in the mud and was still there. Therefore, the battalion had to go back and secure the area while a Sky Hook helicopter lifted it out.[2]

I helicoptered into the battalion laager on May 26 and was not impressed with the security of the battalion NDP. Not only were the security measures poor within the NDP, the ways in and out of the position were restricted to one road. Because of the marshy jungle on both sides of the road, a mechanized unit like the 2-22 (Mech) was extremely vulnerable to ambush whenever it was moving. It was no wonder that most of the casualties within the 2-22 (Mech) were suffered on this road, and why it was referred to as Ambush Alley.

The bridge came in three sections, so it wasn't until 1800 hours that the Sky Hook was able to remove all three sections of the AVLB. Once the AVLB was removed, we moved up Ambush Alley in drizzling rain at dusk to our new night laager position. The new CP laager location was out of the marshy area and near Krek.

LTC Vail assigned me the job of Battalion S-3 Air/Assistant Operations officer until a line company became available. Having served a previous Vietnam tour in both a leg and mechanized infantry unit within the First Infantry Division, I was surprised to see how poor the NDP security and defenses were. Only a few fighting positions were dug and none of them had overhead cover. Since LTC Vail didn't have a previous combat tour in Vietnam; I informed him of the NDP requirements we had in the First Infantry Division. I told him that no matter how tired the troops were, every night LPs were sent out, two-man chest-deep foxholes with overhead cover were dug, sectors of fires assigned, and claymores and trip-flares set out. Although this was LTC Vail's first combat tour in Vietnam, he was a tough infantry officer and knew how to lead men in combat. He had probably already noticed the lax state of security before I mentioned it. Within days he called the company commanders in and established a new set of standards.

On May 27 and 28, the line companies conducted more RIFs, with no results.

On May 29, the battalion had an NVA defector in a clean NVA uniform turn himself in. He said he was an assistant leader of one of the NVA security platoons of two companies from the security battalion of the NVA 9th Division headquarters. He pointed out on the map where the intelligence and supply branches of the headquarters were bivouacked, as well as the exact locations of the caches where their weapons and supplies were sealed in individual tunnels. Although we were suspicious that the man might be a plant, we planned a battalion-size operation to be executed the following day.

Because B-52 strike operations were never established in Vietnam or Cambodia to react to short-notice requirements from ground maneuver commanders, a B-52 strike preparation of the area could not be conducted. Instead only close air and artillery were used on the area prior to the battalion moving in on the morning of May 30. Alpha Company led the battalion into the area and immediately its lead track hit a mine and four men were injured. As Alpha Company continued to advance into the area they were hit by RPGs and AK-47 fire, and suffered five men wounded and two killed. The battalion found a number of huts hidden by the canopy above, but the NVA security battalion was gone. I believe that if a B-52 strike could have been obtained to first prep the area, the battalion would not have had any casualties and the NVA would have suffered heavy losses.

Sun Tzu emphasized the value of using overwhelming combat power in the following statement: "where forces overwhelm can be like a hard rock cast onto eggs."[3]

The Cambodian incursion was necessary. It destroyed a significant number of NVA soldiers and enemy supplies. However, some of the tactics used resulted in more friendly casualties than were necessary. When correct tactics were employed, such as using the element of surprise and preparing the battlefield with a B-52 strike prior to sending in troops, the results usually proved successful.

While in Cambodia, in addition to searching for NVA supplies, the 2-22 (Mech) was tasked to keep Highway 78 and Highway 7 open. This meant clearing the roads every morning before the US resupply convoys could bring supplies over them each day. This obviously set a pattern that was hard to avoid.

On June 1, the battalion's 4.2 mortar platoon moved down Highway 7 to set up a forward firing position to support one of the line company's search operations. At the location they stopped to set up their mortars, they noticed recently dug foxholes along both sides of the road. They called it in to the battalion CP and continued to set up the mortar firing positions. Within an hour, the mortar platoon came under fire from the wood line. The contact only lasted a few minutes and neither the platoon nor the enemy had any casualties. If it were not for the platoon stopping at that particular spot, the NVA most likely would have conducted an ambush on a US convoy or possibly one of the line company platoons clearing the road.

On June 3, the Charlie Company commander went on leave and I was given command of Charlie Company for a couple of weeks until he returned. I continued to search the jungle and rubber plantations in Cambodia for NVA supplies and bases. I stayed off the roads whenever possible and never set a pattern for the enemy to take advantage.

Using a mechanized unit against a guerrilla force required flexibility. There are occasions when it is beneficial to keep all the troops mounted. In other situations, it is best to dismount some infantry to provide advance, flank, and rear security when moving. If contact is made, however, it's important to immediately move dismounted troops back or move the tanks and tracks forward to maximize their heavier firepower. If dismounted infantry troops are to the front or flank, troops manning the guns on the tracks and tanks must hold their fire until their vehicle moves into a position where their fire will not hit friendly dismounted infantry, or until the dismounted infantry pulls back behind or adjacent to the vehicles. Infantry M-16 rifles and M-60 machine guns can't compete with .50 caliber machine guns and tank main guns firing canister or flechette rounds.

The effectiveness of a tank's main gun in guerrilla warfare was demonstrated to me during my first tour in Vietnam, when I had a tank platoon attached to my leg infantry platoon. I was tasked to locate and destroy a small VC base camp that had been discovered by air. I located the base camp. It was deserted. I set out dismounted security and had the tanks button up and destroy the huts. I took the remainder of my platoon and set up in a Vietnamese cemetery to test-fire our weapons across some rice paddies into a jungle area.

We opened up on the wood line of the jungle and all of a sudden we started to receive a heavy volume of fire back from the jungle. Because I just happened to have prearranged that particular clump of jungle to be one of my target reference points (TRP) for the company mortars to fire, I immediately called for mortar fire. Unfortunately, the company mortar platoon failed to continually set their mortars on the correct TRP as we moved during the operation, so they weren't responsive.

I also called the tanks back from the VC base camp and put them on line to fire into the wood line from where the VC fire was coming from. The tanks didn't have flechette rounds, but they did have canister rounds. The tanks opened up on the wood line and within minutes, approximately thirty VC came running out of the jungle, crossing a road that separated the cluster of jungle from a larger jungle area. My M60 machine gunner who was covering the road said he knocked two or three VC down as they crossed the road into the larger jungle. Rather than checking for VC bodies at the initial contact, I had my small tank/infantry task force chase the VC into the larger jungle. Unfortunately, as the tanks crushed through the jungle, one of the tanks smashed into some thick bamboo which camouflaged an old dug-in French tank position. The tank slipped into the dug-in position, threw one of its tracks, and became stuck. It was already late in the day and the battalion couldn't send a tank retriever out to us until the next morning. I set up a perimeter around the disabled tank and spent a long night in the jungle. What I concluded is that APCs and tanks come with additional mechanical problems, but their massive firepower makes it all worthwhile.

After commanding Charlie Company for a week in Cambodia, the battalion captured an NVA soldier walking down a road close to the battalion's night defensive position. When interrogated, he claimed to know where a large NVA underground headquarters and hospital complex was, and gave the Battalion Headquarters the location on the map. Unfortunately, to get to the area, the battalion would have to move down Ambush Alley. Because the road ran through a marshy area, tanks and armored personnel carriers were restricted to the road and unable to maneuver against the enemy; it proved to be an excellent spot to ambush a mechanized unit.

Higher headquarters determined that to locate and capture those in the NVA headquarters and hospital was worth the risk of moving down the road. As Charlie Company was preparing for the mission, we received orders to withdraw from Cambodia on June 13, and fortunately, the mission to search for the NVA complex was cancelled.

As we departed Cambodia, we received a report that a US surveillance aircraft which could detect the heat emitted from human bodies had flown over the road that we would have moved down to reach the NVA complex area. It had detected a large number of NVA soldiers stretched up and down both sides of the road. The captured NVA was apparently a plant, and although I had planned to conduct a dismounted recon of the jungle area on both sides of the road ahead of my track vehicles, and had artillery on call for both sides of the road, we still would have suffered a number of casualties. Our higher command apparently had not read Sun Tzu's warning: "Be aware of the enemy's potential for harming us when conducting combat: With regard to enemy subterfuge [deception]."[4] Certainly, the general's decision to send the battalion down Ambush Alley to look for the NVA command post was a bad decision. Thankfully, God is able to override bad decisions made at any level.

It was truly a blessing that the mission had been cancelled. As I look back at my remaining year in Vietnam, I realize this was only the beginning of God's wonderful protection. God is truly faithful to His word. As Psalm 91:14 says, "Because he loves me,' says the Lord, 'I will rescue him; I will protect him, for he acknowledges my name."[5]

Shortly after we left Cambodia and returned to Vietnam, the Charlie Company commander returned. As soon as I gave command of Charlie Company back to him on June 17, I was immediately given command of Alpha Company, 2nd Battalion (Mechanized), 22nd Infantry. Alpha Company had over 150 men, 22 M-113 APCs with a .50 caliber machine gun mounted on each APC, and three 81mm mortar tracks. Before I took command of Alpha Company, while it was still in Cambodia, the Company was ambushed a number of times by the NVA, and although the men fought hard, they suffered quite a few casualties.

CHAPTER 13

Tay Ninh Province

Seek first his kingdom and his righteousness, and all
these things will be given to you as well.
Matthew 6:33[1]

IT WAS WHILE I commanded Alpha Company, 2nd Battalion (Mechanized), 22nd Infantry for approximately six months in combat that God clearly validated my decision to make the Army my career and to fight those who would deny others the opportunity to learn about Jesus Christ. Validation came by allowing Alpha Company to kill or capture approximately 60 NVA/VC without losing any of our own men. This success did not happen in just one battle, but over a six-month period of hunting and being hunted by an elusive and deadly enemy. Because there were fewer large NVA units operating within South Vietnam and the Army of the Republic of Vietnam (ARVN) was taking over most of the search and destroy missions, there may have been a few other infantry companies that did not lose any of their men during this period in the war. However, I do not know of any other infantry units that had the same level of success at stopping the NVA/VC as did Alpha Company without losing any of its own men.

As discussed in Chapter 2, the Bible tells us that King Solomon asked God to give him wisdom, not to benefit himself, but so that he could lead God's people. Likewise, my prayers in combat were not for wisdom to benefit myself, but for God to give the men I commanded and myself the strength, wisdom, and courage to do His will, and for God to protect us from all harm and danger. God is always faithful to His word. He blessed this request.

Although this book will show how God disciplined the United States as a nation, it will also show how God provided the individual infantry company that I commanded in Vietnam with the insight, innovation, wisdom, and knowledge to achieve an astonishing victory over its assigned enemy. It will identify, on a day-by-day basis, how our God-inspired tactics and techniques took the initiative away from the enemy and resulted in victory.

Once we were out of Cambodia, I moved Alpha Company to a small US artillery fire support base (FSB) called FSB Rawlins, located near the small village of Ap Phuoc Hoa. Ap Phuoc Hoa was located northeast of the major city of Tay Ninh and a few miles south of Nui Ba Den (Black Virgin Mountain), a large mountain that sticks up from a relatively flat area. The area between the city of Tay Ninh and the Cambodian border is Tayninh Province. During my first tour in 1966–67, the Tay Ninh Province sector was the site of the principal Viet Cong (VC) command center for guerrilla operations in South Vietnam and the central office of the National Liberation Front (NLF); enemy resistance was strong. Now, after four years of fighting in the area and the recent destruction of enemy supplies in Cambodia, the area was much calmer.

The US artillery unit that had occupied Rawlins had recently pulled out of the base and was deactivated. Alpha Company was given the mission of taking over the base and securing it until the ARVN could take it over. Other than sweeping a few roads for mines, escorting convoys, and conducting local search and destroy missions, the only action we received while at this location was to assist an adjacent ARVN base camp that was attacked by a company of NVA. I asked if they needed us to come to their assistance, but they said they didn't need help besides indirect fire support, which I provided them.

On June 26, the Vietnamese base commander of the camp we provided with fire support invited me to their base camp for lunch. They were members of the Cao Dai religion, which is a combination of a number of religions, one of them being Catholic. Since it was a Friday, the Vietnamese commander and his staff couldn't eat meat, but they went all out for the lieutenant I brought along, my driver, and me. We were given a Vietnamese delicacy: chickens just prior to hatching out of their eggs. Not to offend our host, we all ate them, but I can assure the reader that I will never order this off the menu in a Vietnamese restaurant. The rest of the meal was quite good. We ate with chopsticks and every time my beer glass was down a quarter, they filled it back up again.

During the lunch, the Vietnamese commander gave me information about the VC in the area. He informed me that there were approximately twenty-five VC within four miles from their camp, and showed me their location on the map. I conducted a search and destroy operation a few days later in the area, but found only a few old bunkers.

During the mission of securing fire base Rawlins, I was also invited to have lunch with the village chief of Ap Phuoc Hoa. He told me the VC came into his village to try to recruit his young men, telling them they had to help the VC drive the American aggressors out of Vietnam. The VC propaganda was that the Americans intended to stay in Vietnam, like the French had, and that the Vietnamese government in Saigon was just a puppet of the Americans.

Unfortunately, some US troops did not present a very good image to the indigenous population; therefore, the VC false propaganda was an effective recruiting tool. Propaganda does not have to be true to be effective; it only needs to be believable. Unless US troops were trained to deal with the local population, as the US Army Special Forces were, US troops should have been kept out of the Vietnamese villages. If a village was suspected of having VC in it, US units could be used to cordon off the village, but a Vietnamese unit should conduct the search within the village.

I believe the US's information program was a complete failure not only in Vietnam, but also at home. The program was never able to convince Vietnamese peasants of the dangers of communism, or that unlike the French, the US had no intention of staying in Vietnam after the war.

On July 8, 1970, I turned Camp Rawlins over to the four ARVN companies who came to secure it. We moved to our rear area base camp Cu Chi for a two-day stand-down to give the troops a little rest and to perform maintenance on our vehicles and our equipment. Then we moved back out of Cu Chi to an area about three miles northeast of Katum. Katum is located approximately twenty-seven miles north of Tay Ninh and four miles south of the Cambodian border.

CHAPTER 14

Katum

*For the Lord gives wisdom, and from his mouth comes knowledge
and understanding. He holds victory in store for the upright,
he is a shield to those whose walk is blameless, for he guards the
course of the just and protects the way of his faithful ones.*
Proverbs 2.6–8[1]

ON JULY 10, 1970, Alpha Company moved northwest out of Cu Chi for
the long trip to Katum. I was familiar with the Katum area from my first
tour and as my company's APCs roared up unpaved Highway 4 northward
from Tayninh , I recognized the site that I believe was one of the most
successful US infantry battles inside Vietnam. It took place in March 1967,
during Operation Junction City, after US Intelligence intercepted an NVA
radio message that indicated they were going to attack the Special Forces
camp being constructed along Highway 4, south of Katum, with two NVA
regiments. The 2nd Battalion (Mechanized), 2nd Infantry, First Infantry
Division, to which I was assigned, was given the mission to protect the
Special Forces camp from the NVA attack.

Seven months earlier, when I was first assigned to the 2-2 (Mech) as an
infantry rifle platoon leader, the battalion was a non-mechanized infantry
battalion; however, after operating as an infantry rifle platoon leader for
four months without tracks, we suddenly became a mechanized infantry
unit on January 1, 1967. Both mechanized and non-mechanized infantry
have their advantages and disadvantages; however, having experienced

both, I preferred leading mechanized infantry in the environment we faced during the Vietnam Conflict. The amount of firepower and ammunition carried by a mechanized unit compared to a non-mechanized unit was significant.

By the time the 2-2 (Mech) was given the mission to secure the Special Forces base camp being built, we had received our APCs and were fully mechanized. Using the camp as bait and drawing two regiments of NVA out into the open to attack a US mechanized infantry battalion in defensive positions was a tremendous opportunity to attrite a significant amount of the enemy.

The defense normally has a passive purpose and the attack a positive one, conquest. However, in some cases it is better to take the defense in order to weaken the enemy. Clausewitz identifies the advantage of being in the defense when he writes, "The defensive form of warfare is intrinsically stronger than the offensive."[2]

The Battalion Commander's idea was to put Charlie Company around the Special Forces camp, Alpha Company, in a laager in a dried-up lake less than a half-mile south on Highway 4 to secure an artillery battery. Bravo Company, to which I was assigned, was to be placed in a dried-up lake less than a half-mile north of the camp on Highway 4 to secure another artillery battery. In this way, the artillery batteries could provide mutual supporting fire for each other, as well as artillery fire for the Special Forces camp.

All companies, as usual, had prepared the required two-man *Depuy fighting positions* with overhead cover, and emplaced claymore mines and trip flares around the perimeter. Infantry fires were interlocking and artillery and mortars were pre-registered. Sun Tzu's advice on defense was well applied in defending the Special Forces camp: "Take advantage of enemy vulnerability: act beyond enemy abilities—in defense ... defend and be certain of safety by defending what they cannot attack."[3]

Within two days, the two NVA regiments attacked the Special Forces camp being secured by Charlie Company and suffered a devastating defeat. It is not known how many NVA were killed the night of the attack; however, in the morning, Charlie Company piled up over 200 dead NVA off the battlefield. Charlie Company was the only unit attacked directly and it only lost three soldiers. Although Bravo Company was not attacked, we could see the NVA moving into staging areas at the edge of the wood line of the dried-up lake where we were located. We were able to bring both direct and indirect fire on a significant number of NVA. Because it was night and a relatively far distance to the wood line, the NVA were able to carry any of their dead out of that area by morning.

Clearly, drawing the enemy out of the jungle and fighting him on our terms was a more desirable tactic than searching the jungle for NVA/VC with large infantry units. Sun Tzu emphasized the value of terrain when he said, "The general who can assess the value of ground maneuvers his enemy into dangerous terrain and keeps clear of it himself. He chooses the ground on which he wishes to engage, draws his enemy to it, and there gives battle."[4]

The only thing I would have changed after reviewing the battle was the design of the Depuy fighting position. General Depuy was the commander of the First Infantry Division at the time of the attack, and he required all combat units to each night dig a specific foxhole that he had personally designed. Depuy's foxhole design required that a dirt mound be built directly in front of the soldier and that the firing port be angled so that the soldier could shoot the enemy coming at the foxhole adjacent to his position. Because the attacking enemy would be shooting at the same position he was attacking, the mound of dirt in front of the defending US soldier would give the soldier protection while still allowing him to engage the enemy soldier attacking the position next to him. The theory was for the soldier in the adjacent foxhole to shoot the enemy attacking your position; you would shoot the enemy attacking his position. This concept looked good on paper, but it didn't take the human factor into account. During the battle, quite a few US soldiers climbed out of their fighting foxholes and fought from behind their positions. In the heat of battle, they wanted to shoot the enemy coming to kill them, rather than the enemy attacking the man in the next foxhole. Consequently, they exposed themselves to fire coming from across the perimeter and shrapnel from above in order to see and kill the enemy coming directly at them.

After we returned to our base in Lai Khe, I recommended keeping the Depuy fighting position with the overhead cover and mound of dirt, but to leave enough of an opening in the front so that a soldier could still move around the mound to see directly in front of him. Apparently, the Army came to the same conclusion, because when I came back on active duty a few years later, the Army's official infantry fighting position was identical to the Depuy fighting position except that it allowed the soldier to move from around the dirt mound in order to see the front.

After arriving in the Katum area, we were assigned a designated restricted area of operation (AO) along the border between Cambodia and Katum that covered about 25 square miles of thick jungle. As defined in an earlier chapter, a restricted area is a control measure that restricts all civilians or friendly military forces from being in or firing into the designated restricted AO unless the commander assigned and responsible for it is informed. I knew that any people within my restricted AO, other than my own men or friendly troops that I knew about, were enemy. Therefore, I was allowed to employ MAs and tactics that would not only defeat the enemy, but also protect the United States' own center of gravity.

The Katum area was heavy jungle and thick with NVA. Shortly after arriving in our new AO, one of Alpha Company's APCs hit a mine in the road. In case it was the beginning of an enemy ambush, and to lower the chance of a direct broadside RPG hit, the other APCs immediately did a herringbone movement (alternating each APC in an opposite direction turn of 25 degrees) and fired into the jungle (See figure 3). It apparently was not an ambush; the mine only blew out a section of the track on the APC and no one was injured. Since the mine exploded under an APC that was in the middle of the convoy, we believed the mine to be command-detonated. We found the wire that had been connected to the mine and traced it back to where the NVA had connected it to the battery. As expected, the battery and NVA were long gone. We were able to fix the APC and continued on our mission.

On July 24, at 1000 hours, one of our mechanical ambushes detonated approximately a half-mile from our company laager. I immediately fired my 81mm mortars on the site, and because we were close to the Cambodian border, I took two of my platoons with me to retrieve any NVA weapons, documents, or wounded. After setting out security, we searched the area and found one dead NVA and one live NVA who had crawled into the brush. The Kit Carson scouts who were with us tried to talk the NVA into surrendering, but instead of coming out, the NVA returned fire. My men reacted with a heavy volume of fire and once ceasefire was called, a Kit Carson scout went into the brush and returned dragging another dead NVA.

As I checked over the spot where the claymores detonated, I realized that since we had fired 81mm mortars into the area, other NVA using the trail would probably think the damage to the ground and vegetation was caused by mortar rounds exploding. I had the men throw a few tail fins of our exploded mortar rounds into the damaged area and had the two dead NVA buried a good distance from the trail. Because the trail came out of Cambodia and was heavily used, I had another mechanical ambush emplaced 200 meters up the same trail. By 1800 hours, the mechanical ambush we had just set out on the same trail detonated, and we recovered another two well equipped dead NVA.

On July 25, a recon airplane spotted two NVA taking a bath in a river approximately four miles north of our position by the Cambodian border. Alpha Company was tasked to check the area out for a possible NVA base camp. Because the area was marshy, I left part of the company to secure our armored personnel carriers. On July 26, the remainder of Alpha Company, with an attached Civilian Irregular Defense Group (CIDG) unit of approximately eighty soldiers, conducted an air assault to search the area where the NVA were spotted. Our LZ was a dried-up lake approximately 500 meters from the Cambodian border. I had the artillery prep the LZ and we came in firing. When we reached the wood line, we discovered NVA equipment and a blood trail. We followed the trail until it crossed the Cambodian border. With all the blood that had been lost, I doubt the NVA survived.

As we moved through an area that was covered in thick bamboo, I stopped the unit for a quick rest. To my surprise, the CIDG troops started collecting bamboo shoots and pulling out pots from their rucksacks to cook lunch. My most trusted and competent Kit Carson scout, who had once commanded a VC company before he became disappointed with the NVA trying to run things in the south, was also surprised to see how undisciplined the CIDG were. I told him that since they were attached to me, I wanted him to get them straightened out before they got us all killed. He gave me a big smile and within seconds he was in their faces. I don't know what he told them, but they had their pots back in their rucksacks and we moved out without a sound. We continued to search the area but didn't find a base camp. I moved the Company to our Pickup Zone (PZ) which was located some distance from our LZ and we were extracted without incident (See figure 12 & 13).

If I had the choice, I would rather have taken three of my best men and my trusted Kit Carson scout with me to conduct that area reconnaissance, rather than the whole company and the CIDG unit. I used every technique I knew of to prevent our being ambushed, but I knew moving my large US/CIDG force through the jungle could never surprise the VC/NVA in their base camp.

After our one-day dismounted search and destroy operation, we returned to our APCs and set up a new night laager. To keep the enemy off balance and to deny him enough time to conduct recons, develop a plan, move forces into the area, or dig in for an attack against us, I moved our company's night laager every one or two days. For security reasons, one should never set a pattern and never stay in one place too long. If you do the same thing more than two times in a row, you can count on getting hit by the enemy.

When moving into a night laager, I would immediately put out Observation Posts (OP) or Listening Posts (LP) to prevent the enemy from surprising our unit. I required my men to dig two-man fighting positions with overhead cover, set up RPG screens (chain-linked fencing attached to poles to stop enemy RPG anti-tank rounds) in front of each armored personnel carrier, and to set out claymores and trip flares every time we moved into a new night defensive position. Moving every day or two was hard work. However, Alpha Company's night defensive positions were never attacked by the enemy.

The policy of not doing anything the same way more than twice was particularly important when we were moving. Whenever possible, I always varied our route and stayed off roads (See figure 19).

While working the AO near Katum, we normally only moved three miles within the AO each time we moved our night laager. Camp Katum was a Vietnamese camp with US Special Forces advisors and it was located astride a major enemy infiltration route into Vietnam from Cambodia. The enemy wanted it removed. They mortared and rocketed it almost every night. Since we were only about three miles northeast of Katum, we were usually able to spot where the firing was coming from and to provide counter-mortar-fire.

Since we were located only a few miles south of Cambodia, there were a lot of NVA in the area. Between July 27 and 30 we had another three mechanical ambushes blown close to the border; however, we found only blood and drag marks. Alpha Company's mechanical ambushes used numerous claymore mines stretched out along each trail, so even though bodies were not found at these three sites, because of the amount of blood found at numerous locations along each trail, at least one NVA was killed and one or more wounded by each ambush. Working in our own restricted AO allowed us to develop some relatively sophisticated techniques for the employment of mechanical ambushes that proved extremely successful not only around Katum, but for future operations.

Alpha Company laagered overnight close to the Cambodian border on July 28. Prior to dark, all fires within the NDP perimeter are extinguished.

This night, an extinguished fire used by one of the platoons to burn their trash during the day flared up for just a moment. Within minutes, an AC-130 gunship that was flying over the area opened fire with their two 20 mm M61 Vulcan cannons. The rounds hit the jungle area only a few hundred meters from the company perimeter. I immediately called the battalion headquarters and told them to call the Air Force to cease fire. The AC-130 pilot said that he was not informed that the area he was flying over was a restricted area assigned to an infantry unit and when he saw the fire flare up he assumed it was NVA/VC. The AC-130 gunship is usually an extremely accurate weapon system; therefore, it was only by the grace of God that Alpha Company did not experience any casualties from friendly fire. I never was able to find out why this particular pilot had not been informed that the area he was flying over was a US infantry company's assigned area of operation. It was a major mistake or incompetence on the part of someone.

On August 1, Alpha Company was happy to receive orders to move out of the thick jungles along the Cambodian border and back to the Cu Chi area where the vegetation was not as heavy. We worked the Cu Chi area for a little over a week and then moved into an area west of Saigon called the Iron Triangle on August 12, 1970.

CHAPTER 15

Iron Triangle

The Lord is with me; I will not fear; What can man do to me?
Psalm 118:6[1]

IN 1966–67, DURING MY first tour in Vietnam, I conducted operations in the Iron Triangle, which is located between two rivers northwest of Saigon. At that time, it was covered in heavy jungle, and considered an NVA and VC stronghold. However, on January 8, 1967, the First Infantry Division, to which my platoon belonged, conducted Operation Cedar Falls. The operation resulted in an estimated 500 VC killed and most of the jungle cut away by rome plows (large bulldozers).

By August 12, 1970, over three years later, some of the vegetation had returned to the Iron Triangle. Still, the jungle was relatively light, and we experienced only light enemy activity in the area (See figure 16).

While in the Iron Triangle, we were kept busy conducting day and night ambushes. One night, I sent out two squads to each conduct an ambush on trails located approximately 300–400 meters away. At about 0100 hours that night, my men on the perimeter of our night defensive position detected movement to their front. To discourage any NVA/VC, I decided to wake everyone up to conduct a *mad minute*. In a mad minute, we fire every weapon we have out to our front. Since we were set up in a circle, it gave us a 360-degree kill zone. My company consisted of twenty-two armored personnel carriers with a .50 caliber machine gun on each and one with a 7.62 minigun (a small, Gatling-like six-barrel cannon) that we removed from a helicopter. Additionally, Alpha Company had four 90mm recoilless rifles which fired beehive (flechette) rounds. A flechette round consists of a thousand flechettes, which are small, dart-shaped projectiles. These flechettes are clustered in an explosive warhead that can be dropped as a missile from an airplane, or fired from a tank main gun or recoilless rifle. It is an extremely effective weapon against enemy troops in the open. When each man in a platoon's individual weapon and the company's twelve .60 caliber machine guns are added to the above firepower, a mad minute looks and sounds like the Fourth of July.

I knew that if the leader of a night ambush patrol was not dedicated to the mission, he may not set up his ambush where he was directed. Rather, he would find the safest spot he could to spend the night. I learned this during my first tour in Vietnam, when I was a lieutenant and led an infantry rifle platoon in 1966. I gave a squad leader the mission to set up an ambush on a trail leading into the village we were securing. In the morning, the village chief came to tell me that the VC came into his village that night and took his assistant, who was a former VC, out to the edge of the village and assassinated him. The chief described exactly how the VC came into and left the village. I told him that couldn't be because I had an ambush on the trail he said the VC used. The chief insisted that the VC used that route; therefore, I immediately separated all the members of the ambush patrol and asked them individually where they had set up that night. Each man told me they set up in an empty house in the village and left one man on guard and the others slept. The last man I asked was the squad leader, and he told me he set up the ambush on the designated trail and the village chief was lying. Needless to say, the squad leader was disciplined, and I learned a valuable lesson in human behavior.

In light of the above experience, before I initiated the mad minute within the Iron triangle, I called the ambush patrols to notify them of what we were about to do. As soon as I did, the patrol who had just received a new squad leader earlier that month frantically shouted over the radio not to fire because they were set up just inside the wood line immediately in front of the company's night defensive position, rather than where they were supposed to be. The terrain around the ambush sites that his patrol was supposed to have set up provided protection and would have been safe from the fire of our mad minute. Because of this squad leader's failure to follow orders and set up next to the company's night defensive perimeter, his squad could have suffered heavy losses. It was by the grace of God that I decided to alert the ambush patrols before giving the command to commence firing.

For a unit to be effective in combat, the leader and his men must know the purpose of the mission. The Army's *Military Leadership Field Manual 22-100* states, "Leadership is the process of influencing others to accomplish the mission by providing purpose, direction, and motivation. Purpose gives soldiers a reason why they should do difficult things under dangerous, stressful circumstances. Direction shows what must be done. Through motivation, leaders give soldiers the will to do everything they are capable of doing to accomplish a mission."[2] I found that if the purpose of the mission was important enough to the troops, then it became their primary motivation to do what must be done.

I believed the reason why many soldiers who served in combat units in Vietnam failed to do the difficult and dangerous things required of them was because they didn't know the *purpose* of the war. Therefore, when a new man was assigned to my company, I would explain why it was important for the United States to be fighting in Vietnam. I would explain to him what communism was and that if North Vietnam took over South Vietnam, the people of South Vietnam would be denied the opportunity to learn about Jesus Christ. I would tell them that because knowing Jesus has eternal consequences, freedom of religion is the most important human right in the world. Additionally, I explained the strategic value to the United States of stopping the spread of communism around the world.

Most young men coming to Vietnam didn't even know what communism was or the reason we were fighting. If they were not told the purpose of the United States' involvement in Vietnam, their only objective was to stay out of harm's way and come back to the United States alive. We cannot expect our troops to risk their lives for a cause they don't understand. It was critical to give every man information about why we were in Vietnam, and also to let them know that God would be with them if they were doing God's will. It is critical for men in combat to trust in the Lord. Psalm 115:9 states, "O house of Israel, trust in the Lord—he is their help and their shield."[3]

I'm not sure if I had had the chance to sit down and talk to the new sergeant who took out the ambush patrol about why we were in Vietnam when he first arrived, or if he just didn't believe what I had to say. Regardless, I did have a long talk with him after the incident, and I never had any more problems with him.

I did have one soldier who refused to go out on an ambush patrol. I gave him every chance to change his mind, but his position was that this was not his war and that his war was back in the United States.

It was a time in our history that the civil rights of African Americans were a major issue, as they should have been. Martin Luther King, Jr. rightly led the African Americans on peaceful demonstrations, and many good changes took place. Unfortunately, King's consuming desire for equal rights for African Americans clouded his understanding of the Vietnam Conflict. Rather than supporting, as a Christian pastor, the effort to stop the spread of communism so the Vietnamese could learn about Jesus Christ and receive eternal salvation, he openly condemned the United States' involvement in Vietnam. This lack of concern by King for anyone besides his own race and his speaking out against the war adversely influenced some African-American draftees well after his death.

Disobeying a direct order in combat was serious. I sent the soldier who refused to go out on the ambush back to the Cu Chi base camp to be court-martialed. Shortly after I sent the soldier back, I was required to come in out of the field to see my battalion commander, Lieutenant Colonel Vail. When I arrived in his office, the military lawyer for the man I was court-martialing was sitting in the office. The lawyer wanted to know if the man could receive an Article 15 instead of a court-martial. He said the man was sorry and wouldn't disobey an order again. Because an Article 15 is only for minor offenses, and at the most, results in a soldier being temporarily reduced in rank, I told Vail that someone else was required to risk his life to take the place of the soldier who refused the direct order on the ambush. It would set a bad precedent if he received anything less than a court-martial. LTC Vail looked at the lawyer, said, "You heard the captain," and dismissed him. The man who refused the order was sentenced to two years in Long Binh prison, and when released, he was required to remain in Vietnam until the length of his normal tour was completed.

I want to make it perfectly clear that most of the African-American soldiers in Vietnam did not share King's anti-war sentiments. In fact, some of my best and trusted soldiers were African-American. The above two incidents were the only discipline problems I had while commanding Alpha Company.

On August 14, I was tasked to conduct search and destroy operations by going up and down the Saigon River on boats driven by the Vietnamese Navy. I left a small force to secure our APCs, and the majority of the Alpha Company loaded onto the Vietnamese Navy boats and spent one full day cruising the Saigon River on the west side of the Iron Triangle. If we saw anything suspicious, we would land and check it out. It was a waste of time, but relatively relaxing (see figure 17).

Other than having one mechanical ambush detonation that only produced drag marks, the Iron Triangle didn't produce much. On August 20, we moved out of the Iron Triangle to look for an NVA 85-man artillery battalion that was supposed to be in the area, on the other side of the Saigon River.

CHAPTER 16

Cu Chi

Be strong and very courageous. Be careful to obey all the law
my servant Moses gave you; do not turn from it to the right or
to the left, that you may be successful wherever you go.
Joshua 1:7[1]

ON AUGUST 20, WE arrived in an area east of Cu Chi, close to the Saigon
River, to search for the NVA artillery battalion that was supposed to be
in the area. We found traces of a few NVA but no 85-man NVA artillery
battalion.

After looking for the NVA artillery battalion for a few days, Alpha
Company moved to an area northeast of Cu Chi and west of the Saigon
River. This area didn't have thick jungle, but it did have a lot of enemy
activity. I always wondered how there could be so many NVA and VC in
an area that didn't seem to provide enough concealment. My question
was answered years after the war, when I watched a documentary on
TV, titled, "The Tunnels of Cu Chi." The NVA and VC had an extensive
underground tunnel system in the area close to the village of Cu Chi that
we never located during the war. In fact, the new communist government
of Vietnam is so proud of the tunnels, they have made them into a tourist
attraction.

We never found the large tunnel complex, but we did eliminate a
number of VC and NVA in the area. On August 24, two mechanical
ambushes went off within thirty seconds of each other. We immediately

reacted and found a dead NVA at each site. Apparently, both enemy soldiers were traveling together, and when the first ambush killed one soldier, the other NVA ran and hit the second ambush. Between August 25 and 28, three of our mechanical ambushes detonated; however, they were too far for us to reach quickly. As a result we only found blood at each site and at one site, a sign saying, "US GO HOME."

On August 29, we apparently killed or wounded two NVA on two different infiltration trails. When we checked the sites where the mechanical ambushes were detonated, we found a large pool of blood at one site, and bandages and blood at the other site.

On September 1, we crossed a trail with fresh enemy footprints. I sent my tracker team and a security element to check out where the trail went. The tracker team consisted of six men, a scout dog, and a tracker dog. A scout dog alerts to the presence of an enemy from scent in the air, and a tracker dog follows the scent on the ground of an enemy. The team returned after about a half-hour. They looked like they had just seen a ghost. I asked what happened and they said that they were going down the trail when both dogs and almost the entire team without knowing it stepped over a tripwire connected to a booby trap. One of their last men hit the tripwire but the pin didn't pull all the way out of the detonator.

I took my most competent Kit Carson scout, the former VC captain, to check out the booby-trapped area. After searching the area, we found that the tripwire was connected to a 155mm artillery round. Additionally, my Kit Carson scout also found a buried US claymore clacker. A claymore clacker is a device which, when squeezed, sends an electric charge to an electric blasting cap attached to a claymore mine. If either the US claymore mine or the 155mm round had detonated, a significant number of Americans would have been killed and wounded. It truly was a miracle that none of the team set off the 155mm round or the claymore.

It is my experience in combat and in everyday life that the time of greatest value is the time spent with the Lord. Every night before I went to sleep, every morning when I awoke, and before every operation, I prayed for God to give us the strength, wisdom, and courage to do His will and for Him to protect us. If we do God's will, He is without a doubt faithful to His word. Prayer to God the Father in Jesus' name for the right reason is a powerful thing. I would pray prior to every operation, but once enemy contact was made, I was too busy orchestrating the battle to pray. However, after the battle was over, I never failed the give the Lord thanks.

James reminds us of the importance of our motives in James 4:2–3, when he writes, "You do not have, because you do not ask God. When you ask, you do not receive, because you ask with wrong motives, that you may spend what you get on your pleasures."[2]

After we found the 155mm round and claymore booby traps, I had them blown up and our own MA emplaced to eliminate the enemy who had set them out. By coincidence, I had scheduled a helicopter so I could reconnoiter the area. After the detonation of the enemy booby traps, the helicopter landed and departed with me on board. When we detonated the enemy booby traps, the enemy probably thought their booby traps had killed and wounded Americans and that the helicopter was evacuating casualties. When we returned the next day, we found that our ambush had been detonated. There was a pool of blood with a number of drag marks. Apparently, the NVA or VC who set out the booby traps to kill Americans had come back to see what damage their booby traps caused, and then ran into our MA.

Counterinsurgency warfare is a deadly game of cat and mouse. To outfox the enemy, we studied their habits and patterns, and then capitalized on them. We knew the enemy used trails at night, so we focused primarily on ambushing trails.

After focusing on trails for a few months, while passing by night defensive positions that we had used in the past, we noticed the NVA and VC were checking them out after we had departed. The enemy was looking for information about us, old ammunition, food, wire, and other things they could use. On September 2, we started to emplace MAs in night defensive positions before moving to new locations. In *The Art of War*, Sun Tzu suggests weakening the enemy through enticement such as showing the enemy gains to lure them.[3] To entice the NVA/VC, we dug only one or two trash pits and purposely did not burn the contents we placed in them. We rigged hand grenades to explode if the contents in the pit were disturbed. Using the MAs in this manner was another example of using bait to kill the enemy.

At the first site, on September 2, we put rigged hand grenades in two different pits. In the first pit we put one grenade and in the other pit we put two grenades under the same object. When we returned to the old site the next day, we found that at the first pit the hand grenade was missing. However, at the second pit a grenade had exploded and we found a pool of blood. I believe the NVA/VC were professional and searched for booby traps prior to pulling out items they could use. In the first pit they found the grenade and may have found one of the grenades in the second pit. However, after finding a grenade in the second pit they probably assumed it was safe and failed to discover the second grenade. Although we killed or at least wounded one NVA/VC, we realized that grenades were not the most effective weapon to use, so we switched to claymores.

Because the senior soldier in the VC or NVA unit checking out the site usually wants to be first at getting anything good left behind, the lower ranking men are put out as security. Consequently, we usually killed relatively senior enemy soldiers at the old NDPs. For example, I set out an MA using claymore mines before leaving our night position on September 3, and returned the next day to find that it had been detonated. There was an NVA bush hat with numerous holes in it so we knew it had killed at least one NVA. I had a tracker team with my company and their dog led us into the woods, where we found a fresh grave with an NVA lieutenant wrapped up in a poncho. In this particular MA, I had set up five claymore mines in a circle so to cover the entire night defensive position area; therefore, although we found only one dead NVA, there may have been others wounded.

On September 4, we heard one of our MAs detonate on a trail. I immediately fired my 81mm mortars into the area and sent out the platoon that emplaced the MA. As they moved towards the site, I shifted the mortar fire farther away. This tactic was used almost every time we reacted to a mechanical ambush that we heard explode in order to inflict additional enemy casualties and to keep the enemy from carrying off documents and weapons. It also allowed us to quickly shift the mortar fire onto the enemy if we came into contact with other enemy forces. This time, we found two dead NVA and two AK-50 rifles. We almost always found enemy weapons when we found an enemy soldier killed or wounded by one of our MAs; normally, though, the rifles we found were AK-47s. In this particular case, these two NVA soldiers were extremely well equipped and carrying new AK-50s. The fact that these NVA had new equipment and the latest weapons was significant information.

It was very important for us to keep the enemy from dragging off those we had killed and from taking away any weapons or documents they were carrying. In actuality, we were required to take a picture of all VC or NVA we killed before we buried them. We would then send the pictures, weapons, and documents back to our division headquarters so that Military Intelligence could identify which unit the enemy soldiers were with. In the rear area at one of the higher headquarters, they had former NVA and VC soldiers look at the pictures and try to identify who a dead enemy soldier was and to which unit he belonged. Along with the weapons and documents, the pictures provided valuable information needed to put together the puzzle that would help our overall effort.

The following night on September 5, we killed another NVA on one of the infiltration routes. It was becoming almost a daily occurrence for one of our mechanical ambushes to detonate. This NVA was apparently some kind of carrier transporting money to one of the NVA or VC units. The squad that I sent out to respond to the MA came back with their helmets full of Vietnamese currency. I sent the money back to our higher headquarters with a picture of the carrier, his weapon and the documents he was carrying. As usual, I didn't receive any information back as to who he was, but a lot of enemy troops or informants were probably very disappointed when they didn't get paid.

Although, we were unable to find a dead or wounded enemy at every single mechanical ambush that detonated, I know of one for sure that was not set off by an enemy soldier. On that occasion, we reacted to the detonation and found a dead bird that unfortunately picked the wrong place to land. There was one other incident, on September 6, we found that one of our mechanical ambushes blown and the battery that sent power to the detonator taken. I'm assuming that the enemy soldier who set off the claymores was probably killed and that a survivor in his unit found the battery and removed the dead body and battery. If they had discovered the MA before they set it off, the enemy would not have detonated the claymores, but rather taken the claymores for their own use.

When we first started using mechanical ambushes, one of my major concerns was the possibility of the enemy finding an MA and taking the claymores and battery, and using them against friendly troops. To address this concern, Sergeant Smith designed a technique that allowed us to employ our MAs so that if an enemy found the ambush, they would be killed if they tried to remove it. No claymores were ever removed from any of our MAs and the only battery taken was the one mentioned above.

Chapter 17

Trung Lap

He who dwells in the shelter of the Most High will rest in the shadow of the Almighty. I will say of the Lord. He is my refuge and my fortress, my God, in whom I trust. Surely he will save you from the fowler's snare and from the deadly pestilence. He will cover you with his feathers, and under his wings you will find refuge; his faithfulness will be your shield and rampart. You will not fear the terror of night, nor the arrow that flies by day.
Psalm 91:1–5[1]

HAVING EXPERIENCED THE ADVERSE consequences of search and destroy operations during my previous tour, I always conducted search and destroy operations with overwhelming combat power, and did not pretend to be able to sneak up on the enemy base camp. As long as the ground was dry and could support it, I would use my armored personnel carriers and attached tanks when searching for the enemy's bases. If I had tanks attached, I would have them lead the way through the jungle. The tanks were able to knock down thicker jungle and detonate booby traps more easily than the armored personnel carriers. Additionally, when tanks or armored personnel carriers move through the jungle, they knock trees and brush down in front of them, helping to deter any enemy ambush. Depending on the area, I would have my infantry dismounted or riding on their carriers to keep any enemy from engaging the tanks from the side or rear. Once an enemy camp was found, I usually had the tanks run through the camp to set off booby traps and destroy any structures.

109

I would have my infantry dismount their carriers, search the area, and blow up any tunnels they found. Before leaving the camp, I would have a number of mechanical ambushes emplaced to kill or wound any returning enemy soldiers.

On September 8, we conducted a search and destroy operation 10km northeast of the village of Trung Lap using the tactic described above, except we only had my armored personnel carriers and no tanks. We found the enemy base camp and as expected, the enemy left the area. Inside one of the bunkers we found nine 82mm mortar rounds, twelve 82mm fuses, and 360 pounds of rice in nine forty-pound bags. We emplaced our mechanical ambushes and pulled out of the area. That night at chow time, several MAs were detonated only minutes apart. A sweep of the area the next morning produced two dead NVA, one AK-47, and a map with valuable information.

Tanks and armored personnel carriers cannot traverse areas that are marshy or mountainous. Search and destroy operations in areas like these should be conducted by small five-man long range patrols that can sneak through the jungle without being detected. Once they find the enemy base camp, they can relay an eight-digit coordinate back to a fire control center for an immediate air or artillery strike. Most US infantry battles with the VC or NVA were enemy initiated, and most of the enemy casualties in these battles were by US air and artillery. Because small five-man undetected patrols can call in air and artillery, large, conventional-leg infantry-unit search and destroy operations are not usually necessary and should be avoided.

The following day on September 9, one of my Kit Carson scouts saw an animal snare in the jungle. We set out an MA. We checked it the next day and found a pool of blood and drag marks. Because most of the Kit Carson scouts were former VC and knew the habits and tactics of the VC, they proved to be extremely valuable.

On September 10, the company participated in a *hammer and anvil* operation with the ARVN, which is an operation in which one unit (hammer) pushes through an area in an attempt to drive the enemy into a blocking force (anvil). The operation took place relatively close to the village of Trung Lap, so the area of the operation was designated a free fire zone rather than a restricted area. Therefore, mechanical ambushes could not be used.

During this operation near Trung Lap, our company was the hammer. As we pushed through what was a lightly vegetated area, our Kit Carson scouts once again proved their value. To reduce the chance of concussion from the detonation of an anti-vehicle mine, US troops had sandbags placed on the floor of their armored personnel carriers, and the troops rode on top of the vehicle. Since I had ten Kit Carson scouts assigned to my company and we normally had twenty-two armored personnel carriers in the field, I had about one Kit Carson scout on every other vehicle. As we pushed through the jungle, all of a sudden, the Kit Carson scouts on top of a couple of the vehicles started jumping up and down, yelling, "VC, VC!" They jumped off the tops of their armored personnel carriers and threw open a camouflaged hatch to a tunnel that none of my American troops had noticed. They started yelling in Vietnamese for the enemy to come out, and when they didn't, they started firing their M-16s into the tunnel. We pulled out two NVA from the small tunnel. One was an NVA lieutenant who was wounded by the scouts firing into the tunnel and the other was an NVA woman. We learned later that they had just come down from North Vietnam about a week earlier.

My medic bandaged the wounded NVA lieutenant and I interrogated the NVA woman through a Vietnamese interpreter (see figure 4 and 5). In figure 4, notice the compassion on the face of my medic giving the wounded NVA a cigarette. Unlike some US combat commanders in Vietnam, I taught the men in Alpha Company not to hate the enemy soldiers, and that they were to treat them well when capturing them. Although Alpha Company killed more NVA/VC than most US infantry companies, I did not believe, nor do I believe, that any of my men killed any enemy out of hate or revenge. Although the VC/NVA were trying to kill us, I think most of us felt somewhat sorry for those we had to kill in order to protect the South Vietnamese. However, Alpha Company knew what the tragic consequences would be if we failed to stop the NVA/VC attacks against the South Vietnamese. Certainly, we wished NVA/VC aggression could have been stopped through diplomacy rather than war. Because the men of Alpha Company knew they were doing their God-given duty, they all returned home without any remorse.

Overall, US military units in Vietnam had a reputation of humane treatment of prisoners. This was evidenced for me when a VC soldier who turned himself in to my unit told me he walked fifty kilometers to find a US unit in which to surrender, rather than surrendering to an ARVN unit.

The hammer and anvil operation didn't produce any other enemy. However, on the way back to our assigned restricted AO, we came upon a B-52 bomb crater with crystal clear water in it. I set out security and allowed the men to take turns swimming in the crater (See figure 6). After returning to Alpha Company's AO, we set out MAs. In the morning, we found one dead NVA at one of our old laager sites. Because of additional blood found at the site, at least one more NVA was probably wounded.

On September 11, I had seventy Vietnamese soldiers attached to my company to conduct a search of an area five kilometers east of the village of Trung Lap. The area was heavily booby trapped; therefore, to detonate the booby traps, I called in an airstrike to drop napalm. It set the jungle on fire and one could hear numerous explosions. When the fire burnt out, we searched the area, but didn't find anything except a few old bunkers.

On September 12, Alpha Company moved back to the restricted AO to which we were assigned ten kilometers northeast of Trung Lap. While conducting a search back in our AO, we discovered a trap door to a tunnel. Concerned that it might be booby trapped, I had it blown open. My men thought they heard some enemy in the tunnel, but I didn't want to risk a soldier's life by sending one into the tunnel to find out. As per my policy, I had the men stick a bangalore torpedo in the tunnel and blow it up. A bangalore torpedo is a long metal tube filled with an explosive. It was primarily designed to cut through barbed wire and detonate buried mines; it also worked extremely well at destroying enemy tunnels and bunkers. In general, my policy was to never, ever risk any of my men's lives just to claim an NVA/VC body count. Every man in my company was like a son or brother to me.

I still resent the time when I was just a rifle platoon leader during my first tour in 1966, when my battalion commander told my company commander to have my ambush patrol return to a night ambush site to retrieve NVA bodies that we may have killed. At the time, my battalion was a leg infantry battalion, and we had been operating out of a dried-up lake in triple canopy jungle that we had air assaulted into, deep in enemy territory. From a helicopter reconnaissance earlier in the day, I detected a trail that led into the dried-up lake that our battalion NDP was located. The jungle was triple canopy jungle, which meant it had extremely tall trees and very thick vegetation. If a person was on the trail that I detected and looked up, he could not see the sky. However, from the sky looking down one could see the trace of a line that ran across the top of the jungle trees that had a little darker color than the rest of the tree tops. Because the NVA/VC probably thought the Americans could not see the trail and therefore did not know it was there, it was safe to move on. Thus, I thought this would be a good trail to ambush. When I returned from the reconnaissance, I planned and prepared an ambush for the trail.

That night I took out an eleven-man ambush patrol to ambush the trail. Because one cannot hear the enemy while one is moving, I would stop the patrol often to listen for any enemy movement. As we approached the ambush site, I could hear the movement of a couple of soldiers walking down the trail, and behind them I could hear a large group moving. We were still in single file; I passed the word back that no one was to fire except my point man and me. Because the jungle was triple canopy, I could only see a few feet in front of me. I was determined to let the enemy walk into the barrel of my rifle before firing; however, when the movement was only around fifteen feet in front of me, one of my men halfway down the ambush patrol file coughed! My point man and I both opened up full automatic ankle level fire at the movement. After I fired five full magazines on full automatic, my M-16 jammed—the chamber would become too hot and cause the ammo casing to expand and jam on the M16 rifles issued during the early years of the Vietnam Conflict. The close-in movement had stopped, as well as the larger movement further down the trail. I pulled my men back behind an old B-52 crater. Since it gave me some clearance from the trees, I threw four hand grenades into the jungle where we had heard the movement. I then moved the patrol back into the battalion NDP located in the dried-up lake.

I reported to my company commander that we had heard movement that sounded like an enemy force moving down the trail. Because of the cough, we initiated fire before we could be sure. Since the movement had sounded like men walking (rather than an animal moving) and because of the larger movement further down the trail, I was almost certain it was an enemy force. Regardless, I was not going to risk the lives of my men by sweeping through the area to see if we had killed anyone just so we could claim a body count.

Unfortunately, someone up the chain of command did want to be able to claim a body count. I was ordered to take my patrol back out to recover any dead NVA. Even though I explained to my company commander that it was a bad idea to return to the ambush site, he indicated that the order came from above and it could not be changed. I knew if I refused the order, I would be replaced, and my patrol would have to go out anyway, but with a different leader. Consequently, I gathered my patrol together and we quietly moved out of the NDP.

As soon as my patrol entered the wood line, one of my men said he saw an NVA crouched down at the edge of the wood line. I moved back to where my man was and asked him to point the NVA out. He showed me where he had seen him, but said that he had moved. I threw a grenade at the spot. Unfortunately, it was one of the old pineapple grenades from the Korean War and a dud. I threw another grenade, which exploded, and we did a quick sweep of the area. After finding nothing we continued the patrol. We had moved approximately a hundred meters when the NVA opened up fire on the patrol, killing one of my men. We returned fire, broke contact, and moved back into the perimeter of the NDP. The movement that we heard at the ambush site earlier was certainly an NVA force. We probably had killed a couple of NVA, but risking our own soldiers to prove it was, in my view, criminal.

Regarding the problem I wrote about with my M-16 rifle jamming, I provide the following additional information: I wrote to the Military's Material Command about the problem soldiers were having with their M-16 rifles jamming when I returned from the field. I told them that I had tested the AK-47 rifle by firing over ten thirty-round magazines of relatively dirty ammunition on full automatic, and could not make it jam. I told them that I believed the reason the M-16 jammed and not the AK-47 was because the chamber of the AK-47 rifle and its ammunition had a greater taper compared to the M-16 round and chamber. Clearly, the more the taper, the more easily the round will eject from the chamber. The Material Command wrote a letter back, saying they agreed, but explaining that it was too expensive to change the taper in the chamber and the ammo. They wrote that instead of changing the ammo and rifle chamber, they were chrome-plating the chamber and slowing the automatic rate of fire to eliminate the problem. A later congressional subcommittee report asserted that the M-16 had malfunctioned "seriously and excessively" due to jamming. The report concluded that the jamming was happening primarily because the gunpowder that was being used sent an unacceptable amount of residue down the gas-tube recoil system to the bolt. The subcommittee said the sloppiness of the testing "borders on criminal negligence."[2] It is unknown just how many American soldiers died because their weapons jammed while fighting in Vietnam.

On September 11, 1970, after I completed the operation with the 70 ARVN, I sent my First Platoon to work with the 2nd Battalion, 34th Armor. While they were there on September 12, my First Platoon emplaced a mechanical ambush in the 2nd Battalion, 34th Armor's old night laager which successfully eliminated an NVA. The following night, they did the same thing at a different old night laager site, killed another NVA, and captured an NVA who was wounded from the MA.

On September 14, I brought the company back to Cu Chi base camp for a two-day stand down. That night I received a call that five of my men had been picked up by the military police while trying to sneak some prostitutes into the Cu Chi base camp. The men had taken out one of our armored personnel carriers and picked up the women prostitutes in the village of Cu Chi. I sent my executive officer to get them out of jail. Because they were all good soldiers in the field and because they had never been in trouble before, I gave them a stern verbal chewing-out, letting them know how disappointed I was in their actions, but handed down relatively light punishment.

It wasn't until seven years later in 1977, when I was assigned to Germany and receiving my household goods into my quarters in Germany for a three-year tour there, that I found out the full story of the NVA money carrier that we killed September 5 and how that related to the men trying to smuggle prostitutes into the Cu Chi base camp. The customs sergeant who was responsible for inspecting household goods at the camp that I was assigned to in Germany said to me, "Sir, you probably don't remember me, but I was in your company in Vietnam, and something has been bothering me all these years. You know when we brought back all that Vietnamese money from the mechanical ambush that killed the NVA money carrier?" I said yes. He said, "That wasn't all the money that he was carrying. We each kept over $3,000 and it has always bothered me." I told him that although it was wrong not to have told me then, I commended him for his honesty now, and more importantly, that God forgives those who are truly repentant. I told him that if the men in the squad had asked me at the time if they could keep the money, I'm not sure what I would have told them. The money that the enemy was carrying did not belong to either the South Vietnamese or US government any more than it did to the men who risked their lives preventing its use by the enemy. Besides, the money we did send back was now in the hands of the communists. That seemed to take a big load off his conscience. I guess that explains why when we returned to Cu Chi, those five soldiers from the squad he was in had the money to hire the prostitutes they tried to sneak into the base. I didn't bring up the incident or ask the sergeant if he was one of the men. There were about ten men in the squad that retrieved the money. The $30,000 the men kept, plus the $20,000 I sent back to headquarters, added up to $50,000 being carried by the NVA.

CHAPTER 18

Ben Suc

Do not be afraid or discouraged because of this vast
army. For the battle is not yours, but God's.
2 Chronicles 20–15[1]

UNLIKE LEG INFANTRY UNITS that normally conducted a three- or four-day mission in the field and then returned to their base camp to wait for another mission, mechanized infantry units stayed in the field and only returned to their base camp for a couple of days for maintenance once every two or three months. On September 16, Alpha Company moved out of Cu Chi base camp and was assigned another restricted AO thirty miles northeast of Cu Chi and ten miles northeast of Ben Suc.

Alpha Company was given the mission to provide security for Rome Plows that cut down the jungle in the area. Rome Plows are large bulldozers. They operate in a group of five to eight in a staggered line, and cut down trees and then burn them in large piles. They can successfully level thirty acres in a matter of weeks. Denying the enemy concealment for base camps and infiltration was an important mission in counter guerrilla operations. Additionally, the bulldozers were used to cut back the jungle from most of the roads in Vietnam to prevent the enemy from conducting close ambushes on convoys. Because of the three-day warning the VC and NVA received prior to B-52 strikes, my Kit Carson scouts told me they were more afraid of being buried alive in a tunnel by a Rome Plow than a B-52 strike. In fact, one of the Kit Carson scouts said that he had been buried in a tunnel by a Rome Plow and it took him three days to dig himself out.

To secure the Rome Plows required only part of Alpha Company to physically provide a perimeter around the operation while the remainder conducted recon missions to prevent an enemy surprise attack.

On September 22, we located a VC base camp during the day and emplaced an MA in the camp before leaving. We returned to our night laager, which was only 800 meters away, and within forty minutes after returning we heard the ambush detonate. We immediately fired 81mm mortars into the area and moved back to the enemy's base camp, where we found a VC with wounded legs. He said that there were three other VC, two of whom were also wounded. We searched the area, but had to return to our night laager because of darkness. The next morning, we returned to the area where we had wounded the VC to try to track down the other wounded VC soldiers. We saw numerous tracks; there looked to have been approximately twenty-five VC in the area. However, we didn't find anyone. We emplaced a few more MAs and departed the area.

On September 23, we started to use bangalore torpedoes for the MAs' explosive when employing them in our old night laagers. Since bangalores didn't have the large killing zone that claymores had, we were able to leave manned stay-behind ambushes to ambush the enemy carrying away any weapons and documents from our mechanical ambushes. The first night we used the bangalores, we also set out a manned ambush. When the bangalores detonated, they killed two VC; however, it was such a violent explosion that the other VC were frightened. They ran, rather than policing up their dead comrades and weapons. Because our manned ambush was prepared to ambush the enemy retrieving bodies at the mechanical ambush site, the M-79 gunner within our ambush patrol replaced his canister round with a 40mm grenade round. When the VC ran out of the area, one of the VC almost ran over our manned ambush. The M-79 gunner fired his grenade round at the VC hitting him in the back. Because the VC was too close for the grenade to arm itself, the grenade stuck in the VC's back without exploding. It knocked the VC down, but the heavy vegetation and darkness allowed the VC to crawl away.

When you command a mechanized infantry company, you realize that the enemy is keeping you under observation most of the time and can easily follow you through the jungle. Knowing that they were usually following us, on September 25, I put out an MA on the tracks we were making through the jungle with our armored personnel carriers. No more than an hour after I set out the ambush, it detonated. We immediately returned and found a dead NVA mortar sergeant. He had on him a letter to his commander asking for an award for inflicting heavy casualties on the Americans when he mortared their battalion headquarters a week earlier.

Because the NVA that was following Alpha Company was a mortar sergeant, he was most likely planning a mortar attack on our company. Killing him may well have prevented Alpha Company from suffering numerous casualties. This example serves to emphasize the constant presence of dangers that were unknown to Alpha Company, and how God intervened to protect us. It was as though God provided a shield around Alpha Company for protection.

If we are consciously doing God's will, we need not be afraid. In 2 Kings 6:16–17, the king of Aram sends a great army to surround the city where the prophet Elisha is staying, in order to seize him. When the servant of Elisha awakes in the morning, he sees the Aram army and is afraid. Elisha tells his servant not to be afraid because "those who are with us are more than those who are with them." Elisha then prays to the Lord to open his servant's eyes that he may see. "Then the Lord opened the servant's eyes, and he looked and saw the hills full of horses and chariots of fire all around Elisha."[2]

While in the field Alpha Company not only had approximately ten MAs set-out at all times, but we also employed two manned ambushes each night. Both emplacing MAs and conducting manned ambushes took men of courage. Unfortunately, sometimes one does not know how much physical courage he has until he is tested in a combat environment.

Alpha Company received a new infantry lieutenant while operating in the field. He was number one in his college ROTC class and seemed to be knowledgeable of infantry tactics. I assigned him a platoon leader position in one of Alpha Company's three infantry rifle platoons. Regrettably, after observing his platoon for a few weeks I noticed that his men were not performing at the level they previously had. Both my first sergeant and I talked with the men within his platoon and found that they thought the new lieutenant lacked courage. I already suspected the same; therefore, to confirm that the lieutenant lacked the courage to be an infantry officer, I told him that I wanted him to personally takeout the next ambush patrol. I told him that it was on a heavily used enemy trail, so I wanted an officer in charge of the ambush. The lieutenant turned pale and came up with every reason in the book as to why his platoon sergeant should take it out rather than himself. Although, he did not refuse to lead the ambush patrol, it was obvious to my first sergeant and me that he had no business being an infantry officer and leading men in combat.

To be effective in combat, leaders must not only be competent, but they must be respected by their men. Therefore, it is imperative for combat leaders to demonstrate both moral and physical courage. Because the lieutenant lacked physical courage, I requested that he be assigned to a noncombat unit and that the Army change his branch to a noncombat arms one. The lieutenant was reassigned to a rear area unit for the remainder of his tour and performed well.

The VC also had a practice of sneaking up to our night defensive positions and turning around the claymore mines we set out at night. On the night of September 26, we set out an MA along with our claymores and killed a VC trying to turn around one of our claymores.

On September 28, we located a tunnel that was exposed by the bulldozers and found a large cache of enemy ammunition. We found 170 rounds of 57mm recoilless and 17 rounds of 75mm recoilless anti-tank ammunition (See figure 7).

After we blew up the enemy ammunition, we stopped by one of our old night defensive positions where we had emplaced an MA. We discovered the ambush had killed two VC.

On October 1, we killed one VC by using an MA at an old night defensive position, and again on October 2, we had another mechanical ambush kill a VC at another old night laager position.

On October 8, the Battalion Scout platoon asked if we could show them how to use mechanical ambushes. I sent my best man, Sergeant Smith, for the job. The MA that Sergeant Smith set out as a demonstration killed three NVA and wounded another NVA, whom we took prisoner.

On October 13, we killed another VC using a mechanical ambush in an old night laager.

On October 19, we set up an MA on a trail that killed one NVA and wounded another two NVA, whom we took prisoner. Additionally, we found one RPG launcher with RPG anti-tank rockets, and three AK-47s (see figure 8). One of the prisoners said he was part of a nine-man squad that came from an NVA unit of approximately 100 soldiers only twenty minutes away. I maneuvered the company in the direction of the 100-man unit and emplaced another MA on a trail that we crossed. On October 21, it detonated and we found two dead NVA.

On October 24, we killed another NVA using a trail with a MA. A few days later, we received word that the NVA we had killed had been identified from the picture we sent back as a notorious assassin in the Saigon area.

I believe the phenomenal success and protection Alpha Company experienced was the result of Christ's divine intervention, and nothing less than a miracle. This experience of God's divine power deepened my faith in God's power and protection, as it did David when he fought Goliath. When he was only a boy, David had the courage to fight the Philistine's giant champion, Goliath, because he had previously experienced God's power and faithfulness when, as a shepherd, David killed a lion and a bear. David tells King Saul in 1 Samuel 17:37, "The Lord who delivered me from the paw of the lion and the paw of the bear will deliver me from the hand of this Philistine." [3]

Years later in life, as a Special Forces Officer, I would not have had the courage to do many of the things I did if I had not truly believed in Jesus Christ's loving faithfulness and power. When I look back at my past experiences, I clearly see how God compassionately nurtured my spiritual development and confidence in His overriding power as He did King David.

October 26, I received a message in the field that I was the father of a baby girl born October 24. Unfortunately I wouldn't be able to hold my little girl for another six months. Regardless, I was a very happy new dad.

CHAPTER 19

Alpha Company's Deactivation

The Lord has driven out before you great and powerful nations;
to this day no one has been able to withstand you. One of you
routs a thousand, because the Lord your God fights for you, just
as he promised. So be very careful to love the Lord your God.
Joshua 23:9-11[1]

ON NOVEMBER 2, I brought my company in out of the field for the last time. President Nixon's Vietnamization concept of turning over the fighting by US ground troops to the Vietnamese was halfway completed, and it was now time for the 2nd Battalion (Mechanized), 22nd Infantry to depart Vietnam. Instead of sending the entire battalion back to Hawaii, the unit's equipment was turned over to the Vietnamese, most of the troops were reassigned to other US units still operational within Vietnam, and only the battalion colors returned to Hawaii.

I do not know of another infantry company in the Vietnam Conflict that killed or captured as many enemy soldiers as Alpha Company without losing any of its own soldiers. I truly believe that God provided the men of Alpha Company with the wisdom to defeat the enemy, and that He protected them from harm. Therefore, in our closing troop formation, we thanked God for Alpha Company's success, and gave Him all the honor and glory.

Having made the above statement, I am not suggesting that units that lost men during combat were less faithful at doing Christ Jesus' will. During my first tour in Vietnam, I think we were doing God's will, yet I

123

lost three outstanding soldiers from my platoon in combat. I cannot judge what is in one's heart; however, I believe all three of the brave men who were killed in my platoon during my first tour accepted Jesus Christ as their Lord and Savior, and therefore they are in heaven.

Certainly, it is God who decides when a person leaves his life on earth. Those who believe Jesus is their Lord and Savior know that when they die, they will go to a better place than earth. Paul explains this in Philippians 1: 21–24: "For to me, to live is Christ and to die is gain. If I am to go on living in the body, this will mean fruitful labor for me. Yet what shall I choose? I do not know! I am torn between the two: I desire to depart and be with Christ, which is better by far; but it is more necessary for you that I remain in the body."[2] Simply stated, we have been created by God and for God. Although this sounds similar to a dictatorship, God is a loving and benevolent dictator.

One must understand that we who receive Jesus Christ as our Lord and Savior become children of God, and God loves us even more than our own parents do. It is God's pleasure to do what is best for each of His children, be it bringing a person home to Him in Heaven or allowing a person to continue to bring Him glory and honor here on earth. Acts 7:54–60 tells us that God allowed Stephen to be stoned to death early in his life because of his testimony about Jesus. His death has been an example to the world of true martyrdom in contrast to those false religions that would erroneously claim that a martyr is one who is killed, while killing innocent civilians.[3] All but one of Jesus' apostles were also killed for being obedient to God and witnessing to others that Jesus Christ is the Messiah. Out of love for us, Jesus allowed himself to be tortured and killed, to pay for our sins so that we can be in heaven with Him.

We should honor those who have paid the ultimate sacrifice so that others may have freedom to worship and know Jesus. Because knowing and believing in Jesus Christ has eternal consequences, there is no greater cause to risk one's life for than for religious freedom. In John 15:12, Jesus states, "Greater love has no one than this, that he lay down his life for his friends."[4] Although Jesus is referring to His own sacrificial death for us, it is true for all mankind.

In light of this, one cannot claim that it is necessarily any particular person's disobedience or the lack of faith in God that results in a tragedy. We obviously do not know the overall plans of God. However, we can take comfort in knowing that those who are children of God through Jesus Christ and who have died in combat are with Jesus in Heaven. Jesus tells us in John 3:16, "For God so loved the world that he gave his one and only Son, that whoever believes in him shall not perish but have eternal life."[5] Additionally, Paul tells us in Ephesians 2:4–10", "But because of his great love for us, God, who is rich in mercy, made us alive with Christ even when we were dead in transgressions—it is by grace you have been saved. And God raised us up with Christ and seated us with him in the heavenly realms in Christ Jesus, in order that in the coming ages he might show the incomparable riches of his grace, expressed in his kindness to us in Christ Jesus. For it is by grace you have been saved, through faith—and this not from yourselves, it is the gift of God—not by works, so that no one can boast. For we are God's workmanship, created in Christ Jesus to do good works, which God prepared in advance for us to do."[6]

After the deactivation of Alpha Company, the members of the company fell into two groups. If a soldier had less than two months remaining on his tour he was sent home early. Those who had more than two months were reassigned to other US units within Vietnam. I was reassigned to the 1st Battalion (Mechanized), 5th Infantry of the 25th Division.

Apparently, Alpha Company's success in the field and high morale was well known within the 25th Infantry Division. I was not aware of Alpha Company's reputation until I arrived at the 1-5 (Mech) and I was introduced to a 25th Infantry Division chaplain, who was visiting the battalion. When he heard my name, he said that he had heard about my company at a 25th Infantry Division chaplain's conference held in Saigon. He said another chaplain within the Division addressed the conference and said that he visited most of the units within the 25th Infantry Division and found that Alpha Company's morale was extremely high and that the troop's attitude towards America's mission was more positive than in most units.

It is a humbling experience to be entrusted with the lives of men in combat. It is a tremendous responsibility and one that I did not take lightly. Understanding that true wisdom and protection comes from God, I stayed in continuous contact with our Heavenly Father through Jesus Christ, and asked Him for wisdom and protection for Alpha Company. The Lord knows the motives of what is in men's hearts; consequently, He provided the men of Alpha Company with wisdom to achieve incredible success.

God blessed Alpha Company with extremely competent and intelligent soldiers; I was able to use the *participating leadership style,* or what the business community calls *participatory management,* when determining what to do and how to do it. Although I made the final decision, asking my subordinates for information and recommendations provided Alpha Company with valuable initiatives that led to remarkable successes not experienced by other units. For example using a helicopter Gatling gun on an APC rather than the standard .50 cal. machine gun was an innovation from one of my troops (See figure 9). Additionally, when troops participated in decisions, they tended to support the final decisions.

Lieutenant Colonel Vail, the 2-22 (Mech) commander, realized the importance of the participating leadership style used within Alpha Company in Keith Nolan's book, *Into Cambodia: Spring Campaign, Summer Offensive 1970*: "Vail was happy to welcome aboard Captain Jim Schmidt, a quiet, mature, competent veteran of a previous tour. This tall, blond-haired captain won his grunts' respect by being completely involved with them, asking their opinions and explaining why he did what he did, so Alpha Company ... continued to be the company Vail could always count on to come through."[7]

In addition to asking for my men's opinions, I explained to them why I did what I did. Explaining the reason for specific operations included providing the men with the purpose of our overall involvement in Vietnam. The men knew that they were fighting to provide the South Vietnamese with the freedom to know and worship Jesus Christ; this had a powerful positive impact on their attitude towards the mission.

Sometimes our leaders forget that when we go to war, we not only ask our men to risk their lives, but also require them to kill other humans. It is imperative that our objective for going to war is a righteous one, approved by God, and that our soldiers know and believe this. If infantry soldiers know the purpose and importance of their mission, which is to find and eliminate the enemy in order to protect the innocent, then their motive for killing the enemy becomes one of duty, not hatred. It is my opinion that hatred and revenge are not necessary, and have no place in combat. There is a vast difference between the lasting effects on a soldier for killing out of hate and for killing to defend the innocent.

Similarly, because my lieutenants and sergeants supported the goal of defeating the communists in order to allow the Vietnamese the freedom to know Jesus Christ, I was able to employ the delegating leadership style as well. This allowed me to delegate smaller AOs within Alpha Company's larger AO to the platoons, thereby, increasing the area that we could effectively control.[8]

CHAPTER 20

Special Task Force

No one will be able to stand up against you all the days of your life. As I was with Moses, so I will be with you; I will never leave you nor forsake you.
Joshua 1:5[1]

THE BATTALION COMMANDER OF 1-5 (Mech) was an excellent commander and a Rhodes Scholar, but his battalion had not killed or captured hardly any NVA/VC. While at the same time the battalion was continually losing men to booby traps, mines, ambushes, and sniper fire.

When I first arrived to the 1-5 (Mech) I was assigned the position of Assistant Operations Officer (Asst. S3) and was heavily involved in planning and directing the day-to-day combat operations. I told the battalion commander about the success my company had with the use of mechanical ambushes and asked if they had used them. He said the scout platoon started to use them, but their platoon sergeant was killed while setting a mechanical ambush out, and after that no other unit within his battalion had attempted to use them. I told him that mechanical ambushes were extremely safe as long as one followed the correct steps while emplacing them. The battalion commander asked if I would give a class to the scout platoon on mechanical ambushes, and of course, I said yes.

The scout platoon was initially hesitant to have anything to do with mechanical ambushes; however, after I gave them a class and demonstration, they became more receptive. After the class, the Battalion Commander told me to take command of a small task force consisting of the Scout Platoon and Flame Platoon and show them how to employ the mechanical ambush in the field. He asked if I wanted anything else and I told him I would like one 81mm mortar section that could fire immediately into the area of any mechanical ambush we employed. He attached a mechanized 81mm mortar section to the task force and assigned to my small seven-APC task force our own restricted AO. The AO was southeast of Saigon, between Phu My and the coast.

The leaders of the Scout Platoon and Flame Platoon were both extremely competent lieutenants and their platoons were well trained. We moved into our AO on December 12, 1970, and I started emplacing MAs on the trails in the AO. However, because the AO wasn't astride any major NVA infiltration route, we didn't have any results from the ambushes set up on trails. I assumed we were being kept under observation by local VC and they were staying off the trails in the area. The only activity we encountered was some harassing fire from the wood line during one of the nights.

As I had done when I commanded my company, I moved the task force's laager every one or two days. Assuming the local VC were following us, I emplaced an MA within the perimeter of a laager site as we were evacuating it. We moved to another laager only a few kilometers away. I had the 81mm mortar section lay their mortar on the old site and told them to have a man watch in the direction of the site for black smoke. It was only about an hour later that we heard the explosion and saw the black smoke rising from the old site. I immediately requested permission to fire the 81mm mortar and sent two of the Scout Platoon squads mounted on their armored personnel carriers to sweep back through the site.

The Battalion Commander was airborne with his helicopter at the time. He picked me up so we could fly over the area. By the time we arrived over the old site, the two APCs from the Scout Platoon were already there. The men from the platoon were waving two AK-47s in the air and we could see two dead VC. Apparently there were three VC who came to the site, because the following day, a VC soldier went to the village of Phu My and surrendered. He said that his two comrades were killed by a large US explosion and that he had enough of the war.

The Battalion Commander was so pleased with the success of my small task force that he wanted to give me one of his line companies to command. He asked the battalion S3 how much *command time* I already had in Vietnam and the S3 told him six months. The battalion already had six or seven infantry captains who didn't have any combat command

and they were begging for a chance to command an infantry company in combat. Additionally, the three current company commanders had only been in command for a little over a month; therefore, the Battalion Commander didn't pursue the issue any further. The decision was in God's hands; therefore, I was content to do my best in whatever job I was given.

CHAPTER 21

Teaching Mechanical Ambushes

Now to Him who is able to do far more abundantly beyond all that
we ask or think, according to the power that works within us.
Ephesians 3:20[1]

DECEMBER 29, 1970 I went on a two week Rest and Recreation (R&R) in Hawaii with my wife Joyce. We had a fantastic time and it was certainly hard to return to Vietnam.

After I returned from R&R, the Battalion Commander assigned me to the position of Battalion S4 (Logistics Officer). This allowed me to be off line, but because we would be standing down the battalion soon, it would become one of the most important and hardest jobs in the battalion.

The fact that most of the NVA/VC now being killed by ground forces were killed from mechanical ambushes finally caught the attention of II Field Force, Vietnam (II FFV) headquarters. Although I was now a battalion S4 in the 1-5 (Mech), because of the astounding success that Alpha Company, 2-22 (Mech) had attained when I commanded it, I was tasked to teach a class to some of the senior officers within the II FFV headquarters on MAs.

On January 12, 1971, I gave a two-hour class and demonstration out in the field to Major General Wagstaff and Brigadier General Roberts on MAs. General Wagstaff was so impressed with the concept and class that he told me he was going to recommend Lieutenant General Davidson, the II FFV Commander to attend my class.

I never did give General Davidson a class, but II FFV tasked me to give a class on MAs on January 20 to approximately forty Vietnamese officers from the 5th ARVN Cavalry Brigade before they conducted an incursion into Cambodia. I presented the class to the ARVN using a Vietnamese interpreter, and it went extremely well. Because there was always the danger of ARVN units being infiltrated with VC spies, and to protect US troops, I didn't teach the ARVN the classified techniques we used to keep the NVA/VC from stealing our MA claymores if they were discovered.

On February 4, 1971, Major General Wagstaff wanted me to teach all the Vietnamese forces in Binh Doung Province on how to use MAs. I believed the Vietnamese needed to know how to employ mechanical ambushes in order to win the war; I would have liked to teach them. However, the Battalion Commander didn't want to lose his S4 at this critical time.

Because the Battalion Commander complained so much when he found out that General Wagstaff wanted me to personally teach the ARVN, the Brigade Commander told General Wagstaff that I had already trained the Brigade Training School on the use of mechanical ambushes, and asked if the school could teach the ARVN instead of me. Additionally, the Brigade Commander told General Wagstaff that I was now the Battalion S4, and with the upcoming stand down of the Battalion, I wouldn't have time to teach the ARVN and accomplish the mission of turning in the Battalion's weapons and equipment.

A few days later, General Wagstaff visited the Battalion forward area and asked the Battalion Commander, "What did you do with Schmidt?" The Battalion Commander just laughed because he was aware that the General already knew I was the S4. The General told my commander that he didn't realize that I had a new assignment prior to making the request for me to teach the Vietnamese forces in Binh Doung Province.

I respected Major General Wagstaff for his interest in what tactics were being used in the field at company level. He was the only general I met who visited any of my units in the field and asked for my opinion.

I would have liked to have trained more ARVN on the use of the mechanical ambush. However, I hope those who did receive the training were able to spread it throughout South Vietnam's military. It is likely that the mechanical ambush contributed to the success South Vietnam's military experienced in their counterinsurgency struggle prior to North Vietnam's 1975 invasion. Sadly, the mechanical ambush, while a great weapon to use against guerrilla fighters, is not very effective against large conventional infantry and armor units conducting a full scale attack. Against these units they needed US airpower.

Although I never gave any more classes to the ARVN, I did continue to provide classes on mechanical ambushes to various other US units within our area until I departed Vietnam in May of 1971. These classes not only taught the mechanics of the actual construction of the MA, but also included the tactical and operational concepts for their emplacement.

After leaving Vietnam in May of 1971, I taught the mechanical ambush only to United States Special Forces units and infantry units that I was assigned to (see figure 10). Returning from Vietnam I was assigned to the Army Infantry School at Fort Benning to attend the Infantry Advance Course. Because the course was not to start for two weeks the Tactics Committee tasked me to enter some of the more advanced techniques into the military's classified Booby Traps manual. Consequently, it would behoove all infantry officers to obtain a copy and study its contents.

CHAPTER 22

Part II Reflections

*The Lord said to Gideon, 'The people who are with you are too
many for Me to give Midian into their hands, for Israel would
become boastful, saying, My own power has delivered me.'*
Judges 7:2[1]

To VALIDATE THE IMPORTANCE of finding God's purpose for your life and
then living it, I started Part II of this book with information on how I came
to make the military my career. The decision to surrender my life to Jesus
Christ resulted in God blessing my company in Vietnam; however, I can
assure the reader that Vietnam was only the beginning of a life full of joy
and true success (in God's eyes) beyond my wildest dreams.

The intent of this book is not only to provide a warning about the
adverse consequences of disobedience to God, but also to present evidence
of God's blessings on those who obey Him and follow His will. I have
provided this evidence by providing a genuine account of the day–by–day
combat operations of the infantry company I commanded in Vietnam.
As God blessed Israel, as stated in the above verse from Judges 7:2, God
also graciously provided Alpha Company with the wisdom to employ
tactics that resulted in protection and an extraordinary victory over its
adversary.

It was God who provided Alpha Company with the wisdom to establish
an automated battlefield by studying the habits and patterns of the enemy,
then systematically employing mechanical ambushes. The chronological

events of Alpha Company from May to December of 1970 reveal how the use of a few mechanical ambushes on trails evolved into a highly sophisticated and effective automated battlefield.

God truly blessed Alpha Company with success and protection. Alpha Company killed or captured approximately sixty NVA/VC soldiers while never losing any of their own men. This was a success not experienced by many (if any) other infantry companies in the Vietnam War.

A commander must always strive to accomplish the mission with minimal losses. They should treat each man as if he were his own son or brother. Sun Tzu said, "So a commander who advances not for glory, withdraws not to evade guilt, and cares for only the people's security along with the lord's interests is the country's treasure."[2]

Part II described how God used me to train South Vietnamese and other American troops in many of the effective techniques that Alpha Company developed. The use of the mechanical ambush was extremely effective as a counter guerrilla weapon, and probably contributed to South Vietnam's success in their counterinsurgency fight after America withdrew from Vietnam. However, it had little value against a conventional attack that consisted of large infantry and armor units.

Technology is always advancing; therefore, tactics should take advantage of it. In Vietnam, I tried to develop an automated battlefield that could keep my men out of harm's way whenever possible while still accomplishing the counter guerrilla mission. I envision that more and more unmanned weapon systems will be used in future wars. The current use of drones against al Qaeda and the use of improved anti-personnel landmines such as the XM-7 Spider Networked Munitions in Afghanistan are two good examples. It is God who provides innovation for developing new systems and wisdom to effectively use them. We must do as Jesus tells us in Matthew 6:33: "seek first his kingdom and his righteousness, and all these things will be given to you as well."[3]

Therefore, even though the effective tactics and techniques identified in this book may not all work in future conflicts, the wisdom, insight, and intuition necessary to successfully accomplish future missions will always be available to those who follow the will of God and call upon the Lord Jesus Christ. This is the real lesson to be learned from this book.

In light of the challenges our military will face in future wars, it is imperative for our leaders to trust in, pray to, and give thanks to the Lord for all things. 1 Thessalonians 5:17-18 states, "Be joyful always; pray continually; give thanks in all circumstances, for this is God's will for you in Christ Jesus."[4] Similarly, it is written in Philippians 4:6, "Do not be anxious about anything, but in everything, by prayer and petition, with thanksgiving, present your requests to God,"[5]

However, it is important for America to understand, as individuals, and as a nation, what is written in James 5:16: "The prayer of a righteous man is powerful and effective."[6] If we expect God to answer our prayers, we must return to God. The important and encouraging lesson from this verse is that each one of us can individually have a powerful effect on our nation through prayer, depending on our own righteousness. This verse also stresses the importance of electing people who are God fearing and obedient to Him to positions of authority within our government.

History shows that a nation's disobedience to God can result in its downfall. God loves his people; as a father disciplines his child, God will chastise us for our own good. However, when we are disciplined, we should learn from our mistake and repent. Hebrews 12:10–11, reminds us, "Our fathers disciplined us for a little while as they thought best; but God disciplines us for our good, that we may share in his holiness. No discipline seems pleasant at the time, but painful. Later on, however, it produces a harvest of righteousness and peace for those who have been trained by it."[7]

Where Do We Go from Here?

For God did not give us a spirit of timidity, but a
spirit of power, of love and of self-discipline.
2 Timothy 1:7[1]

AS ONE WHO HAS been a soldier almost all my life so that the citizens of the United States and other nations can have the freedom to know Jesus Christ, it saddens me to see the citizens of Vietnam being denied this important freedom. However, it saddens me even more to see the increasing number of Americans who have the freedom to read the Holy Bible, but are too busy with the pleasures of the world to read it. Failure to know what is written in the Holy Bible has eternal consequences. Additionally, as shown in this book, failure to be obedient to God not only has adverse consequences for the nation in war, but also for all aspects of life. God's discipline is not limited to war, but includes natural disasters, crime, illegal drugs, plagues such as AIDs, economic breakdowns, etc.

One can clearly see that there is not only a battle to be fought for freedom of religion around the world, but also a spiritual battle taking place within the United States. The Bible tells us that the sword of the Spirit to fight this battle against evil is *the word of God*.[2]

At no other time in America's history has the government so blatantly left God out of the decision-making process as it does now. Decisions made by our nation's military and civilian leadership pertaining to moral issues, such as allowing homosexuals in the military and claiming it is the right thing to do when the Bible clearly identifies it as a sin, is an indication that they either do not know what is written in the Bible, do not believe it is the word of God, or do not believe God's position is important.

It is astonishing that I had not once heard a congressman quote what the Bible says about homosexuality during the hearings on the issue of allowing gays in the military. Likewise, I never heard anyone from the media ever ask the President or a congressman if they knew what the Bible says about homosexuality or even if they believe the Bible is the word of God.

The Bible clearly states that homosexuality is a sin in Romans 1:26–28, "Because of this, God gave them over to shameful lusts. Even their women exchanged natural relations for unnatural ones. In the same way the men also abandoned natural relations with women and were inflamed with lust for one another. Men committed indecent acts with other men, and received in themselves the due penalty for their perversion."[3]

In the above verse St. Paul writes that because many of the citizens in Rome were not worshiping the one true God, He gave them over to homosexuality. Therefore, one must ask the question: is the current increase of homosexuals and the health problems associated with it also due to the world turning away from God?

Certainly, homosexuality is not the only sin the United States is being disciplined for. The following verse provides only a small sample of some of the sins identified in 1 Corinthians 6:9-10: "Do you not know that the wicked will not inherit the kingdom of God? Do not be deceived: Neither the sexually immoral nor idolaters nor adulterers nor male prostitutes nor homosexual offenders nor thieves nor the greedy nor drunkards nor slanderers nor swindlers will inherit the kingdom of God."[4]

As with any addiction, the addict must first admit that he has a problem. Surely, we do not do any favors to individuals addicted to homosexuality, fornication, drugs, alcohol, and other sins identified in the Bible by telling them that these things are not sins. We should love the sinner, but hate the sin. If we love them we should tell them what God says about the sin and warn them of the consequences. This is not being judgmental, but only stating the word of God which is the Holy Bible.

In an effort to obtain acceptability, homosexual advocate groups are attempting to bamboozle society into not only believing that homosexuality is not a sin, but also that the addiction cannot be changed. According to the Bible and the latest research on the ability to change homosexuality, both positions are false. Contrary to the American Psychological Association's

(APA) flippant and scientifically unsupported opinion that, "homosexual orientation cannot be changed," current scientific research actually shows that the majority of homosexual Christians that truly want to change are able to change their sexual orientation.[5]

Comparing the Chairman of the Joint Chiefs of Staff, Admiral Mullins' testimony to Congress in 2011 against George Washington's unpublished letter which he considered sending to Congress in 1789 shows how much our nation's current leaders' obedience to what is written in the Holy Bible has fallen since the United States' beginning. In 2011, Mullins stated to Congress, "I believed allowing homosexuals into the military is the right thing to do," while George Washington's 1789 unpublished letter to Congress said, "The blessed Religion revealed in the Word of God will remain an eternal and awful monument to prove that the best institutions may be abused by human depravity; and that they may even, in some instances be made subservient to the vilest of purpose."[6]

It should be noted that Congress and President Obama claim homosexual conduct is an acceptable lifestyle and demand that American soldiers and sailors respect those blatantly performing homosexual acts. This has, for the first time in the history of the United States, told the entire world that the government of the United States does not believe the Holy Bible is the word of God. As the world's most influential country, their action has caused immense harm to the world. I have never seen such unashamed disobedience to God from American government officials. Isaiah 5:20 provides the following warning for those responsible: "Woe to those who call evil good and good evil, who put darkness for light and light for darkness, who put bitter for sweet and sweet for bitter."[7]

Because victory in war rests with the Lord, God must not be left out of the decision to go to war, and if war is declared, God's guidance and protection must be sought. It is, therefore, imperative for the United States to elect Godly civilian leaders who will pray to our Father in Heaven through Jesus Christ for wisdom to make the right decision when considering going to war. If the decision is to send our men and women into battle, then it is equally important to appoint Godly military individuals to lead them.

Since God is in control of all things, combat leaders must not only be competent in the art of war, but they must know what is written in the Holy Bible, believe it is the word of God and be obedient to it. America's leaders must understand the following verse from Psalm 81:13–14: "O that my people would listen to me, that Israel would walk in my ways!

Then I would quickly subdue their enemies, and turn my hand against their foes."[8]

When Abraham Lincoln was president, he was given a Bible as a gift. When he received the Holy Bible he said, "In regard to this Great Book, I have but to say. It is the best gift God has given to men. All the good the Savior gave to the world was communicated through this Book. But for it we could not know right from wrong."[9]

Not knowing what is written in the Bible is to fight the battle without a weapon. Although I believe most Americans still believe the Bible is the word of God, I think only a few actually have read and studied it to know what the Bible says about various important issues. Many Americans who profess to be Christians and have the freedom to read and learn what is written in the Bible seem to be too preoccupied with making money and pleasing themselves to want to know God and learn what pleases Him. Can we as a nation, therefore, expect God's blessings?

The Lord allowed my company to achieve victory; however, He denied victory to the nation. I truly believe the Holy Bible is God's word and God has demonstrated to me that He is faithful to what is written in the Bible. For over two hundred years our nation has considered the Holy Bible the word of God and our moral compass. Unfortunately, since the sixties, much of our nation has lost its moral compass, and if the United States expects to be blessed by God, its people must return to the Holy Bible. It is written in Joshua 1:8, "Do not let this Book of the Law depart from your mouth; meditate on it day and night, so that you may be careful to do everything written in it. Then you will be prosperous and successful."[10]

Although Christians have victory over death through Jesus Christ, God calls us to bring others to Him. The following paragraphs call Christians to action.

> You are the light of the world. A city on a hill cannot be hidden. Neither do people light a lamp and put it under a bowl. Instead they put it on its stand, and it gives light to everyone in the house. In the same way, let your light shine before men, that they may see your good deeds and praise your Father in heaven.
>
> Matthew 5:14–16[11]

God blessed the United States and it became the light of the world, "A city on a hill." However, as the United States continues to fall away from Christ, its light is becoming dimmer. In fact instead of America's deeds bringing praise to our Father in heaven, they are bringing dishonor. The defeat in Vietnam should have been a wake-up call to America and a warning that there are consequences for disobedience to God.

The defeat is also a warning to Christians about the consequences of Christians failing to take a more active role in America's government, policies, and the education of our youth. Jesus tells us above in Matthew 5:14 that Christians are the light of the world and we should not put our light under a bowl, but rather let it give light to everyone.

Certainly, we who believe that Jesus is our Lord and Savior will receive eternal life; however, Christians are also called to bring glory and honor to God. Each of us has been given specific gifts to accomplish His will. Because God loves us, He also disciplines us Christians when we fail to do His will.

It is important to note that the verse quoted below does not guarantee that God works good for all that call themselves Christians; he only does for those who love God and who have been called according to God's purpose.

> And we know that in all things God works for the good of those who love him, who have been called according to his purpose.
> Romans 8:28[12]

This verse is certainly comforting, but how does a Christian know that he loves God enough to qualify as one of the people in which the above verse applies? Jesus' answer to this question is provided in John 14:23–24, "If anyone loves me, he will obey my teaching. My Father will love him, and we will come to him and make our home with him. He who does not love me will not obey my teaching. These words you hear are not my own; they belong to the Father who sent me."[13] Since Jesus requires us to obey His teachings, we must find out what they are.

> For you were once darkness, but now you are light in the Lord. Live as children of light (for the fruit of the light consists in all goodness, righteousness and truth) and *find out what pleases the Lord* ...
> Ephesians 5:8–10[14]

The only place we can find Jesus' teaching is from the New Testament of the Holy Bible; therefore, those who truly love God should have a desire to read and study the Bible.

It is my experience that when I ask people within the United States what God's position is on current issues such as homosexuality, fornication (sex outside of marriage), drunkenness, abortion, etc., many either do not know or do not care. Basing our values and morals on our own sinful human nature and shallow human understanding rather than finding out what the Lord desires is a major reason for our nation's decline. The Bible tells us in Proverbs 3:5, "Trust in the Lord with all your heart and lean not on your own understanding."[15]

Although I think most citizens of the United States are primarily Christian and believe the Bible is the word of God, most Americans give reading and studying it a low priority.

Additionally, there are a number of people who claim to be Christian and who know what is written in the Bible, but these people lack a strong enough faith to believe that the whole Bible is the word of God. These people tend to only believe those parts of the Bible that satisfy their own human desires and limited human reasoning. Saint Paul's letter to Timothy clearly states, "All Scripture is God-breathed and is useful for teaching, rebuking, correcting and training in righteousness, so that the man of God may be thoroughly equipped for every good work." [16]

Saint Paul explains why some do not believe all that he says in the New Testament is inspired by God in a letter to the Christian church of Corinth. Paul writes, "We have not received the spirit of the world but the Spirit who is from God, that we may understand what God has freely given us. That is what we speak, not in words taught us by human wisdom, but in words taught by the Spirit, expressing spiritual truths in spiritual words. The man without the Spirit does not accept the things that come from the Spirit of God, for they are foolishness to him, and he cannot understand them, because they are spiritually discerned. The spiritual man makes judgments about all things, but he himself is not subject to any man's judgment: 'For who has known the mind of the Lord that he may instruct him?' But we have the mind of Christ." [17]

Saint Paul also provided us the following prophetic warning in 2 Timothy 4:3: "For the time will come when men will not put up with sound doctrine. Instead, to suit their own desires, they will gather around them a great number of teachers to say what their itching ears want to hear."[18]

I would remind those who claim the commands given within the New Testament no longer apply today and call those who do "dinosaurs" that Hebrews 13:8 states, "Jesus Christ is the same yesterday and today and forever."[19] Jesus Christ said in Matthew 5:18, "I tell you the truth, until heaven and earth disappear, not the smallest letter, not the least stroke of a pen, will by any means disappear from the Law until everything is accomplished."[20]

In light of the fact that Jesus has not changed, America needs to revisit our current morals and positions on issues that the Bible clearly identifies as sin, such as fornication, adultery, homosexuality, hard-core pornography (including child pornography), greed, and even killing God-created children developing in the womb. Christians must take an active role in changing the current laws of America that allow the entertainment, media, and government to promote these immoral acts.

Many within the Christian clergy need to stop worrying about upsetting some within their congregations and become more vocal about the moral issues that are facing the United States. As stated above, most people who profess to be Christian do not read the Bible on their own; consequently, they do not know what is written in it. It is, therefore, imperative that the clergy teach their followers exactly what is written in the Holy Bible.

The Vietnam War was used in this book to provide evidence that victory rests with the Lord. This was done by first showing that the war would have been winnable if the right tactics had been used. Specific flawed tactics were discovered to have caused unacceptably high US casualties, causing America to lose its resolve. It was argued that it was God's intervention that denied US senior leaders the wisdom to change these obvious flawed tactics. The reason suggested for God denying victory to the US was the nation's decaying morals. Conversely, the miraculous success and protection of Alpha Company was attributed to God's power and His blessing of those who surrender their lives to Christ Jesus.

This book serves as a testament to the validity of the Holy Bible. It reminds the reader that a nation's disobedience results in God's punishment, while obedience brings God's blessing. Therefore, it calls on all Christians to learn the Holy Bible and elect God-fearing individuals to govern our nation who have the same knowledge of the Bible and faith in Jesus Christ as our nation's past great leaders such as Washington and Lincoln.

Notes

Introduction

1. Proverbs 21:31, *The Holy Bible (NIV)*.
2. Abraham Lincoln, quoted in K. McDowell Beliles, *America's Providential History*, 225-26.
3. David W. Balsiger, Joette Whims, Melody Hunskor, *The Incredible Power of Prayer* (Wheaton, Illinois: Tyndale House, 1998), 285.
4. Romans 8:24, *The Holy Bible (NIV)*.
5. Mark 8:35, *The Holy Bible (NIV)*.
6. Ephesians 2:8–9, *The Holy Bible (NIV)*.
7. Luke 6:22–23, *The Holy Bible, (NIV)*.

Part I
Chapter 1

1. Psalm 81:13–14, *The Holy Bible (NIV)*.
2. Proverbs 21:31, *The Holy Bible (NIV)*.
3. Leviticus 26:17–18, *The Holy Bible (NRSV)*.
4. Harry G. Summers, Jr., *On Strategy: The Vietnam War in Context* (Strategic Studies Institute U.S. Army War College, 1981), 1.

Chapter 2

1. Hebrew 11:30, *The Holy Bible (NIV)*.
2. Matthew 5:43–45, *The Holy Bible (NIV)*.

3. R.M. Shoemaker, General, US Army, "Dealing with a Just War" (Insert to letter, Headquarters, US Army Forces Command, January 29, 1982).
4. Ibid.
5. James E. Schmidt, Lieutenant Colonel, US Army Special Forces, "Hit Drug Lords' Center of Gravity," *Army Magazine*, July 1992, 18–23.
6. Matthew 8:10, *The Holy Bible, (NIV)*.
7. Luke 3:14, *The Holy Bible, (NIV)*.
8. Peter A. Lillback, *George Washington's Sacred Fire* (Providence: Forum Press, 2006), 574–-575.
9. 1 Samuel 17:49–52, *The Holy Bible, (NIV)*.
10. Carl von Clausewitz, *On War*, edited and translated by Michael Howard and Peter Paret with Introductory Essays by Peter Paret, Michael Howard, and Bernard Brodie and a Commentary by Bernard Brodie (Princeton: Princeton UP, 1976), III:3, 185.
11. James 1:5, *The Holy Bible (NIV)*. 1 Kings 3:12, *The Holy Bible (NIV)*.
12. 1 Kings 3:12, *The Holy Bible (NIV)*.
13. Robert S. McNamara, *In Retrospect: the Tragedy and Lessons of Vietnam* (New York: Times Books, 1995), 313.

Chapter 3

1. Proverbs 9:10. *The Holy Bible (NIV)*.
2. Department of the Army, "The Principles of War," *Operations Manual 100-5*, B-1.
3. Department of the Army, *Counterinsurgency Field Manual 3-24*, June 2006, 1–16.

Chapter 4

1. Dave Richard Palmer, Brigadier General., U.S.A, *Summons of the Trumpet: US-Vietnam in Perspective* (San Rafael, California: Presidio, 1978), 75.
2. Department of Defense, *Joint Publication 1-02*.
3. Clausewitz, *On War*, VIII:4, 595–596.
4. Richard Nixon, *The Real War* (Warner Books Inc., 1980), 307.
5. Clausewitz, *On War*, VIII: 4, 595–596.

6. Lewis Sorley, *A Better War* (Harcourt: 1999), 29.

Chapter 5

1. Proverbs 1:29–32. *The Holy Bible, (NIV)*.
2. Proverbs 15:22. *The Holy Bible, (NIV)*.
3. Harold G. Moore and Joseph L. Galloway, *We are Solders Still: A Journey Back to the Battlefields of Vietnam* (HarperCollins, 2008), 5 13.
4. Ibid., 122–123.
5. Sorley, *A Better War*, 184.
6. Ibid., 140.
7. George C. Wilson, *Mud Soldiers: Life Inside the New American Army* (New York: Scribner, 1989), 38–39.
8. Sun Tzu, *The Art of War* translated and edited by J.H. Huang (New York: HarperCollins, 2008), 67.
9. Ibid., 40–41.
10. David Maraniss, *They Marched into Sunlight: War and Peace, Vietnam and America, October 1967* (S&S, 2004), 217.
11. Ibid., 314 and 341–342.
12. Ibid., 260–261.

Chapter 6

1. Harold G. Moore and Joseph L. Galloway, *We Are Soldiers Still: A Journey Back to the Battlefields of Vietnam* (New York: HarperCollins, 2009), 122–123.
2. Maraniss, *They Marched into Sunlight: War and Peace, Vietnam and America, October 1967*, 217.
3. Moore and Galloway, *We Are Soldiers Still: A Journey Back to the Battlefields of Vietnam*, 122.
4. Ibid., 123.
5. Wilson, *Mud Soldiers: Life inside the new American Army*, 38–39.
6. John S. Bowman, *The Vietnam War: An Almanac* (Bison, 1985), 167.
7. Ibid., 170.
8. Ibid., 171.
9. Ibid.,172.
10. Ibid., 173.
11. Ibid., 173.

12. Ibid., 174.
13. Ibid., 174.
14. Ibid., 174.
15. Ibid., 174.
16. Ibid., 180.
17. Ibid., 189.
18. Ibid., 198.
19. Sorley, *A Better War*, 36.
20. Bowman, *The Vietnam War: An Almanac*, 235.
21. Ibid., 241.
22. Ibid., 250.
23. Ibid., 250.

Chapter 7

1. Sun Tzu, *The Art of War*, translated and with an introduction by Samuel B. Griffith (OUP, 1963), 43.
2. Department of the Army, F*ield Manual 6-20, p. D-5.*
3. Ibid., D-4.
4. John E. O'Neill and Jerome R. Corsi, Ph.D., *Unfit for Command* (Regnery, 2004), 53.
5. Sun Tzu, *The Art of War*, 71.

Chapter 8

1. Lewis Sorley, *A Better War*, 374.
2. Nixon, *The Real War*, 119.

Chapter 9

1. 2 Chronicles 7:14, *The Holy Bible*, (NIV).
2. Proverbs 21:31, *The Holy Bible*, (NIV).
3. Sun Tzu, *The Art of War*, 41.

Part II
Chapter 10

1. General MacArthur, "Farewell Speech to Congress."(April 19, 1951).
2. Charles Stanley, *Success God's Way* (Thomas Nelson, 2000).
3. Rick Warren, *The Purpose Driven Life*, (Zondervan, 2002)
4. Ephesians 2:8–10, *The Holy Bible (NASB)*.

5. United Nations General Assembly, "The Universal Declaration of Human Rights" (December 10, 1948).
6. Mark 8:38, *The Holy Bible (NIV)*.
7. Matthew 25:14–30, *The Holy Bible (NRSV)*.
8. Philippians 4:13, *The Holy Bible (NASB)*.

Chapter 11

1. Proverbs 1:33, *The Holy Bible, (NIV)*.
2. Sun Tzu, *The Art of War*, 57.

Chapter 12

1. Psalm 23:1–4, *The Holy Bible (NIV)*.
2. Keith William Nolan, *Into Cambodia: Spring Campaign, Summer Offensive, 1970* (Presidio, 1990), 296.
3. Sun Tzu, *The Art of War*, 57.
4. Ibid., 74.
5. Psalms 91:14, *The Holy Bible (NIV)*.

Chapter 13

1. Matthew 6:33, *The Holy Bible (NIV)*.

Chapter 14

1. Proverbs 2:6–8, *The Holy Bible, (NIV)*.
2. Clausewitz, *On War*, VI:1, 358.
3. Sun Tzu, *The Art of War*, 63.
4. Sun Tzu, *The Art of War*, 43.

Chapter 15

1. Psalm 118:6, *The Holy Bible (NIV)*.
2. Department of the Army, "Military Leadership," *Field Manual 22-100*, 1.
3. Psalm 115:9, *The Holy Bible (NIV)*.

Chapter 16

1. Joshua 1:7, *The Holy Bible (NIV)*.
2. James 4:2–3, *The Holy Bible (NIV)*.
3. Sun Tzu, *The Art of War*, 40–41.

Chapter 17

1. Psalms 91:1–5, *The Holy Bible (NIV)*.
2. Maraniss, *They Marched into Sunlight: War and Peace, Vietnam and America, October 1967*, 410.

Chapter 18

1. 2 Chronicles 20:15, *The Holy Bible (NIV)*.
2. 1 Kings 6:16–17, *The Holy Bible, (NIV)*.
3. 1 Samuel 17:37, *The Holy Bible (NIV)*.

Chapter 19

1. Joshua 23:9–11, *The Holy Bible, (NIV)*.
2. Philippians 1:21–24, *The Holy Bible, (NIV)*.
3. Acts 7:54–60, *The Holy Bible (NIV)*.
4. John 15:13, *The Holy Bible (NIV)*.
5. John 3:16, *The Holy Bible (NIV)*.
6. Ephesians 2:4–10, *The Holy Bible (NIV)*.
7. Nolan, *Into Cambodia: Spring Campaign, Summer Offensive, 1970*, 407.
8. Department of the Army, "Military Leadership," *Field Manual 22-100*, 69–70.

Chapter 20

1. Joshua 1:5, *The Holy Bible (NIV)*.

Chapter 21

1. Ephesians 3:20, *The Holy Bible (NASB)*.

Chapter 22

1. Judges 7:2, *The Holy Bible (NASB)*.
2. Sun Tzu, *The Art of War*, 92.
3. Matthew 6:33, *The Holy Bible (NIV)*.
4. 1 Thessalonians 5:16–18, *The Holy Bible (NIV)*.
5. Philippians 4:6, *The Holy Bible (NIV)*.
6. James 5:16, *The Holy Bible (NIV)*.
7. Hebrews 12:10–11, *The Holy Bible (NIV)*.

Epilogue

1. 2 Timothy 1:7, *The Holy Bible (NIV)*.
2. Ephesians 6:17, *The Holy Bible (NIV)*.
3. Romans 1:26–28, *The Holy Bible (NIV)*.
4. 1 Corinthians 6:9–10, *The Holy Bible (NIV)*.
5. Stanton L. Jones & Mark A. Yarhouse, *Ex-Gays? A Longitudinal Study of Religiously Mediated Change in Sexual Orientation* (InterVarsity, 2007).
6. *Lillback, George Washington's Sacred Fire*, 564.
7. Isaiah 5:20, *The Holy Bible (NIV)*.
8. Psalm 81:13–14, *The Holy Bible (NRSV)*.
9. Dr. Jerry Newcombe, *The Way Out: God's Solution to Moral Chaos in America*, DVD, (Truth In Action Ministries, 2011).
10. Joshua 1:8, *The Holy Bible (NIV)*.
11. Matthew 5:14–16, *The Holy Bible (NIV)*.
12. Romans 8:28, *The Holy Bible (NIV)*.
13. John 14:23–24, *The Holy Bible (NIV)*.
14. Ephesians 5:8-10, *The Holy Bible (NIV)*.
15. Proverbs 3:5, *The Holy Bible (NIV)*.
16. 2 Timothy 3:16–17, *The Holy Bible (NIV)*.
17. 1 Corinthians 2:12–16, *The Holy Bible (NIV)*.
18. 2 Timothy 4:3, *The Holy Bible (NIV)*.
19. Hebrews 13:8, *The Holy Bible (NIV)*.
20. Matthew 5:18, *The Holy Bible (NIV)*.

Jɪᴍ Sᴄʜᴍɪᴅᴛ ɪs ᴀ retired US Army Special Forces lieutenant colonel with over twenty-six years of active military duty. Commissioned an infantry officer, Schmidt served a tour in Vietnam in 1966–67 as a rifle platoon leader and again in 1970–71 as an infantry company commander. The infantry company he commanded in Vietnam for six months killed or captured approximately sixty enemy soldiers without losing any of its own—a success only a few infantry companies achieved in Vietnam.

After returning from Vietnam, Schmidt served in various Special Forces, Infantry, and Joint Special Operations positions. As chief of operations for Special Operations Command, Pacific and J-3 for United States Pacific Command's on-call Joint Task Force for critical and sensitive contingency operations from 1987 to1990, he was not only instrumental in the development of Special Operation Forces concepts for regional contingencies and general war, but he was also instrumental in the planning and employment of combat forces during crisis response exercises and actual contingencies in the Pacific theater. Many of Schmidt's concepts have become doctrine within United States Special Operations Command and have proven effective throughout the world.

LTC Schmidt holds a Bachelor of Science degree in business from Southeast Missouri State College and an MBA from the University of Missouri. Jim and his wife, Joyce, live in Fort Collins, Colorado, and have two grown daughters, a grown son, and nine grandchildren.

Printed in the United States
by Baker & Taylor Publisher Services